The Eucharist

The Eucharist

Origins and Contemporary Understandings

by

Thomas O'Loughlin

Bloomsbury Academic
An imprint of Bloomsbury Publishing Plc

B L O O M S B U R Y
LONDON · NEW DELHI · NEW YORK · SYDNEY

Bloomsbury T&T Clark

An imprint of Bloomsbury Publishing Plc

50 Bedford Square	1385 Broadway
London	New York
WC1B 3DP	NY 10018
UK	USA

www.bloomsbury.com

BLOOMSBURY and the Diana logo are trademarks of Bloomsbury Publishing Plc

First published 2015

© Thomas O'Loughlin, 2015

Thomas O'Loughlin has asserted his right under the Copyright, Designs and Patents Act, 1988, to be identified as Author of this work.

British Library Cataloguing-in-Publication Data
A catalogue record for this book is available from the British Library.

ISBN: HB: 978-0-567-15605-1
PB: 978-0-567-38459-1
ePDF: 978-0-567-03732-9
ePub: 978-0-567-21313-6

Library of Congress Cataloging-in-Publication Data
A catalogue record for this book is available from the Library of Congress.

Typeset by Deanta Global Publishing Services, Chennai, India
Printed and bound in India

To the memory of one of my teachers,
Br A. A. Gilroy
whose theological insights sowed the
seeds that have grown into this book.

TABLE OF CONTENTS

PREFACE

This book has had a very long gestation, and over that time I have accumulated many debts of gratitude. On the one hand I have to thank all those whose advice I have sought on particular matters. I have asked questions of every conceivable kind of theological specialist, and from across the spectrum of Christian belief and practice, but I have also troubled many classicists, historians, archaeologists and anthropologists, along with cooks, food technologists and dieticians, and been grateful for both their patience with my questions and the lengths they went to obtain information from me. On the other hand I want to thank all those who have asked me questions about the Eucharist over the years – whether in the formal classroom setting with undergraduates – or by accident when someone sought an explanation of this or that element of Christian practice: these questions and the discussions they provoked were the energy source that pushed this research forward. As I finish this work my memory goes back to church porches and I can see and hear the question posed, or to the coffee area of a conference centre when a minister – familiar with presiding at the Eucharist – decided that I needed 'setting straight' and proceeded so to do! To all of them, I am happy to acknowledge my debt and my thanks.

I also wish to acknowledge some more specific debts. First, I wish to thank a teacher from my school days in Dublin with whom I fell into my first theological argument. Brother Gilroy, officially an art teacher, had so thought through the nature of eucharistic action, and the implications of *Sacrosanctum concilium*, that he, in the early 1970s, was far in advance of what I later learnt from many of my teachers as a theology undergraduate just as he is still far in advance of much Catholic practice. In the course of a digression from still-life drawing, he took the class through a minute exegesis of the Emmaus story in a way that would pass muster with the best products of NT exegesis, and concluded 'hence the importance of receiving communion from bread that has been presented at that celebration and not from [the reserved sacrament in] the tabernacle'. When I tackled him after class on this final point – I had not been able to see how it followed as a conclusion – he forced me to think my way from what we knew of the actions of Jesus to what would constitute a memorial of that action. The discussion must have gone on for some time – at least an hour – and I remember walking away with that sense of now having a real understanding of what I was doing when I 'received communion'. That was the first of many theological debates with him, and I hope that this book's dedication is a small acknowledgement.

I also want to thank some of my colleagues who have helped me in particular ways to bring this book to completion. A number of friends who are New Testament scholars have listened to me over the years and added sharpness to my thinking; I cannot list them all, but would like to name just two: Prof. D. P. Davies and Dr Kieran O'Mahony – as I returned again and again to certain themes, they both managed to give me the impression that this was the first time they had engaged in the debate. Likewise, I owe a debt to many liturgists – who welcomed me among them despite not being by training one of their fold – and again I would like to name just two of them: Prof. Paul Bradshaw and Dr Juliette Day. Their patience and willingness to share expertise are much appreciated. I would also like to express my thanks to two colleagues, Dr Frances Knight and Dr Francisca Rumsey, who as this work was nearing completion agreed to read it, and have saved me from more than one blunder. Many remain, but for those I alone am to blame; likewise, for the positions taken in this book, I alone am responsible.

Lastly, I owe a debt to many journal editors who published earlier papers that fed into this book – and from whose comments I learnt much. I also wish to thank the University of Nottingham for a semester's study leave, which allowed this book to take shape, and lastly the publishers for their patience in waiting for this book rather than pressing me to finish it on time when I found that there were still issues with which I needed to spend time in research and reflection.

T.O'L
Epiphany 2014

ABBREVIATIONS

AA	*The American Anthropologist.*
ACS	*American Catholic Studies.*
AL	*Archiv für Liturgiewissenschaft.*
AR	*Archiv für Reformationsgeschichte.*
ASR	*American Sociological Review.*
ASYF	*Arv: Scandinavian Yearbook of Folklore.*
ATR	*Anglican Theological Review.*
BT	*The Bible in Transmission.*
BTB	*Biblical Theology Bulletin.*
CBQ	*Catholic Biblical Quarterly.*
CCSL	*Corpus Christianorum, Series Latina* (Turnhout).
CH	*Church History.*
CW	*The Classical World.*
D&L	*Doctrine and Life.*
DOP	*Dunbarton Oaks Papers.*
DS	H. Denzinger and A. Schönmetzer (eds), *Enchiridion symbolorum, definitionum, et declarationum de rebus fidei et morum* (Freiburg im Breisgau, 1976 [thirty-sixth emended edition]).
ER	*The Ecumenical Review.*
ET	*Expository Times.*
ET	English translation.
FS	*Frümittelalterliche Studien.*
IR	*Innes Review.*
ITQ	*Irish Theological Quarterly.*
JBL	*Journal of Biblical Literature.*

JECS	*Journal of Early Christian Studies.*
JEH	*Journal of Ecclesiastical History.*
JMJ	*The Japan Mission Journal.*
JQR	*Jewish Quarterly Review.*
JR	*Journal of Religion.*
JSJ	*Journal for the Study of Judaism.*
JSS	*Journal of Semitic Studies.*
JTS	*Journal of Theological Studies.*
LCL	*Loeb Classical Library.*
LJ	*Liturgisches Jahrbuch.*
M&L	*Music and Liturgy.*
N-A	E. Nestle, E. Nestle, B. and K. Aland, et al. (eds), *Novum Testamentum Graece* (Stuttgart, 1981) [twenty-seventh edition].
NB	*New Blackfriars.*
NEA	*Near Eastern Archaeology.*
NJJWS	*Nashim: A Journal of Jewish Women's Studies & Gender Issues.*
NRSV	*New Revised Standard Version* (New York, NY, 1989).
NT	*Novum Testamentum.*
NTR	*New Theology Review.*
NTS	*New Testament Studies.*
OS	*Ostkirchliche Studien.*
PIBA	*Proceedings of the Irish Biblical Association.*
PNAS	*Proceedings of the National Academy of Sciences.*
PR	*The Pastoral Review.*
PTS	*Patristische Texte und Studien* (Berlin).
QL	*Questions Liturgiques.*
RQ	*Revue de Qumran.*
RSR	*Revue des Sciences Religieuses.*
RSV	*The Revised Standard Version – Catholic Edition* (London 1966).
RTAM	*Recherches de Théologie Ancienne et Médiévale.*

SCE   *Studies in Christian Ethics.*

SE   *Studia Evangelica.*

SF   *Social Forces.*

SL   *Studia Liturgica.*

SP   *Studia Patristica.*

SR   *Studies in Religion/Sciences Religieuses.*

SVTQ   *St Vladimir's Theological Quarterly.*

TD   *Theology Digest.*

TF   *The Furrow.*

TS   *Theological Studies.*

TW   *The Way.*

VC   *Vigiliae Christianae.*

VJCT   *Vision: A Journal for Church and Theology.*

WTJ   *Westminster Theological Journal.*

ZNW   *Zeitschrift für die neutestamentliche Wissenschaft.*

INTRODUCTION

Whether the Eucharist, under any of its names, is a central, perhaps dominating aspect of your discipleship or a peripheral, occasional worship activity, the fact remains that its study cannot be avoided in any assessment of faith that pays attention to Christian history. It is a practice that has attracted not only enormous devotion and great energy, but also unparalleled levels of sustained argument and in-fighting. It is this irony of the Eucharist being hailed as 'the sacrament of unity' while its practice promotes bitter divisions among Christians that underlies this book. How did we end up with a claim to have an event, a practice that celebrates and promotes the unity of Christ's body, yet no sooner do we begin to engage in the activity of Eucharist than divisions of various ages – some decades old, some several centuries old, some over a millennium in age – take hold of our thinking and we exclude one another, condemn one another or even deny the reality of what other Christians are doing? Yet, surely, all claim to be offering thanks and praise to the Father through Jesus Christ in the Spirit. Or is that how they see themselves and their activity, or do they even see the Eucharist as their activity?

This book is an exercise in historical theology. This theological approach takes what various groups of Christians have, over the years, believed and done, alongside what they have formally theorized and written down, as providing a basis for critical reflection. This, in turn, can form a background for asking more traditional theological questions such as what is the basic core of Christian understanding regarding the Eucharist, as well as providing a starting point for discussions of Christian practice today such as whether or not there is a way out of inherited points of impasse between churches, and whether or not looking back at our past can help us see alternative futures. So this book deliberately does not confine itself to the study of the past – in particular the earliest period – such as might be found in a study of Christian origins (whether that study is carried out under the banner of 'NT studies', 'origins of the liturgy', 'early Christian studies' or 'patristics'), nor of the present such as might be found in a work of doctrinal theology or an attempt to form an ecumenical bridge between inherited bodies of doctrine. In all these areas there has been an amazing flowering of scholarship in the last 50 years, and this book seeks to make links between these areas. But to draw attention to these links between areas of investigation, it takes as its starting point the question of what Christians have done and have thought they were doing when they celebrated the Eucharist – what are they doing not only as disciples but as human beings. This is possible because at the core of eucharistic activities is the activity of eating and drinking which are themselves basic within our humanity. So can this human dimension of eating together, which stands both at the foundation of human culture and at the historical practice among the followers of Jesus, be seen as a theological basis for the Eucharist? This book will argue that assuming that there are some common traits in human activity in relation to food and the sharing of food – that indeed we are food-sharing animals – helps us to appreciate parts of our inheritance from the practice of Jesus and that of the early communities, while also being rich in potential for Christian renewal today. But from being food sharers at a common meal in an early church to what happens in a church building on a Sunday morning today is a mighty jump in both practice and understanding, so at every step this book seeks to be aware of how this chasm in experience arose by identifying other aspects of Christian inheritance that are best seen as cancerous growths – and perhaps that now need to be left behind.

This book does not claim to show a path to the future, but it does seek to clarify our view of our inheritance (the good, the bad and the simply confusing) from the past. At the same time, it argues that the basis of eucharistic activity – celebrating the meal of Jesus in which we, in union with him, thank the Father – must take account of our human nature, and in particular our nature as animals who share meals and feast together. Why? Because the location of praise chosen by Jesus was a meal: a reality at the very heart of our humanity. Here is the complex location of the Eucharist: the Christian thanksgiving is, since the time of Jesus' activity with his followers, located within a meal, but meals have their own structure, grammar and existing share values among us as humans. I, as a Christian, see this location of a central act of discipleship, that of praising the Father for his goodness, in the very centre of specifically human activity, sharing food together, not only as part of the genius of Christianity but as uniquely appropriate given belief in the Logos who came to dwell among us and who is the risen Lord present when two or three gather in his name. But this location of the Eucharist has been deeply troubling – both practically and theologically – for many churches down the centuries. In the face of these fears over the location of the Eucharist, this book asks whether one can celebrate the Eucharist if one does not value sharing food with other human beings, and if the Eucharist is about sharing food while acknowledging the Father's creation, then is there any meal that is not somehow eucharistic?

This question of location is also crucial for Christian practice in worship. If the Eucharist is going to hold a genuinely central position within discipleship – as many churches hold it should – then the nature of its form, eating and drinking, must surely be a key to its place in Christians' lives and form a basis for both its practice and theology. Alternatively, if the Eucharist is considered a peripheral activity in the worship of Christians – a position also widely held among Christians today – then there must be some account as to why if Jesus chose to thank the Father from within the domain of human eating, and the first disciples saw this as part of their specific inheritance; this practice is now marginalized. For both groups, it cannot be explained on the basis that our cultural experiential base has changed because there is abundant evidence that food sharing has always been, and still is, at the core of what it is to be human. So the questions become these: first, what is specific about food sharing in the fashion of Jesus; and, second, because food sharing can build up different forms of human world, what sort of world should Christian food sharing bring into view?

Finally, the Eucharist is an activity that we experience, for better or for worse, and when we ignore this, we falsify our theological reflection. We often express this positively, at a pastoral level, by stating that good celebrations help to deepen faith and understanding, but forget that many of the theological misunderstandings of the Eucharist are just as much based in experience of liturgy. So this book will give priority to the manner in which the Eucharist was experienced, and which *then* formed the basis of theological reflection, rather than seeing the practice as a spinout of theology. The Eucharist is an *ergon* before it is *logos*. And indeed, given that, it could be said that the proof of a theology of the Eucharist is the extent to which it illuminates that activity of the People of God, which is thanking the Father.

1

Starting points for a study of the Eucharist

Anyone embarking on a book on the Eucharist needs to ask him/herself at the outset whether there is any need for yet one more book on the topic: 'of making many books there is no end, and much study is a weariness of the flesh'.[1] As it stands, no one today can keep abreast of the quantity of material written either on its history, its current praxis or the theological speculation that it generates. Moreover, because the Eucharist has figured so prominently in both Christian preaching and worship, as well as a source of bitterness in controversies between Christians, there is for every historical event, be that a practice or a text or a point of teaching, and for each period and tradition, a wealth of material that produces specialties within specializations. Conversations cutting across disciplines are rare. Meanwhile theology, in its explanatory mode, produces a steady stream of textbooks, alongside works of pastoral communication and spirituality, such that anyone wanting material on 'the Eucharist and . . .' need never look far. Indeed, any new work can be little more than an added whisper in a crowded discussion! It is this question that animates this first chapter as I seek to set out my stall while trying to make a bid for a perspective on the Eucharist that I do not hear, or hear only dimly, when I listen to historians, liturgists and doctrinal theologians.

Historical contingence

This book's perspective takes as its starting point the actual practices of Christians in their historical particularities, here and there, in this culture and that, in this period and in another. It holds that these should always have

---

[1] Qo 12.12.

primacy in theological investigations; not least because the Eucharist belongs
to the domain of human 'doing' before that of 'believing' or reflection.
It will assume that within the study of such particularities an approach can
be found towards examining not only the larger questions that not only
animate theologians today, but also those questions which affect the way
that we Christians behave and understand ourselves and our activities in
churches. So my approach, beginning with the succession of Christian praxis,
gives priority to what actual followers of Jesus have done, their activity
as disciples and their self-understanding of what they were/are doing. This
involves assuming that 'theology' – formal doctrine and preaching – emerges
as a way of making sense of that discipleship and communicating that
identity. Doctrinal formulation is thus viewed as a function of the activity
of discipleship, and which to be appreciated properly must be located
within the situation of its formulation within a specific context of living as
Christians.[2] I am, consequently, distancing myself from the notion that any
specific theological presentation of the Eucharist can be seen as 'classic' or
held to have within itself the basis for an absolute claim to be 'the theology
of the Eucharist'. Similarly, I am distancing myself from the notion that
there was any 'original' (and thereby privileged) doctrine of the Eucharist
that could form an *a priori* in discussion today. The starting point is among
'the pieces' of what we find in the activity of Christians, and which, taken
together, can be seen as the legacy of generations of effort, practice and
thinking.[3]

This starting point is not only radically historical, but also deliberately
subordinates formal reflection and doctrine to praxis and common understanding on the basis that the activity of disciples we refer to by the term
'Eucharist' belongs within Christian praxis and is never, despite the pleas
of many systematicians, actually studied apart from such activity. The
Eucharist is, first and foremost, a *doing* both conceptually as the act of
'thanking' the Father, 'offering' praise and 'sacrifice', and also empirically
as an action performed by Christians: the doing of liturgy, the carrying out
of a ritual, the performance of that action which is part of the living out of
discipleship whether it is held to be central or peripheral or granted status
for some other reason. It will, at once, be objected that no action is free of its
conceptual framework – which is true: we act with purpose and deliberation
as human agents – and that that framework is supplied by faith given form
as doctrine or theology, and so the Eucharist is a working out of that

[2]So, for example, someone who lived in feudal village will have a different way of imagining
both human authority – the lord in his castle – as hierarchy and the way of behaving towards
'the Lord' than someone in an urban culture today where democracy is seen as a political ideal
which Christians sometimes claim as deriving from their insight that all God's children are
equal (an insight few Christians would have recognized as 'Christian' a couple of centuries ago
except in that both poorest and greatest stood equally answerable for their sins).
[3]This is the starting point for which, on occasions, J. H. Newman longed; see O'Loughlin
1995.

understanding, and, consequently, we must start with doctrine! However, practical activity has its own dynamics within human societies, and it is this that is the primary communication between those who take part, and it is the demands of practice that shape developments. Doctrine does play a part but as we shall see, time and again, it tends to follow practice – as explanation – and when it is used as the rational driver of practice – most famously in the period after the Reformation – it often merely mutated practice and produced practical ends very different from those intended.[4] Moreover, the Eucharist is a ritual action, and within the sphere of human action ritual has a specifically repetitive function of its own – the Eucharist is acted out repeatedly with a constancy and consistency that is quite independent of theological reflection upon the action.[5] In short, Christian praxis has an integrity and dynamic of its own, and this deserves to be seen as a key to understanding what the Eucharist has meant to groups of Christians over the millennia. This approach will strike many Christians as strange, indeed suspect, who, by contrast, would wish to designate the Eucharist as a 'mystery' to be grappled with from their perspective as observers. This reifies the Eucharist while ignoring the fact that its development, both in practice and explanation, has been within the structures of community action and repetition. Hence that legacy of practice cannot be excluded from a study of the Eucharist.

At this point an example may clarify the approach. The Venerable Bede (673–735) never elaborated a formal theology of the Eucharist while his exegesis of 'eucharistic passages' is not very enlightening theologically; yet it is clear from his historical writings that the Eucharist was at the centre of not only his own life and identity as a priest-monk, but also his community's liturgical practice, while he saw it as central to the work of the church and the salvation of the English people. However, before one see this centrality in terms of the centrality ascribed to the Eucharist in Vatican II, one should note that the two key reasons for interest were radically different. First, a Mass, and so by implication a multiplicity of Masses, was the most sure and powerful spiritual force by which someone in painful waiting *post mortem* for the Second Coming could be transferred to 'sweet and pleasant pastures' while waiting for all purgation to be complete. Therefore Masses, note the plural,[6] allowed one to rest in peace, literally, while awaiting one's final entry to paradise. Second, all nations, baptized

---

[4]For this reason, Anton Baumstark in the 1920s saw the period from the Reformation onwards within the Latin churches as one that stood apart in its centralized standardization from the normal 'organic' development of liturgy; see Baumstark 2011, especially 230–43.

[5]This consistent repetition is the basis of much study of liturgy (we have just mentioned Anton Baumstark (1872–1948)) and more will be said about this as a tool in investigating early liturgy later in this chapter; but for a study of the importance of repetition, see J. Z. Smith 2001.

[6]See O'Loughlin 2009a for this point within Bede's authoritative sources: the praxis of Gregory the Great.

or not, had a system of sacrifice: it was part of human cosmology, but these were either defective (in the time of the Old Testament) or deranged, that is, offered to demons (among pagans); and these were replaced by a system by which sacrifices could be offered that were pure, holy and acceptable.[7]

Returning to the starting point of this book with actual practice, we could note that the reasonableness of such a starting point follows from the fact that when we look at the earliest historical references we possess having a bearing on the topic – the references by Paul when writing to the church in Corinth – we have *an account of a memory of an activity* by Jesus which is intended as *giving guidance to the performance of an activity* in the community in Corinth.[8] It is the activity, rather than anything that can be said about it, that has primacy: Paul can encourage, explain, justify and correct, but these actions only have significance given that there is a recurrent activity in that community which has caught Paul's attention. The key concern then in Paul's letter, as in the *Didache*,[9] or the Letter of Jude[10] is that the activity be performed properly, and references to significance are tied to appropriateness of activity. Likewise, today, a theological position is only as good as it is an adequate expression of what a group of Christians believe about the nature of their activity in celebrating the Eucharist. The Eucharist is located in the realm of Christian praxis, irrespective of the status of that activity within the larger framework of discipleship, and so 'eucharistic theology' exists as reflection on practice, and, as shall be argued later, needs to be tested, revised and envisioned in terms of that relationship.

But such a starting point carries within it many other implications. Discipleship is a matter of tradition: it endures over time and it changes as an individual's life and the make-up of the group to which she/he belongs changes; while the context of discipleship relates both to the social situation of the church to which one belongs and the history that church has inherited. The concerns about the Eucharist of a Christian growing up in a western Reformed tradition, except as a matter of academic appropriation, will not be those of someone who grew up in an eastern Orthodox church. Indeed, an outsider observing a modern western liturgy of any of the main western denominations and then an non-western liturgy – be it Greek, Armenian, Coptic, Syriac (of either form) or Ethiopian – would probably not recognize that all concerned would make claims to being engaged in an activity they all would trace to a common moment: the ecclesially formed 'origin' moment of the meal of Jesus before he suffered which became, as a memory, a standard

---

[7]See O'Loughlin 2014.

[8]1 Cor. 10.14-22 and 11.17-32; and see Murphy-O'Connor 1976 and 1977. See also Hollander 2009 for a context for passage; and see Keightley 2005 for the view of memory underlying that passage which will be used throughout this book.

[9]*Didache* 9–10 and 14; see O'Loughlin 2010, 85–105.

[10]Jude 12-13; the work of Smit 2011 on James throws light on the references in Jude.

part of the common *didache* of the churches[11] in the early second century (if not earlier).[12] Likewise, many of the debates and actions that have caused bitter divisions between Christians since the tenth century (between Greek and Latin Christians) or the sixteenth century (between various groups of western Christians) were not even issues a century or two before some specific development in practice emerged which then acted as the spur to comparisons and so one or other side being seen as deficient by the other. The subsequent work of theologians then justified those differences and so embedded them within their own group's identity that they became issues on which they would rather see the body of the Christ rendered than to give way on them! What became bastions in controversy were often accidental, and idiotic, developments in practice, but which were transformed into 'doctrines' when fought over with all the tools that forensic rationality, philosophical insight and spiritual rhetoric could provide. The debate over the cup and the laity – 'Subutraquism' – which emerged in the west with Jan Huss (c. 1372–1415) in the early fifteenth century[13] and which rumbles on still among Roman Catholics[14] – is just the most obvious example from many instances of this phenomenon.

Such disputes should remind us that the Eucharist not only exists in the realm of praxis as a human activity, but also alert us that as such it changes over time. It is a phenomenon open to all the factors, good and bad, intended and unintended, which shape human lives and activities. This means that every manner of celebrating the Eucharist, and the theologies produced alongside those activities, needs to be identified as the product of a particular setting with a unique set of possibilities and limitations. Moreover, when this

---

[11]This part of early Christian life is often translated as 'teaching' with the meaning very similar to the modern notion of 'doctrine'; however, *didache* is better understood as 'training' – that which is learnt to practice within the group – and as such it invariably involves ritual; see O'Loughlin 2011.

[12]It was part of the memory of the Pauline churches (see Keithley 2005) and those visited by Mark – but we do not know the extent to which these groups overlap; and it was taken up in the narrations of Matthew and later Luke – at which point we can say it was well on the way to becoming 'standard'; but note that the *Didache*, John's gospel, and the even later evidence of actual Eucharistic Prayers (see Ligier 1973) all show the Eucharist without a 'final supper' dimension. So as a standard explanation, it is identical with the canonical gospels becoming the standard history of Christian origins; but it was several centuries before that memory became part of the actual Eucharistic practice of the churches (and in some – the East Syrian – it never did become so).

[13]See Cook 1975.

[14]It is still not the normal expectation of Catholics to share the cup at a celebration of the Eucharist: this is a matter of the ordained ministers only. England and Wales form an exception to this practice, but even there the merest hint of difficulty is enough to curtail the practice while younger 'conservative' presbyters present the practice as one more of the baneful 'Protestant' influences of Vatican II. Most Catholic theologians do not see any real difficulty in the so-called doctrine of concomitance which arose merely to justify an omission in practice that had become widespread and embedded over time without anyone paying much attention until it became a matter of controversy with the east.

is inherited by another time and situation; it is then received as a *datum*, and like it or not, with the potential to be as much a distraction from a fruitful understanding of Christian tradition as it is to being the bearer of further enlightenment. All celebrations being the work of a moment are deficient in one way or another; and every group, whether as small as a specific gathering or as large as a denomination, has much to learn from each other and from the experiences of communities in the past. The churches are, to paraphrase Karl Rahner (1904–84), always remembering and always forgetting.

While the notion that doctrine is a function of communities' histories is often acknowledged within the history of theology as a fact (hence there can be a history of theology and a history of liturgy), the key implication of that obvious assertion is less frequently grasped. A practice that was once life-giving and an expression of the best inheritance of the churches can become corrupt, while that which was at one time an imperfect expression of discipleship can, in a different world, hold out precious insights for renewal. Both practice and reflection can both improve and decay – and while there have been many desperate attempts to claim immunity from the ups and downs of history in the form of appeals to infallible traditions or inerrant texts, or more vague appeals to the work of Providence or the Spirit's presence, the fact of the rich diversity of practices and understandings sets the factual limits to such doctrinal claims. Many valuable insights have been lost; many crucial aspects of Christian experience in relation to this practice have fizzled out as historical dead ends. While many of the developments that have gained prominence can be seen, by comparison with other practices, to have been mistaken paths.

There is a misleading tacit assumption in many theologians' works to the effect that 'our now [perhaps with a little tweaking] is as it was intended to be'; but even a cursory scan of the diversity of Christian practices shows that this cannot be the case – we have to accept that our practice may have gone down side-road after side-road – and have embedded results in both practice and debate which are far from the best practice of the churches. It was this recognition that 'the now' could not simply be assumed as the ideal – and such an assumption is the human default setting: that which I have done since childhood must both be 'ok' and in continuity with the ideal moment I associate with it – that was the driving force behind such work as John Henry Newman's tests for 'authentic developments' in the nineteenth century.[15] But while those tests might have seemed adequate to many then, they fail now given our far more complex understanding of the history of the churches, our more nuanced perception of how 'theology' is formed within human understanding, and the manner in which we approach the early literary products of the churches that form the anthology labelled 'the New Testament'.

---

[15]Newman 1845.

But surely the historians can come to the rescue by establishing the original moment that can then be used as a measuring rod amidst the diversity of history – surely that moment was privileged! And, before going any further, it is worth noting that anyone writing on the Eucharist today – or indeed celebrating it in many of the ritual forms promulgated in the twentieth century – stands on the shoulders of several centuries' worth of labour by historical theologians with just that desire of finding the key to the diversity in the perfect moment from which it all grew and developed. However, the more we learn of the world of the first followers of Jesus, the more the notion of there being a single, original 'theology' recedes into the background. Indeed, the very notion that there is a 'firm' doctrinal *datum*, or a perfect causal moment such as 'the Last Supper' which institutes both the practice, the fundamental form, and perhaps the core theological values, appears as itself the product of the desire of later ages to resolve difficulties by an appeal to a pristine original moment whose description has all the characteristics of a supra-historical axiom.[16] The activity of the followers of Jesus emerged in a fluid multi-cultural environment and their discipleship took from the start a wide variety of expressions, and this complex of activities and explanations became our common legacy. Given that fact, my starting point looks back to the activity of thanksgiving in the earliest communities, and their memories of Jesus in relation to this activity, rather than to 'the teaching of Jesus' (as if that could be separated from the variety of presentations of that teaching for which we have evidence), 'the fundamental doctrine' (as if that could be identified in some way such as an archetypal catechism which might then evolve as so justify later positions as 'legitimate' developments) or 'the scriptures' (as if they can be seen as presenting a consistent or coherent position). By contrast with the quest for origins, as historians and scriptural exegetes have recognized since Bauer's work,[17] this book will presume variety and be as interested in what apparently disappeared as it is in what became 'standard' in the sense of Vincent of Lérins' dictum: *quod ubique, quod semper, quod ab omnibus*.[18]

Because there was a range of praxis among the earliest groups of followers – it would be anachronistic to call them 'Christians' or to imagine we know how that name distinguished them from 'Jews'[19] – and an even greater variety of explanations of the significance of their following, the notion that any one position today might be claimed as 'the true position' – in the sense of the original, genuine, the obligatory doctrine or the praxis demanding adherence

---

[16]See O'Loughlin 2012a where some of these assumptions as factors in post-Reformation theology are examined; and see Daly-Denton 2008 for an indication of the direction being taken in contemporary scholarship.

[17]Bauer 1971 – the original German edition appeared in 1934.

[18]*Commonitorium*, 2, 5 (p. 149); and see O'Loughlin 1991.

[19]The continuing debate over the identity of 'Jewish Christianity' should be sufficient to warn us off the quest for any consistent theological position prior to the later second century; see Jackson-McCabe 2007.

– or as a standard by which other approaches to the Eucharist are rejected is itself rejected. Although this book presumes a variety of practice and explanation as the normal situation among Christians, but because elements from that variety both in activity and teaching survived piecemeal into the later standard models, as we see them in their historical relics,[20] it will not privilege any one strand or moment as a paradigm. To isolate one tradition as preserving a core continuity would assume that the outcome of contingent factors has an internal consistence and overall coherence that is rare in any produce of human history. Once again, treating any particular moment as normative would invoke the notion that the history of the church or its doctrine is somehow preserved from vicissitudes of time or that it could be seen as evolving with the teleological certainty with which acorns grow to be oak-trees. A serious commitment to the praxis of the churches involves an equally serious affirmation of the serendipity of historical change. A concept produced in a moment can gain such notoriety that it becomes both a pillar of a theology and a millstone for generations who treat it as 'that which must be'. The implications of the notion of 'transubstantiation' in western theology is a case in point – that notion could just as easily have remained in obscurity or disappeared without trace.[21] Likewise, something that did disappear need not be a lost 'dead-end' in theology: it might be that a practice or perspective disappeared through misunderstanding, neglect or human crassness. So the investigation of forgotten areas can be that which recalls for today otherwise lost insights or highlights the deficiencies of some of those practices or doctrines that can be taken as 'normal' simply because we have inherited them and have not questioned them in centuries. Bad practices and bad theology fare just as well in time's blind sieve as do noble practices and creative theologies.[22] There are forgotten things we need to recall afresh and to embed in our living discipleship, and well-remembered things we need to let slip from our active memories and practices to become shadows existing in libraries.

If diversity is, moreover, a key note of eucharistic origins, praxis and theology, then because Christianity is conservative of its past – it is always looking backwards in liturgy and in study – then complex diversity is the living reality of Christian activity no matter how boldly a group either denies the fact, strives for uniformity or makes exclusive claims for a particular theological vision. While some insights developed, and certain actions and

---

[20]The word 'relics' is chosen to cover not just memories recorded in texts, but practices both those recorded in texts and those found in later liturgies which can be seen as survivals from earlier times, and also material objects, some cultic some iconographic, connected with the Eucharist.

[21]See Goering 1991; and Macy 1994.

[22]It was this assumption, held tacitly, that underpinned the notion of *ressourcement* in Catholic theology in the mid-twentieth century: they assumed there were wonderful aspects that had been lost (and could now be recovered), while many corrupt notions had growth deep roots (and should be allowed to wither).

understandings gained prominence, other practices and verbalizations were passed over or receded into the background, yet most of them, both 'the winners' and 'the losers', left traces in the ecclesial record. This fact – that practices and doctrines which did not become widespread were not completely obliterated – has meant that in so far as Christians look backwards, earlier 'bits of experience' keep re-emerging to confront later practices and explanatory consistencies. Whenever this happens within a theological culture that assumes that there must be a single orthodox 'position' (either in practice or doctrine, or in both), then the result is a clash where both sides claim the authenticity of continuity with the past or with 'origins'. And such clashes, when, first, both sides see themselves as well founded in 'origins' or 'tradition'; secondly, both appeal to a paradigmatic moment of institution, and, thirdly, both claim that their theological position is exclusive, end in futile deadlock. The lack of uniformity of practice and consistency in teaching in the earliest churches has been the bane of later Christian discourse for centuries where those two qualities were not only highly valued culturally and theologically but, indeed, *were assumed to have been present in the originating moment*. The conflicts among western Christians since the sixteenth century are a stark reminder of this phenomenon – and, ironically, the more each side sought the 'neutral witness' of history, the deeper they entrenched their conflicts.[23] Thus at the root of many controversies between Christians – usually each contending for the 'originality' of their position – lies the awkward fact that Christian experience is multiform not just today, but it has always been so. So notions of historical investigation uncovering the pure noble metal beneath accumulated accretions and grime are very wide of the mark. Actual historical investigations are more like a tour around a jumble sale: confusion here, a large heap slowly builds up there, some useless experiment there, but also gems that can be taken and reset within a new praxis and expounded in a renewed theology.

However, one must not press 'the jumble sale' analogy too far because Christian history is a very layered affair and one can trace evolution over centuries. One of the most arresting moments for anyone studying the Eucharist is that of her/his encounter with Justin's account of the Christian Sunday gathering (c. 150).[24] One can tick off the details one recognizes – readings from the Old Testament, a 'gospel',[25] a homily, a Eucharistic Prayer concluded with an 'amen' followed by sharing of the food, and even a collection. The recognized items are ticked and the familiar form is validated: we are doing as was done! We have been faithful! This sense of continuity and historical coherence has animated some of the most influential studies of

---

[23]See O'Loughlin 2012a.

[24]*First Apology*, 65–7.

[25]Part of the problem of reading early texts can be seen in this word 'gospel', which as a term of the written narratives of such authors as Matthew, Mark, Luke and John only comes into use *after* the time of Justin Martyr; see Koester 2007, 69–70.

the Eucharist that appeared in the aftermath of scholasticism, and generated such powerful notions about the constancy of the essential forms underlying the undeniable variety of historical record. The most famous example of this approach in English is that of Gregory Dix (1901–52) who believed that beneath a surface confusion he could find an ever-present 'classic shape' of offertory, president's prayer of thanks, fraction and communion.[26] Not only has this approach been found to be wanting historically,[27] but as with all structuralist groupings it created an illusion of order without proving that such an order exists, while by bolstering our sense of continuities, it blinds us to discontinuities. To return to the example of Justin: did you notice that he assumes that the prayer of thanks is *ex tempore*, that its setting is still within a real community meal, there is no mention of who leads the prayer – and certainly no notion of ordination – or that the leader (*proestós*) has been conferring with any special authority within the group, the 'memoirs of the apostles' are not treated as a sacred text, the collection is for the poor not of the upkeep of the clergy or the apparatus, and the whole event is assumed to be comprehensible to 'outsiders' as the Christian variant of one of the larger society's significant institutions: the *symposium*. While liturgical archaeology is both possible and necessary, when that evidence becomes part of a quest for theological understanding, tracing sequences of developments, over no matter how long a duration, is but a preliminary task so that the evidence can be used as sensibly as possible.

Ritual and routine

Once it is granted that the Eucharist is, first and foremost, an activity, the obvious next points are that it is both a ritual activity and (for most Christians) a regularly recurring activity. The notion of ritual is always problematic: the very word produces for many an 'allergic reaction'. To include anything in the category of ritual is to make it somehow peripheral to reality, a distraction from essentials, and even to place it in the realm of the false: to say someone 'went through the rituals' in a meeting or in welcoming someone is to state that they did not take the matter seriously, they shammed a welcome when they did not really want to greet someone, or that it was an enforced pretence. Ritual in much of our thinking belongs to the world of falsehood.

Moreover, the word has specific derogatory undertones for many theologians and churches. While theology, and so presumably theologians, deals with the

---

[26]Dix 1945, 48 (for a summary of his 'shape'; and then 103–40 for a development of the thesis).

[27]For example, see Bradshaw 2002, 122–6, or Bradshaw 2004, 51–9; Dix was so convinced of 'the shape' that he dismissed as exceptions evidence that did not fit his thesis; most famously he omitted any serious consideration of the *Didache* (Dix 1945, 48 n. 2): see O'Loughlin 2013a.

matters of ultimate concern, the philosophical questions to which faith gives rise, the content of revelation along with its skilled exegesis and explication; ritual, by contrast, is treated as belonging to the world of arbitrary fluff, the gaudy packaging that attracts those who cannot raise their minds above the material and the inessential. While theology, and its history, belong in the study or the market-place; matters of ritual – except when it is studied in lieu of texts by anthropologists – belongs in the sacristy! Moreover, academics, for a variety of reasons, like to think that they stand outside the world of ritual, and they vaguely suspect it as irrational as a topic and pedestrian as an interest. When, so the story goes, Dean W. R. Inge (1860–1954) was told that a job-applicant was studying liturgy, he retorted: 'And other people collect stamps!' Ritual might merit being studied as an 'it' when it is viewed 'from the gallery' by an anthropologist, but the very notion of 'coming down from the gallery' is seen as a form of intellectual contamination.

This lack of interest in ritual produces some strange effects in books on the Eucharist: while there is much talk of its 'sacramental nature', studies bypass the ritual that is vehicle of that sacramentality; while the notion of 'real presence' is discussed in detail, the ritual's actual presence which is the basis of the discussion is ignored; and while the concept of *lex orandi legem credendi statuat* is frequently invoked, the implication of a concern with the detail of how a community prays is still regarded as the domain of others. Specialists in ritual studies may view it as a human phenomenon, liturgists or specialists in spirituality may be concerned with its practical implications for Christian mission, but it is widely assumed it does not affect theology as such. Indeed, there is a large theological literature, built up over centuries, that discusses what the Eucharist is, or means, for Christians without ever actually looking at what either happens when a group of Christians celebrate, or what actual Christians think they are doing when they 'celebrate', 'take part in' or 'attend', the Eucharist. Indeed, one of the problems facing many churches today, but especially the Roman Catholic Church, is that there is a chasm between how the Eucharist is described in official theological statements and the understanding of the Eucharist ordinary Christians are generating as a result of their participation.[28] In contrast to such non-regard of ritual and forms of actual celebration by theologians and historians of theology, we have this statement by Hans Küng:

> The liturgy is and remains the centre of the life of the church. If this can be successfully renewed, won't that also have effects on all the areas of church activity?[29]

A starting point of this book is that we humans – because we are symbol-using animals – are continually engaged in ritual. Ritual will be treated as a

---

[28]O'Loughlin 2010a.
[29]Küng 2002, 285.

basic category far wider than being simply a subset of religious activity and far more profound than might be suggested by thinking of ritual in terms of formal 'ceremonial' occasions. So while it is obvious, as a basic human feeling, a great gathering such as the Olympic Games needs a 'proper' (i.e. ritual) opening and closing, and it would be rather disappointing if one did not see the medal presentation, the flags and anthems, and the jubilation of the crowd! But ritual is still more basic: it is inherent in the concept of 'the game'. Therefore, without the formalized understandings that one needs to time, for example, the runners, have lanes and starting pistols, and a whole complex set of assumptions on 'how to play the game' one would have no Games at all! Moreover, we have but to look at the TV news to see the ritual power of flags as expressions of collective identity – particularly when an identity is questioned.

But there are even simpler rituals that are basic to everyday communication: our society recognizes the handshake as conveying a great deal about how we want to interact with one another (the proof is the care that politicians take to avoid being seen shaking certain hands) and woe betide someone who forgets a birthday card or an anniversary.[30] Few today frequently wear 'the plain dress' of a medieval cleric (even among clerics), but the graduation ritual is but the most visible part of the larger ritual of formalized 'university' learning that is a key component in education, worldwide, today: the lecture, the module, an examination and a degree are all ritual forms in and through which shared knowing is channelled. One might suggest that these are merely 'conventional' structures, as indeed they are, but if one did not have such agreed conventions, one would have to invent others in place of them! Ritual gives form to our lives and facilitates, indeed creates, interactions at the personal, group and society levels.[31]

Rituals, which preserve and enact the memories and cosmologies of a group, can provide keys to our sense of identity. The apparently simple act of 'Sunday Lunch' – a family around a table, perhaps a roast joint of meat that is carved, extra courses – is not only a ritual that is deeply inscribed in many societies' memories but can be used as an index of secularization or the growth of a multi-cultural society where Sunday as the festival day of the week and the day without work are not shared long-term assumptions.[32] Yet this ritual – perhaps the greatest lost eucharistic opportunity of Christianity – still resonates long after the explicitly religious dimensions of it being 'Sunday' lunch have disappeared: it is still used in advertising foodstuffs (invoking memories), and has mutated now into special 'deals' for this meal in many pubs in the British Isles. The ritual is still potent and indeed, as human activity, is more enduring than the formal Christian narratives of which once it might have been presented as a material expression. But a ritual like 'Sunday lunch'

---

[30]These are the habitual actions that build society, see Connerton 1989.
[31]Rothenbuhler 1998.
[32]Brown 2009, 133–4, and 160.

is but a peak in the plane of our ritual behaviour. Travellers, and more recently ethnographers, have long appreciated how the rituals surrounding food and eating can give profound insights into a society, its values and its concept of itself as a group.[33] Mary Douglas, in 1972, showed how we could 'decipher' a meal implying that every meal was a code: a set of symbols and rituals which meant that it was far more than a pause in activity for alimentation.[34] Implicit also in her work was that eating as a ritual activity was not confined to the great ritual meals such as the wedding banquet (in Jesus' time this was the meal of meals in that the wedding day was the day of joyful days),[35] the formal meals in messes and refectories with consciously ritualized elements, or even that annual family meals such as Christmas Dinner or, in the United States, Thanksgiving: ritual is part of every meal. And, therefore, as was shown in detail by Margaret Visser, eating, drinking and sharing meals is a primary ritual activity of human beings.[36] Given that the Eucharist – no matter how celebrated – invokes the language of a meal and involves, at least potentially, eating and drinking; this ritual dimension of human food consumption will form a basic perspective of this book.

Given that we are condemned to be ritual animals – as social and linguistic animals – we can discover our identity in our rituals, and recalling what we said about the Eucharist as an activity, it will be clear that these are overlapping, mutually supporting perspectives.[37] To know what the Eucharist is for Christians involves a study of what they do, how they ritualize, and then how they explain that action to themselves. But 'the ritual turn' has other benefits for the theologian. This was brought home to me most forcefully when I was present at the presbyteral ordination of a friend in the Orthodox Church. The congregation were, naturally, standing in the pew-less building, and so packed was it that a father, standing next to me, stood his small son on his shoulders so that the little boy could see what was happening. Then during the imposition of hands, the boy leaned down and asked: 'why are they doing that?' The father immediately gave an answer – which no theologian, east or west, would ever publish – and this young representative of the tradition's next generation was perfectly satisfied. Ritual is relatively stable, it copies and repeats itself, it forms continuity and shapes memories; but explanation is multiform, and changes with situations and cultures. This stability of behaviour has been utilized by some New Testament scholars as

---

[33]For a classic early example of an anthropologist studying eating, see Powdermaker 1932.
[34]Douglas 1972.
[35]Hence the significance of the wedding meal at Cana in Jn 2.
[36]Visser 1993.
[37]I say 'condemned' for I am keenly aware that there is a long inheritance in academic theology that imagines that theology, or perhaps rationality, can bypass ritual and myth; but those who flee ritual find themselves making 'non-rituality' their key ritual expression – in abandoning ritual, the Quakers evolved a new ritual, while 'demythologization' is itself one of the great myths of modernity. However, it is often not easy to appreciate that every decoding is another encoding!

a way of finding a pathway through the various theologies of the Eucharist we find in early Christian documents[38]; and, in this book, that approach will be used as a methodological assumption. This is how it will be understood: it is assumed that once a given way of doing something is developed, that practice impeded the development of alternatives.[39] However, that practice needed to be verbalized for those who took part in it, explained to neophytes, and passed on as teaching to new groups in new situations. So what is handed on is not just a ritual, but a ritual narration. And at this point we come to the complexity of ritual and doctrine in Christianity, which is both a ritual practice and explicitly formalized corpus of handed-on teaching. The practices tend to be conservative of their form,[40] and the teaching tends to follow on from them and explain, and justify, them. But there is both noise and feedback within this system. The 'noise', if that is what it is, takes the form of every individual who takes part creating for her/himself an explanation of what is happening. This explanation, my 'take on it', may be common and shared with others around about and may be long-enduring, but its relationship with the group's 'official' teaching at that time may be rather tentative and there is always interaction between such private and official meanings. Meanwhile, there is also another form of 'noise' in that most teaching claims for itself exclusivity: this is what we are doing, this is what our ritual means, this is what the sacrament is sacramental of. . . . But there is always more than one theology/explanation in use in that no matter what the dominant theology is, there is the variety of theologies implicit in the words, actions, gestures and objects of the activity of celebrating the Eucharist.[41] Moreover, the very people who propound the teaching about the Eucharist, pastors, have usually been those who presided and determined much of the form of the ritual: so often the ritual was adapted by being seen as a material expression of theology. While historically formal teaching has followed from ritual; for many teachers it is the 'theology' (seen as tantamount to revelation) that has, de facto, been perceived as primary, and then the ritual has been seen as a subsequent manifestation whose exact utility is often hard to tie down. This tension can be easily observed in that most participants are able to make a shrewd guess about the theological 'flavour' of their leader by simply watching his/her ritual style – and this is usually far more revealing than formal statements of adherence. All Catholic clerics subscribe to Vatican II and likewise Anglican clerics subscribe to the

---

[38]Nodet and Taylor 1998, 88–125.

[39]In this pattern, that what was an accidental pattern the first time tends to become the established way of doing things; ritual parallels learning; as Milavec 2006, 472 has noted: 'Once a given recognition is developed, it positively impedes an alternative'.

[40]This has been an underlying assumption in the study of liturgy since the work of Louis Duchesne (1842–1922) and Adrian Fortescue (1874–1923) and became central to the work of Baumstark; on the anomalies that occur due to this conservatism of form, see O'Loughlin 2009.

[41]On these competing theologies, see O'Loughlin 2008.

Thirty-nine Articles; but watching 2 minutes of presidency will normally be enough to know what they really 'feel' – in the sense of believing in their depths – about those doctrinal events.

In short, religious ritual is never free of theology, but this work will argue that there is a certain priority in actual human engagement and that we are able to break out of our inherited paradigm by making fresh contact with the realities we have been trained to serve.[42]

One very obvious aspect of ritual is often passed over in the study of liturgy: ritual relates to routine.[43] This study will see this as both a boon and a problem, but also, first and foremost, as an inevitable part of being human. As we have just stated, once a given way of doing something is developed, that practice impedes the development of alternatives: so having chosen a particular breakfast cereal once, it is likely that that will become my 'default' or, at the very least, if I do make a change, it will be between cereals rather than for a completely different sort of breakfast![44] So routine cannot be seen as decay from a pristine early time when there was a complete charismatic freshness,[45] nor can it be seen as the result of decrepitude or laziness. This has several implications for any study of Christian history. First, it means that actions which we have been repeating, in this way of that, for centuries, even millennia, may have come into existence quite pragmatically. Something was done, or done in a particular way, not as the result of some careful planning, but as the result of what happened, or was convenient, on a particular occasion, and then it set the pattern for routine, and soon it had the authority of being 'our tradition' – and as such it became inviolable and, quite literally, 'sacrosanct'. The tendency then is to see what happened as that which was 'intended to happen' and indeed as *a domino institutus*; and so study, especially historical investigation, becomes the quest for the perfect original moment. Moreover, the ritual now is seen as an insight into our humanity guaranteed by Providence; by contrast, it is our humanity as ritual beings that allows us to understand ritual and through ritual those aspects of our humanity. So while we must examine the origins of a ritual as a key to what it was that became routine, that does not mean that the moment of origin should be treated as a perfect archetype ever to be imitated. Second, routines can preserve earlier forms, both good and ill; for example, the Roman rite preserved a fraction even when it had lost all doctrinal contact with that action and all practical connection with the

---

[42]This draws on the insights of Michael Polanyi 1958, 322–3 whereby all knowing takes place within societies and traditions, yet we have a calling to discover more adequate understandings than that which we have inherited. See Milavec 2006, 475.

[43]I am deeply indebted to Paul Connerton for his notion of how habitual memory of bodily practices, actual doings, produces routines that can be transmitted from one generation to another – see Connerton 1989 – and so is the very basis of 'tradition'.

[44]The exception proves the rule: when I go abroad, and my everyday routines are set aside, I may have a completely different kind of breakfast.

[45]See Draper 1998.

ceremonial due to the invention of pre-cut individual 'altar breads'; while that rite also preserved forms of language and action that made perfect sense within the stratified world of late antiquity despite the fact that making such 'distinction of persons' came to be frowned upon in formal theology. And lastly, routine has its own in-build decay mechanisms whereby actions become tokens rather than disappearing completely, and this invites new justifications. These 'explanations' driven by the existential need to make sense of what is perceived as a brute fact – the notion that one would drop actions that have become tokenized and incomprehensible being ruled out by the very nature of ritual as routine – often produce, cumulatively, a general theological scene that is radically different from that understanding in which the original action made sense. In routine's lack of change lies the greatest danger of the betrayal of the original insights! So attention to routine, and the implications of routine within understanding, will be one of the characteristics of this book's approach.

One of the effects of thinking of the followers of Jesus as continuously involved in ritual – and so routines – is that it allows us to appreciate from the outset that as this movement arose within the Galilean perspective on, what we call, 'Second Temple Judaism', spread within the Judaisms of the Mediterranean world, and continued with ritual routines almost without the loss of a beat. So in the actual living of discipleship, continuities formed the matrix for new insights and departures that was part of their following of Jesus. It has been all too easy for those who study the history of Christian theology to look back to the earliest followers of Jesus and imagine the Eucharist as a Christian institution with 'inheritances from Judaism' – it is not so long ago that this was the dominant perspective of most writing on the history of liturgy and its legacy is still potent – and the process of inheritance is described almost like the work of a church committee. In that way of looking at the past, there was a fixed background element, the Passover Meal, a new institution by Jesus within, or perhaps against, that 'background context', a new sacrifice intended to replace the older sacrifices, and the need to continue the memory following the Lord's mandate; and within this, one can find bits and pieces which we kept, adopted and adapted. So any reference to the religious world of Jesus and his followers became, in essence, an appeal to something other than the Eucharist (albeit to something that might throw light on it), while, at best, the Eucharist is to the ritual and routine of Jews of the period as text is to context. But while such a neat cleavage between, and juxtaposition of, Christianity and Judaism may have a place in later Christian kerygma (as when we sing Aquinas's *et antiquum documentum novo cedat ritui*), it only creates confusion if we are intent on understanding an activity among the early disciples of Jesus. The reality of routinized ritual means that continuities are primary, and we have to be more concerned with discontinuities either in practice or verbalized theology. The first communities who engaged in 'eucharist' – the name is, of course, later – were, first and foremost, communities that were self-consciously Jewish but who had some regard for Jesus; and they were people already formed in the ritual and patterns of their religion who, quite naturally, continued in those routines.

In fine, trying to make a study of the Eucharist without reckoning on communities and their routines is merely to study an *ens rationis*.

Memory and community

How one values and understands the past is one of the determining issues for how one approaches the Eucharist. If the past is but prologue, or bunkum, then the Eucharist has to have its existence solely in terms of what it can be demonstrated to do *now*. This can be seen in any number of explanations such as 'it is the perfect prayer' which then generates the question: but can I not pray – or the more utilitarian: can I have my prayers heard – without having to go to it? Alternatively, if the past is the source of the perfect moment of divine contact, then the past becomes so important that the Eucharist becomes some sort of revival of the past, a re-enactment, a mode of escape from the present into a meta-historical moment (such as those moments Eliade would designate '*in illo tempore*') which ironically claims to be the most historical of moments: the moment of the Last Supper or the 'un-repeatable' moment of the Cross.[46] Likewise, those who emphasize the Eucharist as 'sacrament' are often so concerned with a future, transcendent or eschatological 'reality' that the actual, present activity becomes almost an irrelevance. Those Catholics brought up in the era of 'private Masses' and the accumulation of 'Masses for the Dead' will know that the actual liturgy (just over one-quarter of one hour in virtual silence with only a server 'to answer' by rote) became a cipher, and all interest moved towards the otherworldly 'outcome' of these actions.[47] The otherworldly dimension of the *opus operatum* led to the downgrading of the present, and the eclipse of the activity as an event within the domain of human meaning and action. What 'it' might 'mean' as a liturgical event might be of interest to some peripheral specialist called either a 'rubrician' or 'liturgist', but the focus was upon its effect before God, while the human actions could be bracketed as the *sacramentum tantum* – and treated as virtually irrelevant.[48] Similarly, an approach that stresses the *mysterium* – a dominant

---

[46]Heb. 9.28 – the unique and un-repeatable sacrifice of Jesus – has been contrasted with the repeated celebrations of the Eucharist as a sacrifice to create a long-tale of Christian dispute through a failure to recognize the difference between ritual language and theology as an imaginative process which employs ritual language.

[47]See O'Loughlin 2009a; the actual liturgy became simply a necessary process so that its 'product' – a pleasing sacrifice to God and – and 'commodity' – sanctifying grace among humans – might come into existence.

[48]The 'mere sign' value was contrasted with the *res tantum* – its final reality (union with God); and when 'liturgy' was compared with such a momentous reality, it was but natural that it should be seen as transient and of no great importance (except in so far as doing certain actions was a demand of divine positive law).

eastern approach – virtually denies history and, with it, the community role in the celebration except in so far as their attendance is a religious act quite distinct from being a participation in an act of eucharist to the Father taking place within their own history as a community and as individuals. The iconostasis not only shields the table from the eyes of the gathering but also marks it off from human history. And most churches have similar barriers: the Tridentine ritual did this for Catholics through its retention of Latin, while making the Lord's Supper into an out-of-the-ordinary ritual event did it for many Reformed churches.

However, instead of approaching the Eucharist in terms of time divided into past, present and future (despite the fact that this approach has a long history and the arguments it has generated have, for centuries, kept theologians busy), this book will invoke the notion of *memory* as one of our starting points in any attempt to appreciate the Eucharist. Why this is a valuable starting point is, however, not at all clear. On hearing the word 'memory', our immediate image is of memory as a database of past events or of intimate individual reveries. In the first case we approach memory as akin to a TV camera that has been left running and which we can replay in real time to see what happened then – and so we can say to someone: your memory is mistaken, it did not happen on the Tuesday but on the Monday! But this sort of memory of details (albeit of great value when the police are trying to solve a crime) is not the memory that constitutes us as distinct individuals and communities with identities. Anyone who grew up in Ireland, as I did, knew that the memory of the Famine and Easter 1916 could form both a community and a whole framework of explanations for a world; while for others, often living just meters away from the first group, the Covenant of 1912 and the first day of the Somme in 1916 could be, equally, fundamental facts that explained the world and one's place in society. Two sets of memories, each seemingly complete, forming two communities. Memory creates the present and the future, and indeed the past, for it is through memory that we have identity and purpose, and search out and evaluate the past. The present is, more often than we realize, the prologue to the past!

Likewise, on hearing of 'memory' we think primarily in terms of individuals: my memories are different to yours; my memories are what are most intimately 'mine'. But as social beings, who live in real historical communities, memory is a social phenomenon.[49] It is memory that constitutes communities, and a community without a shared memory simply cannot exist as such. Memory, and how it forms us (and it has formed communities of the followers of Jesus since the beginning),[50] will feature on every page of this book. Memory is a present reality, but in this present exist all the pasts that make us who we

---

[49]This book will take its perspective on social memory from the work of Maurice Halbwachs (1877–1945), see Halbwachs 1992; especially as this was linked to commemoration within communities in the work of Barry Schwartz, see Schwartz 1982.

[50]It was in such communities that the memories of Jesus were recalled and their identity as his followers was built up, see Kirk 2010.

are; and it is this memory-enriched present that makes us who we are as we move forward out of our memory into our projected future. Likewise, it is this memory that evaluates what we find in our past and why that past is, so often, not shared despite our illusion that there is a moment 'then' common to us all. This 'present', 'past' and 'future' belong not to me but to us whether we call ourselves a community, a church, 'the church' or more vaguely those who seek to follow Jesus.

By highlighting 'memory' as distinct from thinking in terms of ontological distinctions between a moment today, a moment in Jerusalem so many centuries ago, and a 'future' moment, we can understand why many issues that have arisen over the course of Christian history in relation to the Eucharist have proven so intractable of solution. Moreover, a focus on memory allows us to search out ways that can resolve traditions/memories without continually re-fighting old battles in the hope that 'our side'/'orthodoxy' might finally be able to land a winning blow against an opponent. Because memory is, of its nature, multiform – and *de facto* has always been that way: even in the earliest historical evidence we see the interplay of the variety of memories of Jesus[51] – so also is theological explanation. Once one form of the memory of Jesus, or more precisely of the eucharistic meal, is imagined as 'genuine' (to the exclusion of other memories), as has happened all too often in eucharistic controversies, then the primary reality, practice, is disrupted by the secondary activity of reflection and explanation. Then the abstraction becomes the blueprint for activity; and the problems for later clashes embedded within the tradition. Eventually, the diversity of the *corpus* of memory collides with the insistence on a particular detail, and the result is a division into factions in conflict. And groups with sundered memories – which include all Christian denominations today – find it difficult to imagine that others who do not share their memories are engaged in the activity they hold so dear. Attention to memory helps us approach how the Eucharist developed in the churches, why it was placed at the centre of ecclesial *anamnesis*, appreciate the structure of Christian disagreements, and with the task of helping Christians engage in thanksgiving with one another.

It will become clear over the course of this book that a community's rituals, memories and identity are closely intertwined realities: indeed, they only become distinct within the process of analysis by which we seek a deeper appreciation of what is experienced as single reality. At one level this is a trite observation: one has but to look to the vehemence with which liturgical 'innovations' are resisted within churches, particularly if the innovation it imagined as making 'us' more like 'them', to see that rituals and identity (especially if that identity is felt to be under threat) are almost

---

[51]This can be illustrated by the variety of theologies in the first-century documents that eventually became canonical: the most glaring example of this is the three synoptics that are historically related not only in their target time – the period of Jesus on earth – and in their historical development in that both Matthew and Luke used Mark, but they form three distinct events of memory – and three different theologies of Jesus.

interchangeable words. I am reminded of the young Anglican and Roman Catholic clerics who I encountered recently. The Anglican is an evangelical and deeply antagonistic to modern worship trends exemplified by *Common Worship* which he sees as 'High Church Romanism', while the Roman Catholic is deeply antagonistic, though not verbally so, to the reforms of Vatican II which he described as 'Protestant-izing heresy'[52]: the moment of maximum agreement between them was that they would severally quietly ignore Church Unity Week. Embattled and fearful memories, formed as ritual and expressed as theology, prevent each of them both from (1) growth in understanding (not to mention mutual understanding) of their traditions' rich complexities and (2) being able to engage critically and creatively with their own traditions – and, consequently, being able to help those traditions to evolve within the ever-new situations we find ourselves, with our historical inheritance, as disciples of Jesus. Tradition consists in, as Picasso remarked, having a baby, not wearing your grandfather's hat!

But if memory is the possession of the community, and group identity takes physical form within the ritual routine of the assembly, does that not mean that liturgy is no more than an atavistic declaration of difference, at one extreme, or, at another, no more than a passing performance of what we think is 'relevant'? And it is worth noting that actual Christian liturgy often falls into one or other of these extremes. Equally, among many emigrant or oppressed groups the adherence to the familiar forms of liturgy becomes a matter of cultural defence and defiance: and any challenge to its form or language is resisted as akin to treason.[53] Likewise, there are many communities who, while often valuing the Christian 'holy book' as a sacrament, cannot envisage a community activity which is not 'spontaneous' and, apparently, without memorialized form.[54] But between these extremes lies the vision of the purpose of Christian liturgy that inspired it down centuries. Liturgy is an expression of a community encountering the living God and seeking to make progress on a way towards him, and, as such, should both model and help it in the establishing of the Kingdom. Robert Taft expressed this well: 'Liturgy is not a thing but a meeting of persons, a celebration of the expression of an experiential relationship'.[55]

---

[52]He was able to perform this piece of intellectual gymnastics of 'affirming the council' while considering the reformed liturgy as 'tending towards heresy' by positing a distinction between 'the council' and 'the spirit of the council' (assuming thereby that an event can be isolated from time)! On such anti-ecumenical trends in relation to the Eucharist, see Johnson 2006.
[53]For example: the Russian Orthodox Church was contemplating a reform of the calendar and the adoption of the living language in the early twentieth century, but abandoned plans in the light of the 1917 revolution.
[54]Many western churches whose origins lie in the eighteenth century pride themselves on not having a formal worship book akin to the *Book of the Common Prayer*, but they often fail to recognize that a pattern of worship has, unbidden, arisen among them: the participants unconsciously recognize the shape their assembly takes each Sunday – and they often defend it against what it sees as innovations.
[55]Taft 2000, 141.

This being the case, it is never enough to trace a liturgical form back to its earliest form (however instructive that process is for our understanding of Christianity), but rather we must evaluate all forms in terms of the finality of liturgy. This purpose links our need to recall the memory of Jesus, and to affirm our belonging to his community who seek to progress on the path which he initiated for his disciples, while fulfilling the task of all liturgy: the worship of God (which, for Christians, is offering praise and petition to the Father 'in Christ'). Our belonging is, therefore, not to an original past, but to the original future vision, ever unfulfilled historically, which is inaugurated through participation in the Paschal Mystery. So we look backwards in our ecclesial memories not to reinvent the past, but (1) to understand afresh the original vision of the future and (2) to grasp how we arrived here today, and so assess how far we need to travel in the future to be more fully members of the community of the Christ.

The theologian's vocation

All knowing takes place within traditions whether this is acknowledged, as is often the case among theologians, or not. The fundamental assumptions of our knowing form 'the tacit dimension' within which we question, discover and make sense of the world.[56] However, and this is something particularly true of theologians, while many see their task as that of repeating, codifying, simplifying that tradition through its transmission – and have gloried in that role vainly proclaiming that they have not 'innovated' anything in the process[57] – this is not the sole task of the theologian. Polanyi spoke of the researchers' 'sense of calling' that working within a tradition, which they have been trained to serve, that they not only repeat common learning, but also seek to make renewed, fresh contacts with the realities that are valued and explicated within that tradition. The researcher is seeking a fresh encounter with the real. So the task facing a theologian is not to reframe what has been said, but to seek anew the fundamental realities which the tradition codifies – so in the case of this book the task is to make fresh contact with that activity that is 'eucharist': the blessing of the Father in the shared Christian meal.

It is this effort to confront afresh the fundamental realities, which develops historically in the tradition through practice and doctrine, that constitutes the ultimate purpose of historical theology. This aim can easily be confused with the search for origins, as if having found the 'original kernel' from which all practices stems, one has in hand the solution to all problems; but it is far more involved than that. The result of the search to elaborate as fully as possible the history of the activity is the preparation for looking at what is involved in this activity within the structure of the disciples' lives;

---

[56]See Polanyi 1966.
[57]See O'Loughlin 1999, 273–95.

and from this hoped-for confrontation with reality, with its warts and its gems, its flashes of insight and its confusions, will come, hopefully, a fresh appreciation of this particular activity.

In effect, this means that the theologian has to respect all her/his sources, while at the same time refusing to grant any particular historical moment paradigm status. Each to some extent, greater or less, refracts the Christian understanding of the activity of being 'eucharistic', and it is the theologian's task to construct an appreciative understanding from the fragments that are those individual historical moments. The result is neither a synthesis nor a summary of the history, but a new vision of what is contained in the traditions regarding the Eucharist which can inform the ways we go about, and talk about, the activity of being eucharistic in our actual situations. So if one can talk about an ideal of eucharistic activity, it is as a result of the study of umpteen actual celebrations and theological reflections, without identifying any one of them as 'the ideal' which we can access by some process akin to exegesis. History provides the fragments and the historian's craft determines the manner of assessing those fragments with accuracy, but it is the theologian who seeks out what is the significance of each for our understanding of this central activity of believers while we look to the future. This action is, when well done, not bound by the repetition of 'common knowledge' contained within the paradigm, but seeks to be a fresh encounter with the reality of Christian existence and must also somehow provide a vision for disciples as they confront the need to be eucharistic both in this moment and for the future.

Theological approaches

This approach is not one with a long history in the churches. Over the last four centuries, the desire to find the original theology of the Eucharist has taken three paths. The first to emerge was the exegetical (the matter of the exegesis varying with the sides of the Reformation debate). The Last Supper – as found in the scriptures – was seen as the perfect event and the absolute paradigm: if one could fully understand that meal (i.e. in effect, those sacred texts which were themselves inspired, inerrant and sufficient) then one had all one needed as the core.[58] The second, emerging in the nineteenth century, was the notion that the perfect Eucharist existed not only in the Last Supper but also in the 'apostolic church' – and so the quest became one of finding the earliest evidence, a perfect early time, and treating it as normative. The problems inherent in this approach were legion and need not concern us

---

[58]Such works as Higgins 1952 or Jeremias 1966 are classic expressions of this method, but it still emerges whenever the 'New Testament' is thought of as a reality within Christian understanding distinct from being the products of communities: for example LaVerdiere 1996 or Witherington III 2007.

here,[59] but the by-products of this quest (such as an awareness of the rich diversity and difference of early practice) have transformed our ways of looking at the Eucharist. Moreover, this research has impacted on the manner of the celebration of the Eucharist in many churches, and this is a process that continues steadily to make ground.[60] The third approach has been to take a church's present position – defined in councils, law and catechisms – as that which is the mind of Christ, and then to see history as an apologetic arm of its catechesis showing that while there may be differences between the present and the past, this is simply the passing of time in the process of bud, acorn, sapling and mighty oak. There has, it is admitted, been 'development' but this is defined in such a way as to make it the opposite of real historical change. This latter approach has had its greatest exponents in the Catholic Church – and while the approach seemed to be disappearing in the mid-twentieth century, it is now undergoing something of a revival – and it continues to be used extensively in Orthodoxy.

These older approaches are still practiced, in a variety of ways, by many theologians; and for many they come together in concerns about one 'event': the Last Supper.[61] It is as if this meal is somehow immune to all the problems, long recognized, about the historicity of events in the life of the historical Jesus.[62] Therefore, gospels – all four of them – and Paul are read as if they could be mined for a 'real-time' narrative of the evening before the death of Jesus: one can appear to know when specific events happened, the words and actions of Jesus, and the sequence of actions. Moreover, one can know who was there and who was not, namely 13 men with Judas leaving before the crucial moment, and that this was a uniquely significant event of formal 'institutions': obviously of the Eucharist, and, for some Christians, of an ordained 'priesthood' who could continue this 'sacrifice' and also continue the chain of ordinations which is imagined underlying 'apostolic succession'.[63] So much seems to hang on this evening, reinforced by the now habitual use of the institution narrative in eucharistic celebrations – with the exception of the East Syrian rite which preserves earlier practice[64] – and

---

[59]See O'Loughlin 2012a.

[60]The Liturgical Movement's great advances in historical understanding which paved the way for reforms of liturgy in many western churches in the latter half of the twentieth century began as the search for the 'perfect' liturgy of 'apostolic times'.

[61]See the interesting approach of Meier 1995.

[62]The perception that the Last Supper is a moment of almost real-time narration is no doubt a result of the frequency with which it is invoked in the liturgy as just such a moment, and because it is one of the most recognizable events in the life of Jesus in art; but, ironically, the problems of its historicity are among the oldest concerns regarding the historicity of the gospels; see O'Loughlin 1997.

[63]That is, all that is contained in the *liturgical memory* for the celebration of the 'Mass of the Lord's Supper' at the beginning of the Easter Triduum in the Roman Rite on Holy Thursday evening.

[64]See Taft 2003.

given visual expression in Christian art, that it seems almost impossible to distinguish history and theology.

Unpicking the elements of memory and kerygma that made 'the Last Supper' stand out as the final meal in a sequence, and so the moment of passing on the fundamental image to the communities who employed this memory as part of their foundation narrative of their distinctiveness as disciples of Jesus is one task. Unpicking the significance of those accounts, being retold and mutating in the life of the churches until those accounts became rigid as canonical scripture, for the eucharistic practices of those same communities is a separate affair.[65] An equally distinct historical task is that of unpicking how the later theological edifice took that memory and recast it as 'history'. And we should note that this process of recasting that meal as a conjunction of historical time and theological event took place within a situation where that meal was being historicized, and so theologized, within the annual Easter liturgy – then reinforced on a weekly, if not a daily, basis. However, any theologian approaching the history of the Eucharist must consciously separate these levels of ecclesial memory as his/her starting point in any investigation of either Eucharist or ministry if he/she wants to avoid taking one later theological formulation and then finding it as 'original'. This separation is routinely carried out by those who see themselves as investigators of 'scripture' or 'early Christianity' – who ignore matters of later theology and contemporary practice – but this book will argue that this is a necessary discipline for theologians precisely because of its benefits, first, for setting doctrinal statements about the Eucharist in perspective, and, secondly, appreciating the nature of Christian liturgy as anamnetic rather than mimetic.[66] However, while it is necessary to avoid letting 'The Last Supper' distort our historical perception of the early churches' practice, that does not mean that we can side-step the theological questions that have been generated by that myth. Not to take account of those questions would transform this book from an essay in historical theology into one more properly seen as belonging to the history of early Christian structures. So, for example, it remains important to pursue a question such as the significance of the Eucharist being 'instituted' by Jesus but it is not enough to study accounts of 'The Last Supper' to answer the question.

Theology for much of its history has sought either to break free of the historical conditions in which Christians live (a desire that was often expressed as the wish for a 'classic theology' that was not a reaction to

---

[65]We shall touch on this issue in more detail in Chapter 6.
[66]It might be argued that this is a point that is, today, redundant. However, one has but to note the frequency with which a statement such as 'there were no women ordained at the last supper [because there was none there]' can be enunciated as a factual argument against women as presbyters to see that this view of the Last Supper is still very powerful among a group who would imagine they were not textual literalists.

heresy in some form or other – and so could be seen as 'timeless'), or else seeking to demonstrate that while one could not 'escape history' that it was, nonetheless, of little or no real significance (e.g., notions that stressed changing theological languages and practical manifestations while holding that 'essences' do not change – and so theology 'developed' but its core was immune to temporal alterations). By contrast, this book will take changes for granted, and see whether amidst this variety of Christian actions one can piece together a way of looking at the Eucharist that both accords with our inheritance and the situation confronting us of seeking to be a community of disciples giving thanks to the Father.

2

The focus of eucharistic
thinking: Thanking the Father

The focus of eucharistic thinking can be understood to be about thanking the Father: 'In our prayers for you we always thank God, the Father of our Lord Jesus Christ'.[1]

One of the interesting developments in the latter half of the twentieth century was the number of churches that abandoned inherited titles for the eucharistic gathering in favour of the term 'Eucharist'.[2] These older titles include 'Mass', 'Holy Communion' (as used as a name for the whole service), 'Holy Communion' (as used as an addition to 'Mass' such as in 'Mass and Holy Communion'), 'Communion Service', or 'Lord's Supper' or variants on the theme of 'the Lord's Supper'[3] as the designation of a particular form of liturgy/ceremony.[4] While those older terms still survive in popular parlance, they are rarely used in theological discourse, and increasingly less used in pastoral practice. This, despite the fact that the Greek-based term 'Eucharist'

---

[1]Col. 1.3.

[2]This is, for example, the principal term used in Vatican II's key document on the liturgy, *Sacrosanctum concilium*, in the title of its second chapter: 'The Most Sacred Mystery of the Eucharist'; however, it is used throughout the document interchangeable with the term 'Mass'; for early modern interest in this term it is interesting to note that J. Hastings' *Dictionary of the Bible* (1898) did not have an entry 'Eucharist' but T. K. Cheyne's *Encyclopaedia Biblica* (1901) did have; on the origins of the term and an example of early modern interest in its use, see Hort and Murray 1902.

[3]The German '*Abendmahl*' (literally: 'evening meal') is the invariable Protestant name for the eucharistic liturgy; but note this significant piece of translation: when Jeremias's book *Das Abendmahlsworte Jesu* – originally published in the 1940s (the second German edition appeared in 1949) – appeared in a new English edition in 1966, it was entitled 'the *eucharistic* words of Jesus'.

[4]Some churches try to cover every possibility as if 'Lord's Supper' and 'Eucharist' as simply different names without any shift in emphasis, much less theology; for example, the Church of Ireland in its 2004 *Book of Common Prayer* has a second liturgical formula flagged as 'Holy Communion Two' with this masthead: 'The Celebration of Holy Communion also called The Lord's Supper or The Eucharist' (p. 201).

needs to be decoded into everyday speech, usually as 'thanksgiving'. However, while the early Christian term 'Eucharist' has gained this new popularity as a term expressing what Christians are seeking to do at such gatherings, few have noticed how this word has a completely different theological frame of reference from the set of words it is replacing.[5]

Part 1: We have got problems

Christocentrism and the Eucharist

While many use the word 'Eucharist' as simply a synonym to a word like 'Mass' as the name of a service, the primary intention of the word 'Eucharist' relates to an activity – the act of thanking or giving thanks – as befits a word that is derived from a verb. While such words as 'Mass' and 'Communion' are all too easily linked in our minds with religious objects: the 'Mass' something you attend (or 'hear' or 'get') and 'communion' as something you 'receive' (or 'take'). The actual act of 'taking communion' or being a 'communicant member' might relate to an activity, but it is an activity relating to a ritual object. Moreover, it relates to the historical sphere: if one were to think about it as 'communicating with God' most Christians would expect the activity to be described as 'praying' rather than being present in a building for 'Mass' or 'Holy Communion'. For many the notion of holding the Lord's Supper relates to an event on a particular day which one chooses to attend or not. This event is then linked to the words and actions of Jesus, seen as fulfilling a Scriptural command, and as an act of teaching: modelling a way of community. Moreover, in contrast to terms such as 'the Lord's Supper', which immediately 'recall what happened on the first Holy Thursday' – and a recollection of that unique moment in the past – Eucharist refers to an event occurring in the present: we celebrate the 'Eucharist' or share in 'the Eucharist' today.

More profoundly, the older terms have their theological focus in Jesus – celebrating his meal, re-enacting his last supper with his disciples, encountering him in 'the sacrament', making him present, entering his presence or our being present at his sacrifice, enacting his sacrifice, receiving his body and blood, . . . – while the focus of 'Eucharist' is the activity of giving thanks to the Father. We thank him for all his generosity in, through and with the Son. Eucharist is an activity directed to the Father by us who are 'in Christ'. In short, titles like 'Holy Communion' are directed towards Jesus – and reflect that common understanding of eucharistic activity; while the term 'Eucharist' is directed towards the Father. We shall see on several

---

occasions in this book an unacknowledged tension between the 'direction' towards the Father that is inherent in the early sources to which Christians constantly return and the 'direction' towards Jesus which is perceived to belong to 'do this in memory of me'.

Significantly, if we look over the history of Christian in-fighting over the Eucharist, we see that it is wholly focused on the relationship of the ritual event to Jesus – is he 'present', how is he present, how did he come to be present, how does our doing relate to his sacrifice and so on. On the focus of the Eucharist upon the Father, if we ignore the issue that sacrifice has to have an object (an aspect of disputes over sacrifice that was not itself disputed), there is virtually no disagreement! That said, there is precious little on the Father as the focus of the Eucharist in our legacy of theological writings. Probably from the time that the 'institution narrative' became part of the Eucharistic Prayer,[6] the interest of participants shifted from the Father to Jesus. The extent of this shift in theological interest can be seen in what is one of the most eminent early patristic studies of the Eucharist: Gregory of Nyssa's (c. 330–95) *Catechetical Oration*, 37.[7] For Gregory, the value, wonder and mystery of the Eucharist lay in its encounter with the Christ in the consumption of the elements.

Stating that the fundamental dynamic of the Eucharist – as with all Christ-based activity – is thanks directed to the Father by us 'in Christ' empowered by the Spirit appears so elementary as a statement of Christian theology as to be hardly being worth mentioning.[8] Is that not the state of affairs brought about by the Paschal Mystery into which each of us is plunged in baptism?[9] This may be a fundamental theological truth, but it is one that only came to prominence in thinking about the liturgy in the first half of the twentieth century,[10] and it has not penetrated very deeply into the consciousness of Christians. In practice, we not only ignore it in most of our activity and thinking about the Eucharist, but often when it is raised with regard to the Eucharist, it generates a dissonance running right through our eucharistic activities. For example, it is noticeable that many of the 'culture wars' regarding liturgy that affect many of the churches today are fought over this fault line (even if this fault line is itself unrecognized).[11]

---

[6]See Ligier 1973.

[7]See Srawley's edition of Gregory 1903, 141–52; this will be dealt with in more detail later in this chapter.

[8]See Verheul 1968 as an elegantly clear statement of the theocentric nature of liturgy.

[9]This is the approach taken in Vatican II (*Sacrosanctum concilium*, 10 – although there is a tension in this section between viewing participation in 'the Lord's Supper' as the expression of sacrifice to the Father and as an end in itself); on the liturgy as the Paschal Mystery, the work of Odo Casel (1886–1948) remains fundamental, see Casel 1999.

[10]The re-discovery of the nature of the Eucharistic Prayer – addressed in all cases to the Father – was one of the major themes in the work of the Liturgical Movement.

[11]It is noticeable that in conservative Catholic circles there is a marked preference for the term 'Mass' and 'Holy Mass' over the term 'Eucharist', while many on the evangelical wing of Anglicanism dislike the use of the term 'Mass' by 'High Church' clergy.

It is as if we can make the statement that all liturgical prayer is directed to the Father whole-heartedly when we engage in the theology of liturgy – or discuss trinitarian theology liturgically – but when we take part in a eucharistic event on the following Sunday morning – be it sign-posted as 'Divine Liturgy', 'Holy Communion', 'Holy Mass' or 'Eucharist' – we are involved in a celebration of, memorial of, recollection of, encounter with the Word made flesh, or with the need to remember the words and deeds of Jesus.[12]

This shift of focus from the Father is such, and so basic to how we might build a theology of the Eucharist, that it is worth noting its extent in our practice. For many strands of Christianity, the word 'sacrament' is a word used in relation to the Eucharist. Thus for those who count 'the sacraments' – implicitly reifying them as distinct sacred objects – the Eucharist is either one of seven or one of just two such objects. But what is this sacrament? It is the 'sacrament' of Jesus Christ. As a sign points to its object, and as a sacrament effects what it signifies, so the Eucharist brings about the encounter with Jesus. The sacrament is that which links me (or perhaps us as a community) with the Christ. The notion that it is the Christ who is the sacrament between me/us and the Father, and that it is him who connects me/us to God, lies below the horizon of thought.[13] How this 'sacramental' linking of me/us with Jesus takes places, the dynamics of the presence of Jesus established by the sacrament may be disputed in all its details (and have been in the west since the time of Berengarius (c. 1010–88)),[14] but that the sacrament related to Jesus has not been an issue. For Catholics, the word 'sacrament' has taken on an additional range of meanings due to the late scholastic method used at the Council of Trent (1545–63) which distinguished between the Eucharist as (a) a sacrament of sacrifice to the Father by Jesus Christ and (b) the sacrament as a sacrament of the presence of Jesus Christ.[15] It was the presence of Jesus Christ – his 'real presence' – that was a primary focus of dispute; consequently, a pattern of theology/catechesis grew up which concentrated on when Jesus became present (the moment of consecration), how this occurred (transubstantiation) and how

---

[12]These two perspectives – expressed in liturgical style, sermons and hymnody – are both focused on Jesus the Christ; and it is some sort of encounter with him which is the activity's purpose.

[13]While traditional christology spoke of the humanity of Christ as 'sacramental' of his divinity, and more recent theology speaks of Jesus as 'the sacrament of our encounter with God', in the theological sub-specialism of 'sacramental theology' the emphasis is on the sacraments being encounters with Christ: being joined to him in baptism, fed by him in the Eucharist, being in him, healed by him, forgiven by him . . . in the other 'sacraments'.

[14]See Macy 1984, 35–53; and Chadwick 1989.

[15]Trent dealt with the 'sacrament of the most holy Eucharist' in 1551 (Session 13) – see DS 1635–61; it dealt with 'the sacrifice of the Mass' in 1562 (Session 22) – DS 1738–54. The greatest concern was on the presence of Christ and its mode (Session 13), and the later treatment of 'sacrifice' built upon it – if Christ were really present in the sacrament, then it followed that it could be his sacrifice.

it endured (after the celebration of Mass).[16] And all these issues were then reinforced in the minds of all participants by their expression in liturgical ritual.[17] Hence, because it was the divine Son of God whose presence had been established by the celebration of a Mass, he was now really present and so could be 'adored'.[18] The celebration of Mass was indeed a work, an activity – the *opus operatum* – whose result was the making present of Jesus sacramentally; and this was 'effected' through the recitation of *canon actionis*[19] (or at least the dominical formulae) by a validly ordained priest *ex opere operato*; and 'proof' that this had been a 'valid' (a concept whose finality was coterminous with 'real') was that the Christ was sacramentally present on the table after the 'consecration'. This possibility that one could 'effect' the Eucharist by simply the recitation of the words '*Hoc est enim corpus meum*' might be seen as arguing from an extreme – but that it was so argued[20] (and in official Catholic teaching the possibility is still held to exist)[21] meant that the Eucharist could be detached from the act of blessing the Father. This meant that the Eucharistic Prayer – in actual reality, eucharistic praying – was, in the final analysis, otiose.[22]

Effecting presence

This raw approach 'to making Jesus Christ sacramentally present' (and the qualifier 'sacramentally' tended to disappear in the concern that eucharistic presence was 'real' presence) was infrequently found in theological textbooks, but because it was the basis of many judicial decisions, it was seen as 'the bottom line' of Catholic theology, and it was certainly the basis of actual practice. Put bluntly, it meant that when an Anglican chaplain aboard a British

---

[16]These concerns of Trent became standard theses for exposition in theological handbooks, see, for example, Gihr 1942 – a manual in use for more than half a century, and typical of Catholic theology prior to Vatican II.

[17]This can be seen in the manner that within Roman Catholic ritual until 1970 (and still to a large extent today) the moment of significance was the moment of 'consecration' – kneeling, bowing, salutes, bells, incense, additional lights – or in the fact that 'communion' was given from wafers 'consecrated' at one Mass and then used over several later occasions (the only wafer consecrated at most Masses is that eaten by the priest himself).

[18]On the origins of 'adoration' of the Eucharist, see Mitchell 1982, 163–84. This needs to be set in the context of 'reservation of the sacrament', on which topic, Freestone 1917 is still a basic text.

[19]This was the rubric describing the Eucharistic Prayer in the missal promulgated in 1570 in the aftermath of Trent.

[20]Thomas Aquinas, *Summa Theologiae*, 3a, 78, 2 is the classic statement of the position.

[21]The current Western Catholic Code of Canon Law, canon 927 states that it is a crime (*nefas est*) to consecrate bread or wine, no matter how urgent the need, outside a eucharistic celebration – but it does not state that such an act is invalid, merely that the one who could do such an action (i.e. someone with presbyteral orders) and has done it, has committed a crime.

[22]See the elegant critique that one can have the eucharistic reality without reference to the Father in Burkhard 1994.

warship during World War II asked if he could 'reserve the sacrament' in a Catholic 'tabernacle'[23], he was refused on the basis that just as live and blank ammunition could not be stored in the same magazine on board the ship, so the result of a real Eucharist (the Catholic 'blessed sacrament') could not be stored alongside the result of an invalid – mock/blank – Eucharist such as that celebrated by the Anglican who was not (according to official teaching) anything more than a (presumably) well intentioned but theologically confused layman![24] One wafer was [sacramentally][25] 'the body and blood, soul and divinity'[26] of Jesus Christ (and it was the Mass that has produced this), the other was a bland wafer of flour and water! Clearly, the focus of the Eucharist within this theological framework was upon the sacramental presence of Jesus, and the encounter with Jesus was the fundamental to it. This polemical Catholic position became the focus of other churches' theologies of the Eucharist as they calibrated their own positions in relation to it,[27] and those who tried to steer other courses became but whispers in the wind.[28] Its very extremity, itself the result of dispute, could be said to have unbalanced most thinking about the Eucharist over the last four and half centuries among western Christians; and not the least problem for all concerned is to find ways of moving on that are not prejudiced by the after-effects of this barren battleground.

---

[23]The term used for the locked box in which the sacrament is reserved; during the Counter-Reformation period, it came to occupy the central focal position in Catholic church buildings.
[24]This story, which may be apocryphal, has 'done the rounds' over the years as an example of one approach to the Eucharist, and it was certainly retold when I was an undergraduate in theology in the early 1980s: faced with explaining why a Catholic could not communicate at an Anglican celebration, the lecturer's final position was expressed as 'it comes down to facts: would you genuflect after an Anglican had recited the formula of consecration?' The lecturer, taking *Apostolicae curae* (1896) as his datum, simply assumed that because nothing had happened, there was no basis for participation. The crime involved, for the Catholic, would therefore be one of 'formal' idolatry – treating a waver as worthy of reverence. This would not be a crime for the Anglicans for, not recognizing their own inability to consecrate, they proceeded in 'good faith' and so committed, merely, 'material' idolatry. In using the latter distinction between 'formal' and 'material' idolatry, that lecturer was invoking a position set out by Juan de Lugo (1583–1660), see De Lugo 1869, 3, 419–20 [= *Tractatus de sacramentis in genere*, 8, 12, 187–91].
[25]What is included in [] indicates the difference between formal theological expression and what was actually believed among Catholics.
[26]This phrase became common among Catholics through its use in numerous catechisms – it is taken from Session 13, Canon 1 of Trent (*DS* 1651) where it is stated that anyone who denied this and said that the Christ was present only in a 'sign' or 'figure' or 'by power' was anathema. As a tag used in Catholic question-and-answer catechisms it was still in widespread use in the 1960s; though, I was still able to find one on sale in a Catholic Church in Nottingham in 2011.
[27]See Pusey 1855 – which is still one of the complete surveys of the origins of a christocentric understanding of the Eucharist.
[28]For example, the approach of Jeremy Taylor (1613–67); see McAdoo 1988.

This Christ-focused approach to Eucharist can be seen, most clearly, in the cult of the sacrament as an object of worship.[29] The feast of Corpus Christi[30] – the celebration of the presence of Jesus in the 'species'[31] – became from the thirteenth century the Eucharistic focus of the liturgical year (with Holy Thursday being seen as the historical re-enactment of the Last Supper). Indeed, the devotions and reflections linked with the feast of Corpus Christi became a central plank in all western practice and thinking on the Eucharist prior to the Reformation; and the *casus belli* thereafter.[32] Theologically, the debate became the question as to whether or not this presence was such that it could be reverenced with the worship due to God alone (*latria/adoratio*). For many of the churches of the Reformation, this was a distraction from the true focus on Christ as the saviour now at the right hand of the Father as the unique interceding priest who offered a unique and unrepeatable sacrifice on the cross.[33] While through Counter-Reformation over-reaction this sacramental presence led to a multiplication of devotions based on the notion of 'adoration' of 'the Blessed Sacrament' which in their popular appeal often were more 'attractive' than Mass itself![34] But wherever one stood on these bitterly contentious issues, there was one point of virtually unanimous agreement: Jesus Christ was the focus of the whole liturgical affair we now call 'Eucharist'.

---

[29]See Mitchell 1982.

[30]The feast originated in the thirteenth century and spread throughout the Latin church; its name was changed in 1969 to '*Corpus et Sanguis Christi*', but this has not changed either at the level of practice, not has the addition of a reference to the cup altered its focus and iconography which is firmly on the reserved sacrament with the monstrance as its icon.

[31]'Species' became a technical term in scholastic discourse on the Eucharist in an attempt to find a term that would cover the physical fact that whatever change took place as a result of consecration, no change was visible with the eyes: what began as bread retained all the humanly perceptible qualities of bread (and likewise in the case of wine). So this term came in to use to describe the object as perceived and handled with the ordinary senses (sight, touch, taste) without making any statement about its extra-perceptual ontological status. Because the term '*species*' was used in scholastic psychology for that which impinged on the mind as a result of sensing an external material object, this term seemed suitable as a way of describing the physical object without committing oneself to a word that could be seen as tantamount to disbelief. So the cleric was to 'carefully consume all the crumbs of the sacred species' left on the paten, whereas if he said 'all the bread crumbs' it could be taken as a statement that is was 'still bread'. The corrosive results of this word game on liturgy will be examined later.

[32]The sermons written by Thomas Aquinas for the liturgy during the octave of this feast (*Officium de festo Corporis Christi*) are far more representative of view of the Eucharist that was preached than anything found in the *Summa theologiae*.

[33]This often expressed itself in concern over the meaning of *ephapax* ('once for all') in the Letter to the Hebrews (7.27; 9.12 and 26; and 10.10) and recurring Christian rituals.

[34]In comparison with the dullness of attending 'Low Mass' – and few ever attended the more elaborate forms which even then were remote from all but those in the 'sanctuary' – being present at the annual 'Forty Hours' or even weekly 'Benediction' was a synaesthetic event of imaginative power, quite literally, full of 'bells and smells'.

A sacrament, the sacrament, sacramentality

Thus, the Eucharist was the Christian sacrament *par excellence* which was
'administered', 'received', 'reverenced' or 'visited'. In each case, the Christ
was coming to his people, present among them, or was 'there' as the object
of their attention, prayer and worship. The whole of this approach to the
Eucharist can be seen in two material objects within Catholic practice. First,
the tabernacle placed (from the seventeenth century onwards) in the very
centre of the 'high altar' in the very centre of every religious building.[35] The
presence being indicated by a burning light; and the presence was there so
that he – the sacrament was always referred to in personal terms – could be
visited and be a real object of private prayer. Second, by a special instrument
for displaying 'the Host' so that it could be easily seen: the monstrance. The
monstrance was used to 'expose the blessed sacrament' when it was the
object of formal liturgical prayer and 'adoration'. Parallel with this focus
on the presence of 'the body of Christ', the majority of Catholics (as was
also the case with members of other churches) only 'received the sacrament'
once a year (even for the pious or for vowed religious, other than priests,
'receiving' only occurred on a handful of occasions each year).[36] So while
formal Catholic theology had introduced a confusing distinction between
the 'Eucharist as sacrifice' and the 'Eucharist as sacrament', in lived theology
there was a three-fold distinction: (1) the Mass at which one was expected
to be present (expressed legally as the requirement *sub poena peccati* 'to
hear Mass on Sunday and other appointed days'); (2) the Blessed Sacrament
which had its own liturgy and spirituality, which one was expected 'adore';
and (3) 'receiving Holy Communion' which was infrequent; but which canon
law demanded should take place 'once a year around Easter'.[37] However,
what the law laid down as a minimum became, as is the way with minimum
targets, an expression of a maximum. Moreover, the act of 'communicating'
became intrinsically problematic in that people feared 'unworthy reception'
and all that was connected with the need to receive 'worthily' and in a
'state of grace'.[38] This fear of receiving Jesus in the Eucharist was itself
much older that the Counter-Reformation period, but continued in many

---

[35]See Jungmann 2007, 108–9.

[36]St Clare (1193/94–1253), founder of the Poor Clares, wrote that her nuns must receive seven
times each year on specific feasts – and this was, though, extraordinarily frequent.

[37]This was known as 'the Easter Duty' and the law extended the concept of 'Easter' beyond
any sensible liturgical meaning of the term as running from Ash Wednesday to Trinity Sunday.
Because one had to be free of 'mortal sin' to receive communion – and such certainty demanded
sacramental confession – the 'Easter Duty was presented – and still often is – as involving
'Confession and Communion once a year'.

[38]The requirement of making auricular confession was never without severe pastoral problems;
it was simpler to seek to avoid 'going to communion' than face the ordeal of confession. So
that which was intended to prepare the individual for the Eucharist became one of the factors
acting as a barrier to communion.

churches until well into the twentieth century,[39] and still persists in popular Christianity.[40]

The irony involved in this legal situation is instructive for anyone thinking about the theology of the Eucharist today in the light of the recent past: the Eucharist was seen as so distant from ordinary Christian desire that one had to make attendance a matter of a penalty – one attended Mass 'under pain of sin' (*sub poena peccati*) – while what could be seen as the ritual culmination of the event as expressed in the language of the liturgy – which was about eating and drinking – was so divorced from practice that one had to be commanded to participate fully, *sub poena peccati*, but the legal principle that 'restrictive law binds minimally' meant that most obedient Christians were involved in the Eucharist only to the most minimal extent consistent with not breaking the law. Simmering beneath the confusion was an irreconcilable notion of the virtual impossibility of mixing sanctity with sinfulness in actual life: so the Eucharist was transformed from being the food of those on the Way into being a reward for the godly. Thus it came to be perceived as something that those aware of their own ungodliness should stay clear away from as far as possible, while those who did not see pursuing a special holiness as part of their life-task simply ignored except in so far as they had to avoid sin.

The distant Eucharist

If the Eucharist was understood primarily in terms of an encounter with Jesus, and was then theologized in a Christ-centred way, it was also a reality to which people related in a distant, indeed fearful, way. The reality of their participation in a celebration of the Eucharist was their attendance ('presence' would not have been used in this case nor would it have expressed the ritual reality) at the making present of Jesus in the sacrament by the priest.[41] Meanwhile, for Catholics this distance was increased not only by the use of Latin,[42] but also by the fact that most of the liturgy took place in

---

[39]To explore the extent of deep-rooted fears about the Eucharist within Anglicanism – a factor that limited the attempts of the Oxford Movement to promote a richer eucharistic theology – see Knight 1995, 53–7.

[40]If one notes the proportion of those taking part in religious events where a celebration of the Eucharist is 'part of the programme', one will notice that many who believe they are participating would never dream of 'going to communion' – which is seen as a step too far.

[41]The notion of the 'priest' both theologically and culturally as the one who was other than the layman (women were *ipso facto* excluded from this debate): the layman, like a woman, could only attend the sacrifice; the priest could celebrate it. We see this distinction worked out culturally in detail in writings such as those of Bede (see O'Loughlin 2014); and it still manifests itself in common parlance among Catholics: the priest is 'the celebrant' (assuming the others present do not celebrate) and 'says Mass'; others 'attend Mass' or 'get Mass'.

[42]On the use of Latin being a factor alienating participants from the event at which they were present, see O'Loughlin 2013d.

either silence (e.g. during the Eucharistic Prayer)[43] or near silence. The time was to be occupied either with silent prayers (such as the Rosary) or, on special occasions in affluent parishes, with music; the aim was to make 'a spiritual communion' – actual 'reception' not even being considered – with Jesus whose presence had entered one's vicinity. Moreover, one was in the presence of the perfect sacrifice. The Mass as a sacrifice was 'the unbloody' (*incruoris*) re-enactment of Calvary. This was not thought of in terms of sharing in Christ's offering to the Father, but as one now standing at the foot of the Cross (along with Mary and John whose stance there was recalled in hymns such as *Stabat Mater*, rood screens and reredos paintings behind altars) while his death took place. To share in the sacrifice was to offer one's own sacrifices to Jesus, and then be present while his sacrifice took place, on the unbloody altar, before which one knelt. As Mary, John, the good thief, and the centurion had stood on the afternoon of the first Good Friday; so now the faithful Christian participated in the sacrifice by presence at Mass. The Mass broke down time's separation, and one was there standing amidst the saints as the Lord gave his life for us all. It is captured in stone on many Tridentine altars where the words, from 1 Pet. 3.18, *iustus pro injustis* were carved on the front of the table.[44] One was not participating in the sacrifice to the Father; one was involved only in the more distant mode of being present and observing, and in so far as one who had made other sacrifices separately.

While the presence of Christ and the individual's presence in the presence of Christ were central to the Eucharist (in Trent's terms both as 'sacrament' and 'sacrifice'), the dominant thinking about the event of physical engagement with the Eucharist was imagined in terms of a sacred commodity. The priest 'confected' the Eucharist, it was reserved for adoration and the sick,[45] it was received when someone chose to receive Holy Communion, and one could 'get communion' 'outside of Mass'. Indeed, this was so standard a practice that there was no provision for anyone other than the priest to 'communicate' in the 'ideal text' (the *editio typica*) of the Roman Missal promulgated in 1570. While at that iconic event of the young independent Ireland, the High Mass of the 1932 Eucharistic Congress in Dublin – famous for the hundreds of thousands present and the singing of a then famous Irish tenor: John McCormack – only one person, the celebrating bishop, actually ate and

---

[43]Then called 'the canon' whose main function was understood as bringing about the consecration of the elements; indeed, this was seen merely as giving accidental form to the words of institution, see above for details.

[44]Pet. 3.18 reads 'For Christ also suffered for sins once for all, the righteous for the unrighteous (*iustus pro iniustis*), in order to bring you to God. He was put to death in the flesh, but made alive in the spirit'.

[45]These two uses of the reserved sacrament have been linked since Trent (*DS* 1645); there the antiquity of one was seen to justify the acceptability of the other – without recognizing that the understanding of the role of sharing in the Eucharist by eating a particle of the common loaf had changed in the intervening period of more than a thousand years.

drank of the eucharistic food. One could gather to honour the Eucharist, discuss the Eucharist, adore Christ in the Eucharist and be present at the Eucharist, but it was not seen as incongruous that the gathering did not communicate at that central event – yet the kernel words of the consecration formula included imperatives of 'taking', 'eating' and 'drinking'.[46] Nothing else was like it, it was the most holy commodity, and when it entered one's body, there must be a clean soul and a clean stomach, and it was not even – according to popular preaching and inherited practice – to touch one's teeth.[47]

The ironical situation was that the Eucharist was declared central by theologians, and certainly was at the centre of a great deal of religious fuss, but it was also distant from people in a variety of ways. Between its own language and its practice, there was almost a complete dissonance, between its claims as the sacrament of love and the reactions it evoked – already in the seventh century the Eucharistic Prayer was referred to as the 'oratio periculosa' (the dangerous prayer),[48] and, indeed, participation in any way at its celebration was peripheral to actual everyday discipleship. This ironical situation deserves careful attention as without an appreciation of this Christ-centred peripherality of the Eucharist, many of the roots of contemporary theology, and not least the need for a thorough-going reform of eucharistic theology and praxis (such as was initiated by the Second Vatican Council's reforms),[49] cannot be understood. This can be explored by looking at how many Catholics in the aftermath of Trent experienced the Eucharist as part of the cycle of life. In contrast to the east, the western churches had long separated Eucharist from initiation: baptism made one a Christian – and a member of Christendom – and the Eucharist was a boon that was, to all intents, a completely separate gift. As such it needed both (1) awareness of what it was (defined minimally as an understanding of what it was not: it was not bread [wine did not enter the picture for Catholics]) and (2) a state of grace for its reception. This led to the development of 'the' special day: 'First Holy Communion'.[50] This was to take place in the early teen years when the recipients were considered old enough to appreciate the

---

[46]This phrase became common among Catholics through its use in numerous catechisms – it is taken from Session 13, Canon 1 of Trent (DS 1651) where it is stated that anyone who denied this and said that the Christ was present only in a 'sign' or 'figure' or 'by power' was anathema.

[47]See McGuinness 1999.

[48]See Jungmann 1955, 2, 205.

[49]There is a considerable body of Catholic opinion that insists that Vatican II did not initiate anything, but made some external changes in the ritual, and that these changes, promulgated in 1969, were to be seen as one completed act; after that there was to be simple repetition of the new arrangement without change. Even if one does not commit oneself to such view of human history as this perspective implies, one cannot make those changes without implicitly recognizing that the inherited rite was flawed – but that one 'hastens slowly' in reforming liturgy.

[50]For a fuller analysis of this most complex eucharistic event, see McGrail 2007.

august gift, but ideally before puberty when 'impure' thoughts might make reception difficult.[51] However, the encounter with Jesus was still a fearful affair and so 'First Confession' normally took place on the day before. First Holy Communion provided the basic Catholic understanding of the Eucharist: one would welcome the body of Jesus into one's own body, and this private and individualized encounter was to be understood as the most sacred possible moment in life. This was a rather different theology of the Eucharist to that found in formal textbooks, but it would be reinforced by culture and repetition – and even if the young First Communicant would later become a cleric, that understanding of the Eucharist, more often than not, remained with him. Eucharist was an intensely intimate, private meeting with Jesus, but one hedged about with fear over worthiness, personal purity, the fears that surrounded Confession as a preliminary to receiving Communion, and even about such practical matters as whether the preparatory fast had been performed correctly.[52] At the other extreme of life, the Eucharist as 'Viaticum' was the final moment in the so-called 'Last Rites' – and, by a curious trail, the formula for the administration of Communion on any occasion was, until 1962, the formula originally intended for Viaticum.[53] Again, the Eucharist was seen as located on the extremities of life – linked to a time of fear, and peripheral and distant from everyday existence. This sense of fearfulness was reinforced at other times. While the medieval practices such as referring to the canon as the 'oratio periculosa' and swearing oaths on the Host might have disappeared, the 'sanctuary' was railed off, and there was a fear of touching the species. It was a sacred commodity which demanded reverence, to be kept separated from ordinary world, and it was encountered as a fearful meeting with Jesus Christ.[54] Indeed, this focus on the sacramental presence of Jesus has been seen as characteristic of Catholic spirituality in the period between the seventeenth and mid-twentieth centuries.[55]

---

[51]Most Catholics now associate 'First Holy Communion' with the first years of school and use the rule of thumb of 'the age of reason' or 'about seven' – but this practice only began in the early years of the twentieth century; prior to that time, 14 or 15 would have been normal.

[52]It has been argued that the reform of the fasting regulations had the greater impact on Catholic eucharistic practice than any other development in the renewal of the liturgy.

[53]'May the Body of Christ guard you unto eternal life'.

[54]The extremes of this position can be seen, on the one hand, in the so-called Eucharistic Miracles when a consecrated wafer became actual flesh and blood before the eyes of the a priest lacking faith in the 'real presence'; on the other hand, it can be found in those who abandoned any willingness to 'receive communion' as they were traumatized by the notion of cannibalism. Between these extremes fell most ordinary Catholics, who might be reminded of this sort of literalism by stories such as that of the saint who, seeing someone leaving the church immediately after receiving communion, sent two acolytes with candles (the normal escort to the Blessed Sacrament being moved from one place to another) to accompany the man: the aim being to show that until sometime for digestion had elapsed, he was irreverently taking the Eucharist into the streets in his stomach!

[55]Jungmann 2007, 93–103.

The origins of christocentrism

It is impossible to identify precisely when this emphasis on encountering the Christ as the object of the Eucharist began, but it was certainly a major theme for Gregory of Nyssa whose *Catechetical Oration* presents a detailed exploration of how the Christian encounters the Word made flesh in the eucharistic elements, and with a corresponding understanding of 'the prayer of blessing' (*tés eulogias*) as having the function of 'transforming the nature of what appears before our eyes'.[56] For Gregory the Eucharist is a locus of encounter between the baptized person and his/her Lord. In all likelihood, the origins of what eventually became this christocentrism lie in the desire that the eucharistic meal be seen as an imitation of the last meal of Jesus. With the inclusion of the Last Supper mimesis – the Institution Narrative – into the heart of a prayer directed to the Father the focus moved from the purpose of the Lord's prayer to the excitement of the participants in being 'present' as the great event. This interest in re-creating a specific gospel moment is not an isolated phenomenon: we see the same process (usually referred to as the process of historicization) in both the development of the liturgical year,[57] in biblical exegesis[58] and in the developing interest in the Holy Places as pilgrimage sites.[59] As is the way with liturgical evolution, this inclusion did not displace what was already there but sat alongside it, and gradually became the major focus of attention.[60] So while the anaphora remained formally addressed to the Father (and in the case of several eucharistic prayers (e.g. the dominant Latin form: 'the Roman Canon') had several repetitions of 'through Christ our Lord'), this focus on the Father receded from attention through the manner in which the canon was recited,[61] and the way it was received,[62] all focused on the presence of the Christ. The pattern once established could then be embellished – the most extreme examples being the introduction of the presentation of the elements along the chant '*Agnus Dei*' after the recitation of the Lord's Prayer[63]; and

---

[56]*Catechetical Oration*, 37, 141–52; Srawley's notes on the text, despite their age, are still invaluable and a great assistance in translating the text; with regard to *tés eulogias* he renders it as 'the prayer of consecration' (p. 152, n.7) which imposes a later western view of the prayer.
[57]See Bradshaw and Johnson 2011, 60–8.
[58]See O'Loughlin 2010b on the process of ensuring that the gospels were historically coherent.
[59]See Markus 1994.
[60]Such evolutions over time usually do not generate much attention, and so few notice how the development actually subverts the original purpose: it was the fact that earlier forms survive and coexist with later disruptive intrusions that was at the very core of Baumstark's method: see Baumstark 1958 and 2011.
[61]For example, bowing while reciting the dominical formula, saying it word by word as effecting the actual conversion of the elements, treating these words as sacred utterances.
[62]For example, it was the moment after the consecration that became the focus of bells, incense, torches and salutes; and it was to that moment that the congregation's attention was directed and 'devotional attendance' was seen as reverence for that moment.
[63]This entered the Roman rite in the last years of the seventh century, see Jungmann 1955, 2, 332–40.

then later in the west the development of the elevations as the moment in the re-enactment of the drama of the Last Supper and Golgotha.[64]

The Eucharist as a private affair

One other aspect of this christocentric approach, implicit in what has already been said, needs to be noted. Although the Eucharist was envisaged as an act of the community, and the Mass was seen as a public legal act regulated in the smallest details by church law, ironically, for both those who 'said Mass' and those who 'heard Mass' it was an intensely private affair where little or no notice of the community needed to impinge. The language of the liturgy was still in the plural, the command *orate fratres* can serve as a sample, but the understanding was firmly in the singular.

From the perspective of the lay participant, this was an encounter in the depths of the soul and as such it did not have any real relationship (i.e. a relationship that affected what was happening) with other members of the church. The only human relationship that had any bearing was the presence of the celebrating priest: if the priest was there, then there was Mass; if not, there was nothing. As regards others, whether it was just you and the priest or you and myriads of other Christians, that was a wholly accidental matter: it made no difference. It was not us who were acting in giving thanks, it was not us who were encountering Jesus, but it was me who wished to link my sacrifice *per accidens* with that of the celebrant, I who was making spiritual communion in my private prayer, and I who might decide to receive communion if I had so prepared myself by confession and fasting. It was then within this private 'space' of my soul that the wonder of meeting Jesus in Holy Communion took place. If this had any implications with regard to others, it was a matter of derived moral implication: having been in the presence of Jesus, I should resolve to live a holy life, and this demanded certain patterns of action.

With regard to the celebrant, at least in Roman Catholic understanding and with roots going back into the early medieval period, it was the high point in the individual's quest for sanctity, and as such was the basis of the unique 'privileges' of the priesthood.[65] The priest was so special, so distinct among Christians and so elevated precisely because of this individual ability to encounter Jesus: his hands were sacred because he, and he alone, handled

---

[64]This entered the Roman rite sometime in the later twelfth century, see Jungmann 1955, 2, 206–16 – note that already, long before the Second Vatican Council, he was calling attention to the appropriateness of worship of the Blessed Sacrament at this point within the liturgy (pp. 214–15).

[65]There is a large literature – although with remarkably little written in English – on this as a problem within traditional Catholic theology: see Rahner and Häussling 1968; Häussling 1973; Vogel 1980, 1981, 1983, 1986; Angenendt 1983; Angenendt and Schnitker 1983; and O'Loughlin 2009a and 2014.

the sacred elements which were handled in 'the sacred and venerable hands' of the Lord himself. He did not depend on others for the celebration, but could perform it alone save his need for someone 'to answer him'.[66] Indeed, he could even say Mass completely alone – despite the fact that the law frowned on the practice.[67] The Mass was the priest's private affair, which he performed for the community or simply for himself. It was, and to an extent still is, true that priests would describe the celebration of Mass primarily in terms of their own spirituality or monk-priests describe it in terms of an extension of their own self-consecration begun in the act of taking vows.

While recent popes would inveigh mightily, and correctly, against a world of individualized consumerism, they did not see the irony that in permitting and promoting older forms of liturgy and older visions of the presbyterate, they were promoting a liturgy that was the apotheosis of such a consumerist individualism. No other aspect of older views on the Eucharist is as clear-cut as the implications of the practice of 'private Masses' (*missae privatae*), and the corresponding lay spirituality, to point out the need for a radical overhaul both of eucharistic practice and theology.[68]

Christocentrism in practice

The legacy of these developments is still with us today and affect *all* the churches, directly or indirectly. Even those churches who might not see themselves as in continuity with, much less the heirs of, those groups of Christians among whom this development took place, one can see impact and aftermath. Go into virtually any church building when a celebration of the Eucharist is taking place, and there is a strange dissonance between, on one side, what the key liturgical actions and texts demand from their very nature and language, and, on the other, what long established prayers, customs and expectations stress as the kernel of the activity. At the heart of the celebration is the activity of thanksgiving – eucharist – and so the prayer of thanksgiving is addressed·to the Father and concludes with the doxology: we make this prayer to the Father through, with and in the Christ. But the practical focus is upon the encounter with Jesus. This encounter may be presented as a recollection of his Last Supper and death, or as the coming of Jesus within the elements however this might be represented theologically, or with the fact that the prayer has as its 'product' that now there is the holy food which – again with a variety of expressions – allows an encounter with Jesus, and especially his death and resurrection. This christocentric focus will be reinforced in many traditions by official texts such as the memorial acclamation, the 'Lamb of God', the private prayers of the president, the

---

[66]See Lysaght 1991 for the extent and depth of this spirituality in actual Catholic belief.
[67]The law still does frown on the practice, but it is a law that was and is frequently ignored by clerics who inhabit this world of individualized spirituality.
[68]See Rausch 1990.

ritual actions of the ministers, and very often by the occasional interventions of the president by way of emphasis or explanation.

This christocentric interpretation of the purpose of the gathering will then be further emphasized in that culmination of the liturgy, the actual sharing in the loaf and cup, is seen as the moment of making communion with Jesus. Because we naturally expect that the finality of any action coincides with the final action in any sequence, this act of 'receiving the sacrament' is perceived as the rationale of the whole event: everything is preparatory for that moment. Nor will anything that precedes the Eucharistic Prayer disturb this interpretation. For example, liturgical theory may declare that the Prayer of the Faithful is a priestly intercession of the community with the Father – a central expression of the universal priesthood of the baptized and as such focused on the Father. But, in practice, this dimension remains below the theological horizon and these intercessions take the form of shared prayers often being addressed to the Son or the Spirit – and in Catholic practice they often include prayers addressed to Mary or the saints to further the theological confusion.[69] Earlier in the liturgy, the readings, in those traditions which use a lectionary, will often be centred on the gospel text – and thus christocentric,[70] while the introductory rites contain the appeals to the Christ (*Christe eleison*), and the president's words of welcome usually dwell on the christological significance of the assembly: they are now in the presence of Jesus just as the first disciples were when they met him in Galilee. This dissonance in liturgy hides a greater theological confusion about why we engage in this activity – and both confusion and dissonance usually go unnoticed.[71] However, Christians continually renew their imagining of their activity by engagement with the memory of the earliest times – indeed for most churches this has its most prominent manifestation at their eucharistic gatherings – and there we see a very different focus summed up in the term 'eucharist'.

Part 2: Is there an alternative?

Eucharist looks to the Father

Our earliest securely datable reference to the religious significance of the meal gatherings of the followers of Jesus comes from Paul's first letter to the

---

[69]See O'Loughlin 2012b.

[70]Most modern western lectionaries are formulated on the principle that each year (over a 3-year cycle) presents one evangelist's view of Jesus; see O'Loughlin 2012c, 66–75.

[71]It used to be argued that the Catholic Church was aware of this problem and seeking, to overcome it gradually as witness the suppression of the theologically bizarre prayer '*Suscipe, sancta trinitas*' (and other formulae like it) from the liturgy, and the abandonment of the notion of 'the canon' as 'confecting the sacrament' in favour of the term 'Eucharistic Prayer' – however, the sanctioning of the unreformed liturgy for continued use implies that a renewed lack of official recognition of the failings of that liturgy for purpose.

Corinthians written in AD 54.[72] The nature of that gathering need not concern us for the present, but simply Paul's view of that church's objective in celebrating their meal in a particular way. Paul, distressed about the implications of certain of the group's practices at their regular meals together, offers a theological reflection on what he sees as the significance of sharing a loaf and a cup (10.14-22) as the eucharistic moment of their common meals. Paul then underlines the theme of a right way of sharing within the whole meal by an appeal to an origin story, focused on the expression of thanking God, as the basis of the practice (11.23-9).[73] Yet while explaining their fellowship (or the lack of it) in terms of their meal being a sharing in the body and blood of Christ (10.14), Paul is clear that the focus of the attention in uttering these blessings is the Father.[74] They offer praise to God, the Father, and can do so because they are in Christ. This community in thanking the Father acts in contrast to those with many so-called gods: 'for us there is one God, the Father, from whom all things and for whom all things exist, and one Lord, Jesus Christ, through whom all things and through whom we exist' (8.6). That being the case, their prayer at the meal must not be idolatrous (10.7), they must flee practices that are tantamount to idol worship (10.14), and then sharing in Christ they can offer the cup of blessing (10.16) – and this blessing is of the Father. Thus, in the act of properly sharing the cup and loaf of the Lord, they offer a sacrifice not to demons but to God (10.20). Gathering for the meal proclaims the Lord Jesus's death until he comes (11.26), but to be waiting on his return is to be waiting for him who 'delivers the kingdom to God the Father' (15.24).

Abhorring idolatry, Paul cannot imagine any true prayer – such as a meal's prayer of thanks – as being directed anywhere but to God – and for the followers of Jesus, this is a prayer placed before God, the Father, through Jesus. As it was through the gift of the Law that Jews could offer God true worship, so it is through Jesus that gentile Corinthians can do so. It is through this meal they participate in Christ and so take part in the worship of God that will come to its finality with the eschaton.

This theme that the thanksgiving at the community's meals is focused on the Father also finds expression in a passage, 14.1-6, in the letter to Romans – and so this passage too must be viewed as relating to early eucharistic practice.[75] It was probably written with 'detailed knowledge of the contemporary Roman ecclesiastical scene' in the spring of AD 56.[76] The context, as in Corinth, is dissentions at the common meal – some feel they can do one thing, others that they cannot, and there seems to be recrimination

---

[72]The dating is that of Robert Jewett 1979, 48 and is widely followed, for example Murphy-O'Connor 1996, 280.

[73]See Hollander 2009.

[74]On 'blessing' as the act of blessing the Father, see Kilmartin 1974, 273–5; see also Burkhart 1994.

[75]I am indebted to Prof. Robert Jewett for drawing this to my attention; see Jewett 2007, 846–7.

[76]The quotation and date are both from Murphy-O'Connor 1996, 332.

and bitterness as a result. Paul seeks to answer these disputes – probably the
first dissention over the ritual uniformity among the followers of Jesus – by
reminding them of the purpose of their meals together:

> Those who observe the day, observe it in honour of the Lord. Also
> those who eat, eat in honour of the Lord, since they give thanks to God
> (*eucharistei gar tó theó*); while those who abstain, abstain in honour of
> the Lord and give thanks to God (*eucharistei tó theó*). (14.6)

Within the community, the purpose of both eating and not eating is that
God be thanked by them – this is reason for gathering for the Lord's Day
(for those who hold to this practice)[77] and the reason why some see such
importance in eating together. However, Paul believes that all these disputes
can be resolved by locating them in their ultimate context: thanking God.

What is perhaps most significant about these passages, written within a
couple of years of one another, is that for Paul the very structures upon which
he bases his teaching in one church, he is quite prepared to relativize in another,
but what is not negotiable is the act of thanking God. This is the rationale
for a properly conducted meal in Corinth, lest there be conduct that amounts
to idolatry; this is the rationale for why the Romans should not be arguing
over the details of eating together in special gatherings, for no matter what
happens, as members of the church, they should be giving thanks to God. This
alone is the purpose of the followers of Jesus having meals together.

Although debating the date of the *Didache* has become one of the sub-
specializations within early Christian studies – especially among English
speakers,[78] one can hardly doubt that its traditions reflect usages that
became well established in the first century, and with regard to its material
on the Eucharist it reflects the situation before AD 70.[79] We have here table
prayers reflecting a clear Jewish context, and equally clear in their focus
of thanks.[80] In the *Didache* we find this prayer supplied as a model for
the householder, who is a follower of Jesus, to offer what is already being
described as 'the sacrifice of praise' – and as such something being offered
to God now addressed as Father[81]:

> Now this is how you should engage in giving thanks (*tés eucharistias*),
> give thanks (*eucharistésate*) in this way. First, at the cup, say:

---

[77]The implication is that these communal meals were taking place more frequently than once
a week – we shall see later that the notion that eucharistic sharing in food can be restricted
to particular occasions (e.g. 'the Sunday Eucharist') is itself a diminution in eucharistic
understanding.

[78]O'Loughlin 2013a.

[79]Milavec 2003, 351–421; O'Loughlin 2010, 85–104; Walker 1980 offers a different route to
an early date and makes explicit links between its eucharistic practice and that of Paul.

[80]All research on the prayers of the *Didache* is in the debt of Finkelstein 1929; and see Draper
2007 who develops the theme in a manner parallel to that being used here.

[81]See Milavec 2003a; and note Audet 1959.

We give thanks (*eucharistoumen*) to you, our Father,

for the holy vine of David, your child (*tou paidos sou*), which you have made known to us.

Through Jesus, your servant (*tou paidos sou*), to you be glory forever.[82]

Then the pattern is immediately repeated:

Then when it comes to the broken loaf say:

We give thanks to you, our Father,

for the life and knowledge which you have made known to us.

Through Jesus, your servant (*tou paidos sou*), to you be glory forever.

Here we see theological self-understanding within the earliest communities when they were engaged in worship – worship which took place in the setting of a real meal: they blessed the Father through Jesus.[83]

Blessing/thanking God – it is God, not the food at hand, that is 'blessed' – in gratitude for food was 'hard wired' into the notion of the covenant. It was God who had given his people 'a land flowing with milk and honey' (Deut. 26.15), and it was this gift of the land that was the basis of all other gifts, including the food it produced. For this, his goodness, God was to be praised. So at a meal, while the food on the table was the occasion of the thanksgiving prayer, the thanksgiving was not confined to what was on the plates, but extended to all God's gifts, indeed the whole creation.[84] The actual meal was a sacrament of all food, and of all of God's gifts to his people.

However, when we look again at the *Didache* we see that three important changes have taken place. First, God is addressed in a formal prayer as 'Father'. This, in itself, is not surprising as it is the basis of the relationship that Jesus established between his community and God.[85] This is the sonship that formed them as a new people who could call out 'Abba! Father' (cf. Rom. 8.15), and it is as such a community that the *Didache*, 8.3 prescribes that they pray the 'Our Father' three times daily. Second, instead of the prayer referring to the gift of the food there before them and, by extension, all God's gifts, now the thanksgiving ignores (verbally) the food and is solely concerned with the Father's gift of his Son. The food in the presider's hands is not even mentioned – yet the food is still the occasion of the prayer – and so has in effect become a sign of the Father's new gift. This sacramentality of

---

[82]*Didache*, 9.

[83]The full dynamic of this is explored by Draper 2007; and see Mazza 1995, 16–26. Both treatments should be read in conjunction with Milavec 2003a.

[84]See Bokser 1981.

[85]On the rapidity with which developed the appreciation of the eucharistic meal as an encounter with the risen Jesus, and thus that he could present the community to the Father; see O'Loughlin 2009b.

the food is then confirmed in the *Didache*'s next verse where the nature of a loaf becomes, itself, representative of the new covenant group with Jesus:

> For as the broken loaf was one scattered over the mountains and then was gathered in and became one, so may your [the Father's] church be gathered together into your kingdom from the very ends of the earth. (9.4)

But just as the prayer is addressed to the Father, so the object of the action of gathering is that the Father's people be united as his new people of God. Third, these prayers in the *Didache* are not simply offered to the Father by the group, but offered *through* Jesus – indeed, we see the familiar later formula '*per Christum Dominum nostrum*' in the course of formation in its repeated use in the text. It is the Christ's prayer to the Father; and the community, transformed and bound together in him by baptism like the grains of wheat transformed and bound into a loaf, are enabled to be there, and pray thus, through him. Although the *Didache* does not employ a priestly language about Jesus, it does see the eucharist as the community's sacrifice,[86] so we can see that their liturgy already contained elements that could form the basis of the priestly christology used by the author of Hebrews: 'Through him then let us continually offer up a sacrifice of praise to God, that is, the fruit of lips that acknowledge his name' (13.15).

The structure of prayer in the *Didache* can be summarized thus: at the community's meal, there takes place their act of eucharist to the Father. God is blessed for the gift of the child/servant who has given them life and access to him, and so this blessing by the church is made in and through this son of David. This was to become, if it had not done so already, the paradigm for all liturgical prayer.[87]

In some quarters, it may cause surprise that I have moved from Paul writing to the Corinthians and the Romans to the presuppositions of the *Didache* without stressing the divisions between the churches: it has been almost a working assumption in much Pauline scholarship that the *Didache* did not represent his style of Christianity,[88] while much of the work on the *Didache* has stressed its locale as being within Jewish Christianity.[89] However, given

---

[86]See Milavec 2003a for a perceptive study of this issue.
[87]See O'Loughlin 2012b where is theme is developed at greater length.
[88]See O'Loughlin 2013a.
[89]Not only would such a dating agree with Audet and Milavec, but would also be in accordance with the work of Niederwimmer 1998, 43 who posits a single redaction of the text 'at the beginning of the second century' assuming that the materials are all older than that time. However, we should note that (a) the pattern found in the *Didache* may well be independent of this document, and simply reflected in it; and (b) the crucial dating fact remains that the Eucharist as imagined in the *Didache* is distinct from the Last Supper origin story, and so prior to its widespread acceptance, which is, at the latest, coterminous with the diffusion of the synoptic tradition and so around the end of the first century: by that time the pattern reflected in the *Didache* was already so well established that it was not displaced by the origin story (and, therefore, the argument is immune to any late dating of the text). We shall return to this topic in detail in Chapter 6.

that we know so little about the period, while we must reject the temptation to imagine a mosaic from a few tesserae, we must also note that there was a body of common opinion among the followers of Jesus, and a good case can be made that the variety among the Pauline churches can easily be shown to have included many of the practices found in the *Didache*. This dispute about the significance of community meals in Rome, to which we have referred, can easily be explained by some in that community taking the practices of the *Didache* as essential to belonging to the church, while Paul's own concern not to be beholden to a church for his living can equally be his awareness of the sort of regulation of visiting teachers found in the *Didache*.[90]

So assuming that the practises of various churches throw light on one another,[91] we can now look at the eucharistic implications for a passage in the letter to the Colossians. While no agreement exists on whether this is Paul or Deutero-Paul,[92] this will not matter for our purposes as the point at issue acts as a summary of what is essential to this question in any formulation of a eucharistic theology that takes account of early Christian understanding, while it also offers a key insight into the perspective on prayer common among the followers of Jesus. The text in question, 1.12-20: the hymn of thanksgiving. The claim, moreover, that this prayer is representative of widely held views is strengthened by the fact that this prayer may be an existing element of tradition – taken as known in the churches by the fact that the author of Colossians incorporated it into his letter. While a good case has been made for seeing this hymn as eucharistic in the sense of its form being linked to Jewish table prayers and so being used at the community's meals,[93] it suffices for my purpose in this chapter to note the structure of its act of thanksgiving.[94] The church joyfully gives thanks to the Father (*eucharistountes tó Patri*) because the Father has made them sharers in the inheritance of the saints in light (1.12) although transferring them into the kingdom of his Son (1.13). This church is gathered and reconciled to God by the Son (1.20), but when it gives thanks, it continues (through the Son) the activity of Israel: it gives thanks to the Father.[95]

Giving thanks – the fundamental form of prayer over food within Judaism, and so the fundamental structure of those meals which were a central community activity of those groups who saw themselves as following Jesus – is an activity that is directed to God the Father; this thanksgiving is for all his gifts but most of all for their being gathered in his Anointed One, for it is through him that they were enabled to offer their thanks. But if this act of

---

[90]See O'Loughlin 2010, 121–3.
[91]I see the work of Thompson 1998 as offering an empirical basis for this assumption.
[92]See Murphy-O'Connor 1996, 237–9; however, the evidence all points to it being Deutero-Paul and it is as such that I read the text.
[93]See Gamber 1960; and Kilmartin 1974, 273, n. 17.
[94]The aspect of thanksgiving receives detailed attention – without any hint of a link between the hymn and 'the Eucharist' – in Lohse 1971, 32–61.
[95]See Robinson 1964.

thanking the Father is so important – whether it is linked with a community meal or not – did those communities imagine this as an activity that was part of the ministry of Jesus, modelled for them by Jesus, and given to them as a possibility by Jesus? To answer that, we have to know how they presented their own history to themselves to help them make sense of their own identity. We can see this in a cameo in the origin story used by Paul in 1 Cor. 11.23-6. There the action of Jesus 'on the night he was betrayed' is presented as their model for activity in that he took a loaf and a cup and gave thanks (*eucharistésas*) to the Father. This action of thanking the Father is presented as the basis for all meal activity by the churches. But if a memory of Jesus's activity was widely seen as paradigmatic of the churches' meal practice of thanking/blessing the Father, then our best evidence comes from the gospels.

Blessing the Father

The gospels are a presentation of history, but they are also part of our actual history in so far as they show us indirectly what the churches thought about themselves as the new people and how the community saw its own life formed in remembrance of Jesus.[96] In short, what the churches remembered – and through repetition emphasized – is the very process of Christian theological formation. However, from the moment we begin to recall a gospel as part of a theological argument, we are all too apt to move from the horizon of what the church remembered to that of what is contained in the memory. It is well to remind ourselves just what we are recalling in using the gospels in theology:

> The canonical gospels are in their primary intent mythical (we have become accustomed to saying 'kerygmatic') rather than historical. What can be known about the historical Jesus lies behind the Synoptics, in Mark and Q, more than behind John. But one must be skeptical as to the historicity even of the Synoptic Gospels, since, as form criticism insisted, they are primarily witnesses to the life of the primitive church and only secondarily witnesses to the life of Jesus.[97]

With this perspective in mind, and assuming on the basis of other sources (such as Paul and the *Didache*) that the communities gathered for meals at which the Father was blessed/thanked, can we read a gospel in such a way that it might illuminate how the churches were imagining these gatherings?

Mark is the obvious candidate in that we can confidently place his preaching before AD 70, and we know that his gospel was widely valued in that it was a basis for the work of Matthew and Luke, known to John,

---

[96]This assumes that the gospels cannot be localized to particular churches but were widely diffused from their outset, see the essays in Bauckham 1998.
[97]Robinson 1991, 177.

and was well used in the second century.[98] As Mark moved from church to church performing his gospel (it was a text for oral performance recorded on papyrus, not simply 'a book'), it is reasonable to assume that frequently the occasion for his performance was within a meal setting – at the community meal of the group he was with. If that was the case, then we can see references to meals within those performances as throwing light on the setting of the performance.[99] So did Mark pick up on this context (as any good communicator would) of a meal – eucharistic gathering when telling his story? What, if any, cues from the meal did Mark bring into his account to give his story immediacy? Did he, in other words, use the fact of what his audience were doing *as they listened* to help him to convey his gospel? Moreover, given that he was talking about Jesus who was known to have 'eaten with tax collectors and sinners' (Mk 2.15), would his audience have heard his story in terms of what they were doing while listening – and to that extent to have heard it in a manner we might term: 'eucharistically'? Did Mark's stories of Jesus' meals influence how they understood what they were doing at the meal they were then eating?

Mark's narrative opens with three domestic scenes, like the ones in which he is preaching. No sooner is Jesus with his followers than there is a supper in Simon Peter's house (1.29-31). Then he is in another house preaching with the group so packed in that the door is blocked (2.1-12). The packed domestic preaching scene may have been a familiar one to Mark when no one in a church had a large house, yet all wanted to squeeze in to hear him! Almost the next scene is another meal in a house: this time it is Levi's table and around Jesus are the rejected 'others' within society; and eating at that table is likened to medicine for the sick (2.15-7). And there is one other meal cue at this point: to participate in the Jesus' meal is to be like guests sharing in a wedding banquet (2.19) – proverbially 'the meal of all meals'.

Further into his gospel, Mark begins to use the very words already being used in the eucharistic dimension of the churches' meals. Mark has two great feeding stories: one of 5000 *men* and another of 4000 *people*. This was not just a bit of unthinking duplication, but a deliberate repetition to bring out a point that would have been obvious to Aramaic speakers but easily lost on his Greek audience. In the first feeding (6.35-44), we find this action: 'Taking the five loaves and the two fish, he looked up to heaven, and blessed, and broke the loaves, and gave them to his disciples to set before the people' (v. 41). Note the comma after 'blessed': we might

---

[98]The evidence for this is the extent of its second-century re-editing (see Koester 2007, 39–53) – a process in which the various endings are but the most obvious symptoms.

[99]The *symposium* structure of group meals in the first-century Mediterranean world made allowance for a performance of some sort – it is the legacy of this structure that has given us a Liturgy/Ministry/Service of the Word as an invariable part of our eucharistic gatherings. There is a large literature on the *symposium*, both as an ancient institution and as part of Jewish and Christian community structures, see Smith 2003.

think he 'blessed the loaves' but what it means is he took the loaves and blessed (*eulogésen*) the Father. In Jewish table prayers, the verbs for 'to bless God' and 'to thank God' were interchangeable[100]; and both terms passed on to the communities following Jesus. Then we move to the second feeding story (8.1-9) and find the other word 'thanking' used: 'and he took the seven loaves, and after giving thanks (*eucharisésas*) he broke them and gave them to his disciples to distribute' (8.6).[101] The two expressions, *blessing* the Father and *thanking* the Father, balance one another perfectly – making his point that both words refer to the one activity. And just in case the point had not been driven home, in his story of Passover meal we find this perfectly balanced pair of verbs: 'While they were eating, he took a loaf of bread, and blessed (*eulogésas*), and broke it, and gave it to them' (14.22), followed by 'Then he took a cup, and after giving thanks (*eucharisésas*) he gave it to them' (14.23).

These feedings are, for Mark, a key mystery his audience must think about. Therefore, after the feeding of the 5000 men, he says, almost cryptically, 'And they were utterly astounded, for they did not understand about the loaves, but their hearts were hardened' (6.51-2). There is more to that feeding than just hungry people getting some miraculous food. Then after the feeding of the 4000 people, Mark has a story of the disciples with Jesus in a boat and having forgotten to bring bread – indeed they have only 'one loaf' (*hena arton*) and think that will not be enough to keep them going! So Jesus gives out to them for letting their 'hearts be hardened' and asks them to remember how much was left over at the two feedings – and they can remember this. And the story concludes with Jesus saying 'Do you not yet understand?' (8.14-21). The point Mark wants his audience to appreciate (he uses the teacher's trick of letting them think they are smarter than those in the story) is that sharing in the one loaf is the key to being disciples of Jesus and sharing in his life. A point made in rather similar terms by Paul in 1 Cor. 10.17: 'Because there is one loaf, we who are many are one body, for we all partake of the one bread'.

It is quite possible that, like Paul, Mark had to deal with arguments about their community meals in churches he visited. We get two hints. First, the

---

[100]On several occasions Paul Bradshaw has drawn attention to the fact that words linked to 'blessing' deriving from the Hebrew *berak* are not synonyms for words relating to 'thanking' derived from *hodeh*, and he notes that they generate two different grammatical structures in prayers (see Bradshaw 1981, 11–16; 2002, 43–4; and 2004, 8–9); however, while he attacks 'the persistent misconception among many New Testament scholars that these verbs are merely synonyms that might be employed interchangeably' he then points out that 'both of the forms were in use by Jews in the first century' (2004, 8–9). The different verbs are significant in a pursuit of the origins of the wording of liturgical formulae, but are interchangeable in terms of their intention and real object in that both relate to God/the Father – as we can see in the way they are used in Mark.

[101]The phrase *eulogésas auta* [fish] (8.7) is a later insertion, note the marks around the words in N-A, revealing later confusion about 'blessing' as Christians moved further from appreciation of these Semitic expressions.

remark that it is 'not right to take the children's bread and throw it to the dogs' (7.27) which parallels the *Didache*, 9.5 'Only let those who have been baptised in the name of the Lord eat and drink at your eucharists. And remember what the Lord has said about this: do not give to dogs what is holy'. Could it be that this rule was being used to exclude people from the common table? If so, Mark puts this answer into the mouth of a triple outsider (a gentile woman in contact with a possessed daughter): 'Lord, even the dogs under the table eat the children's crumbs' – and Jesus healed her child (Mk 7.24-30). This hint at dissention in communities is also found in the dispute about which disciple is greatest (10.35-45). To sit alongside Jesus is to share his cup – cup sharing was as rare then as now: people were shocked that cup sharing was a central part of the eucharistic meal.[102] Drinking the common cup was to assert a common destiny with one another and with the Christ. Moreover, in this group, the leader must *serve*. Mark may have been well aware that people did not like sharing a cup, and the all too real possibility that meal leaders can forget they should serve, not dominate, the community.

Then the story reaches Jerusalem and Jesus is at supper with another outsider: Simon the leper (14.3-9). An unnamed woman anoints him, and Jesus predicts that anywhere in the world the gospel is preached (as Mark was now doing far from Bethany) this would be remembered (so a detail of that meal with Jesus is recalled at another meal). Finally, there is the Passover meal. Mark uses this annual event to provide a paradigm for the weekly meal of the churches he visits. What are they doing when they gather? How might they express what they are doing blessing the Father over a loaf and cup? They are sharing in the Passover meal of the Christ. Their meals and that Passover are the same event: their eating and drinking is eating and drinking in the kingdom of God (14.24). And who is this Christ? The answer is supplied in 14.61: 'Are you the christ the Son of the blessed?' In answering 'I am' Jesus declares his relationship to the Father whom he blessed at the feeding of the 5000 and at the Passover Meal – and at the meal that Mark and his audience have just shared. For the churches visited by Mark – and those who valued his gospel – their common meals were central to their expression of common discipleship. And so gathered, the focus of their attention in prayer was the Father: in this action of blessing they were acting as the Lord had repeatedly shown them.

One other point should be noted about the way the communities were remembering these meals of Jesus. Those which belong to this everyday world – be it a meal in the evening or the great meal in Jerusalem before the passion – all take place indoors in domestic settings very much like those of the later communities' meals; while those that take place outdoors – the feedings, the lakeside breakfast after the resurrection or the 'picnic' with James recalled in the *Gospel according to the Hebrews* – are all miraculous

---

[102]This practice's implications will be examined in detail in Chapter 6.

once-off events and are to be remembered as such.[103] The implication
is obvious: the Eucharist is part of the everyday, domestic life of the
churches.

The sacrament of worship

This sketch of Paul, the *Didache*, and Mark brings out, above all, the
importance attached by the early followers of Jesus to the action of
offering thanks, praise and blessing to God. This thanks was addressed to
the Father not only as an acknowledgement of his goodness as the God of
Israel, but expressed their attitude for the gift of his Christ who was, in the
Didache's words, their life and knowledge. Being eucharistic to the Father
was, therefore, a characteristic of their existence, and one specific occasion
for manifesting this aspect of their life was the eucharistic dimension of
their common meals where they expressed their unity with one another and
the Lord Jesus. That thanksgiving was a core activity, and that it could be
expressed when food was eaten should in no way surprise us. The service of
the temple in Jerusalem was a continual liturgy of praise and thanksgiving –
and so was at the heart of being the People of God, while the Law saw the
act of thanking God for food as a basic act of the people being aware of
their own identity as God's chosen ones: 'You shall eat your fill and bless the
Lord your God for the good land that he has given you' (Deut. 8.10) and
which is echoed in the *Didache*.[104] This centrality of being eucharistic to the
identity of the followers of Jesus should hardly surprise us: without it, one
would hardly be able to claim any continuity in the focus of prayer between
Judaism and the new movement. To offer praise and thanks to God is at the
heart of the covenant, it was the rationale for the temple in Jerusalem, and,
as remembered by the followers of Jesus, part of the time of the kingdom
would be perfect worship of God from the rising of the sun to its setting.[105]
This new movement was shifting its focus from the Jerusalem temple,[106] it
was making claims for its worship as the perfect praise,[107] and it was seeing
itself addressing God with a new intimacy[108]: but in the focus and purpose
of the activity there was no change. The followers of Jesus are eucharistic
to the Father.

---

[103]On the significance of eating indoors/outdoors, see Jones 2007, 111.
[104]*Didache*, 10, 1; see Klein 1908, 142; and Weinfeld 1992, 427–8 which sets the use of Deut.
8.10 in a larger context.
[105]*Didache*, 14, 3 echoing Mal. 1.11 and 14.
[106]*Didache*, 13, 3 shows that they were thinking of the own structures as paralleling the liturgy
of the temple; and see Jn 4.21-3 where the community's worship is equivalent to that offered
in Jerusalem.
[107]*Didache*, 14, 1–2.
[108]*Didache*, 8, 2.

Writing later (most probably more than a generation after the destruction of the temple in Jerusalem), Luke presents us with an idealized image of early liturgical practice:

Day by day, as they spent much time together in the temple, they broke bread at home and ate their food with glad and generous hearts, praising God and having the goodwill of all the people. (Acts 2.46-7)[109]

These 'summaries' are usually studied in terms of why and how Luke created the kind of history he did and we warn ourselves that they do not represent historical accuracy. However, it may well be that this is an historically accurate summary of the *earliest theological perspective* of the followers of Jesus. While they were in a situation when the temple was still functioning, and they were still within its geographical reach, the basic eucharistic activities continued in both the general, public sphere in the temple and in the sectional, group sphere in 'the breaking of the loaf' in their homes. Later this temple setting would become irrelevant, and then the sole eucharistic dimension of their existence would find its expression in the thanksgiving at meals. So they could recall for themselves that while eating food was ideally always an occasion for the blessing of God for his goodness – Deut. 8.10 – now it became for those who followed Jesus an occasion of thanksgiving to God such that it was all that the temple was and more – implicit in *Didache* 14, 3. If Jesus was the new temple, the great High Priest, and the one present among them, then in this activity at the meal they fulfilled all that belonged to the temple.

These meals – as the locus of their eucharistic activity – could be described as 'sacramental' in the sense that it was an action in the historical and created order, but also one that took place, through the action of blessing/thanking as recalled from Jesus's practice, in the presence of the Father. This sacramentality consisted primarily in that here at an event in the everyday world – eating together as a community 'in Christ' – they were also engaged in the activity of entering the divine presence and offering thanks: they were blessing the Father. While we are apt to see these meals in terms of their sacramentality as being 'encounters with the Christ', we must be clear that such an 'encounter' is but the basis of the central, purposeful sacramentality of their eating together: an encounter with the Father. In the light of later developments we could now describe the two sacramentalities in this way. In terms of its finality, the sacramentality of the meal lies in it being the locus for addressing/blessing the Father. And in being the sacrament of our blessing, it established communion with the Father. In terms of its origin, this is the christ-ian blessing of the

---

[109]This is the conclusion of the 'first major summary' in Acts covering the very earliest days in Jerusalem, and it begins with this description of the group's activity: 'They devoted themselves to the apostles' teaching and fellowship, to the breaking of bread and the prayers' (2.42).

Father – and so is an expression of the sacramentality of the Christ: he, Jesus, is 'the sacrament' of our encounter with God.[110]

This perspective of the early churches was well summed up by Kilmartin when commenting on the dynamic of the eucharistic institution narratives and early anaphoras:

> While one or other aspect of the Eucharistic mystery is emphasised in the prayers . . . the relational structure of the accounts of institution remains: thanksgiving to God for His mighty works in Christ is the *sacrificium laudis* of the Church undertaken with a view to obtaining deeper communion with the Father, especially through the sacrament of the humanity of Christ.[111]

In a nutshell, for those baptized into Christ, the activity of celebrating the Eucharist is the sacramental means of engaging in the activity proper to us as creatures which is praising and thanking the Father for all his *magnalia* – most especially for his gift of the Anointed One through whom we encounter him.

Part 3: Reviewing where we now stand

Naming our situation

This chapter has been motivated by the fact that over many decades I have heard it repeatedly asserted that there is little at fault with the inheritance of theology relating to the Eucharist: an emphasis here or there needs revision: some aspect of popular perceptions/celebration might need enhancement or cutting back, or that a few liturgical alterations will set matters aright! Such a conclusion can easily follow if one sees 'theology' (as found in books), pastoral practice (what is believed and expressed in worship) and liturgy (as a distinct study) as quite separate. But when an attempt is made to look at these areas holistically, then we glimpse that matters might be far more problematic. The first part of this chapter has sought to demonstrate this in terms of the individualist, 'encounter with Jesus' focus of most Christian practice, where the meal inheritance from early Christianity is either problematic or metaphorical. Viewed in this light, contemporary Christianity has 'big problems' with its eucharistic understanding and practice. But what is the alternative? This has been the focus of the second part of this chapter. Eucharistic activity originated in the reality of the communities' lives in that they ate together and in that setting carried out, in the way shown them by Jesus, that basic human action: blessing and thanking God. If this

---

[110]See Schillebeeckx 1963.
[111]Kilmartin 1974, 287.

analysis is seen to have value, then Christians today are faced with the need to recognize deep problems in both believing and doing, and must be willing to make changes that are more far reaching than those which have been part of 'liturgical renewal' programmes.

We began with the seemingly trivial observation that many churches had over the course of a century adopted the name 'Eucharist' for their ritual meal gathering. The use of this word – such a perfect coinage, first used in this technical sense in the *Didache*,[112] to express the purpose of their gathering – does not merely express a shift in liturgical emphasis, or even the desire 'to resource the present' by a renewed engagement with the fathers, but drives us to examine the whole focus of Christian worship.

The most obvious result of this re-examination is that it is better to think of 'Holy Communion' and 'Mass', on the one hand, and 'The Eucharist', on the other, as two distinct liturgical events. The former has emerged from the latter – and retained many traces of its origins – but in terms of focus they are distinct. The one is focused on the memory of Jesus and thought of as a sacramental means of encountering him; and this relates both to those who want to affirm these statements and to those, who in the tradition of the Reformation, want to take issue with them. The other is focused on the Father and is the christ-ian sacrament for blessing him.[113] It is the sacrament by which the disciples offer their sacrifice of praise which is announced in Mal. 1.11 in a sacrificial meal.[114]

Sed contra . . .

This claim will generate, at least two, responses. First, that this is nothing more than what is claimed by those churches which have emphasized the Eucharist as unbloody sacrifice of the new law. While there is some validity in this statement, it is an academic response whose primary value is that it protects the claim that 'the church' is in perfect continuity with the apostolic period. In fact, within a christocentric spirituality the Mass was seen as an encounter with the sacrifice of Jesus on the Cross, and his expiation of sin, not our sacrifice of praise in union with him. The relationship between the Eucharist as 'sacrifice' and the Cross as 'sacrifice' is too complex – as we shall see in a later chapter – to simply say that using the scholastic distinction of sacrifice/sacrament allows that withal it being

---

[112]*Didache*, 9, 5.

[113]The latter function was often carried out liturgically in recent centuries by such rituals as singing the *Te Deum* in thanksgiving for some act of divine goodness – if the original function of the Eucharist had impinged on those groups there would have been no need for such additional rituals.

[114]On this distinction between sacrifices, see Milavec 2003a; it will be examined in detail in Chapter 4.

'the sacrament of Christ' it is, as his sacrifice to the Father, focused on the Father.[115]

The second objection is that the liturgy is primarily the work of Jesus Christ and proceeds *ex opere operato*: whether individual Christians were thinking of the Father or the Son is fundamentally irrelevant (although better catechesis should be encouraged and perhaps a few ritual changes considered) as it has, as its *res tantum*, the glorification of the Father by the Son. While no one committed to a sacramental – indeed an incarnational – view of Christianity could really disagree with this lofty viewpoint, it really does not take us anywhere in terms of understanding, and does not take sufficient account of our dignity as human agents who are disciples. While incidentally, if we took this approach consistently, most theological work would be made redundant as in any sense a real search for understanding. We engage in liturgy within our overall cultural grasp of faith and reality – and, consequently, we make blunders, go off at tangents, and sometimes lose the plot completely. Rather than accept this, many Christians engage in drawn out defence of the notion that some core or kernel has been preserved inviolate in perfect continuity with 'the age of the apostles' – but with every added distinction they expose the threadbare nature of their arguments. It is far healthier for our understanding to acknowledge that the church forgets, but the church also remembers afresh.

There is, however, a yet more important outcome of this investigation. When looking at origins and developments, we can be faced with dissonance and discontinuity such that the act of anamnesis establishes a confrontation between our understanding of our origins and the process of tradition that has brought us to the present and given us our legacy of memories. When we look at origins and what later emerged, we discover – perhaps to our shock and surprise – that the relationship, far from being that imagined in studies built upon a notion of development, is actually one of dialectical contrast. So a legacy – perhaps powerful in its appeal to us for aesthetic reasons or because of the eminence of those who have adumbrated it: the cult of Corpus Christi, for example, with its elaborate pageantry, its rich hymnody and its deep cultural memories for those who took part in village, parish or city – may actually be that which has to be held in contrast with the memory of earlier periods if we are to explore the actual bases of our theology either now or in the past. This sense of discontinuity can be unsettling for several reasons. We seem naturally to favour continuity in

[115]Intellectually this holds true, but having discussed the matter some time ago with a friend who passionately held this position, we both found ourselves at a Roman Catholic celebration of the Eucharist: the president's procedure during the anaphora was to race through the words until 'the formulae of consecration' and then to hold the elevated wafer and cup for a full minute for 'adoration'! The Father as the addressee of the prayer, and the role of the Spirit in actualizing the community's act of eucharist were no more than vaguely recalled theological theses.

matters religious and ritual,[116] – and to imagine that our present is as the oak tree from the sapling: so we track backwards noting the continuities. Likewise, for many the notion of discontinuity is seen as the preserve of the churches of the Reformation – and to admit the problem is somehow to sell the pass! Unfortunately, the more historical investigation has progressed, the more it has shown that gradual drift can often change our religious perception to an extent far in excess of what any notorious heretic could. The differences between Luther, Calvin and Trent with regard to the Mass are but technical differences within a single intellectual paradigm in comparison with the theological shifts, such as that we have just explored, that took place unnoticed over centuries.

Anamnesis

If, however, the churches assert – and it is a fundamental strand of Christian worship – that the liturgy is an *anamnesis* of the work of Jesus, then they cannot ignore how they relate to their historical origins. The present and the past have to be brought into comparison, and then a decision taken as to whether the changes that have taken place should be welcomed as 'developments' or whether it is necessary to work for a reversal of those changes that are deemed pathological. This was glimpsed by the researchers who pioneered the liturgical movement in the twentieth century, but in events like Vatican II it was not explored in an open and comprehensive way mainly because the notion of discontinuity/disruption was not openly addressed. Implicit in the liturgy proposed in Vatican II – its Eucharistic Prayers being a good example – is the awareness that the existing rite was seriously flawed and that in many areas its focus was misdirected. However, rather than state this fact, it proceeded on the basis that there was a great continuity: all was well, and things were just going to be improved once more. Whether or not this approach was politically necessary at the time in order for its reforms to be accepted or necessary rhetorically because of the long tradition of asserting that no significant mistakes could be part of the tradition is one matter, but it has now generated unbidden consequences. First, the reforms' significance have often not been understood, and have thus been grafted on piece-meal to the existing edifice creating even more jumble, confusing theologies, and dissonance where what is claimed in liturgical texts is not consistent with praxis and vice versa. Second, failure to identify by name the real problems of the inherited rituals has facilitated a nostalgic backlash where the former rites are seen to have as great a validity, if not more so, than those which replaced them. This has led to the ironical contradiction of those conservative forces who are most concerned with enforcing a uniform praxis as a touchstone of orthodoxy

---

[116]See Chapter 1.

promoting the notion that one can pick one's eucharistic rite, and so one's theology![117]

The current Roman Catholic debacle should be a warning to other churches: historical investigations reveal pathologies in human edifices. Naming those pathologies and bringing inherited ideas into confrontation with earlier practices and understandings is an essential part of a healthy ecclesial, theological and liturgical culture. We will see examples of this confrontation in the subsequent chapters.

However, once that is said, it should become clear that re-focusing on the task of blessing the Father and recovering the basic eucharistic dimension of discipleship – which finds its most explicit form in a celebration of the Eucharist – raises some profoundly awkward questions regarding theology, preaching and practice for many. This is especially so in churches where 'the Eucharist' is traditionally held in high regard as the encounter with the Christ and where that perspective is encouraged through the notion that its central perceived action, eating and drinking,[118] is focused on 'receiving' Christ 'made present' – as if the risen Jesus is not already present in the gathering and its acting – and its extended reality is seen in terms of the 'Blessed Sacrament'. The fears and difficulties inherent in confronting this confusion – in every church a moment's confusion carried over centuries becomes that which is both 'orthodox' and most precious to identity – should not be underestimated! This is all the more so because the confusion of a christocentric theology of the Eucharist seems so satisfactory.

Among some Christians today it has become commonplace to describe the People of God as a 'Eucharistic People'.[119] This is an excellent designation in so far as it identifies a fundamental aspect of our creature-hood: the need to be aware of God's generosity and to offer him thanks and praise for 'even our desire to praise you [Father] is itself your gift'.[120] For Paul this was expressed in his comment to the Romans: whether one eats or not, the important point is to be eucharistic to the Father. This perspective can then

---

[117]See O'Loughlin 2010a.

[118]The attention to who can receive 'communion', who cannot and under what conditions, is a central area of concern for Christians 'in the pew'; moreover, this perception is further enhanced by the recent practice in Catholicism of having communion services in lieu of the Eucharist due to a shortage of clergy (see O'Loughlin 1998a).

[119]When recently I saw this phrase used in some leaflets at the back of a Catholic church-building, it was clear that as used it was intended purely as a variant on the importance of 'the Mass' as an encounter with Jesus, and the most practical expression of being a 'eucharistic people' in the life of that community was that there were regular periods of 'Eucharistic Adoration of Christ in the Blessed Sacrament'. Meanwhile, playing in the background was a recording of the music of a hymn which captures in a couple of line this christocentrism located in the reserved and 'exposed' species: 'O sacrament most holy, O sacrament divine, all praise and all thanksgiving be every moment thine'.

[120]See the Roman Rite of 1970, Preface of Weekdays IV: *Quia, cum nostra laude non egeas* [Father], *tuum tamen donum quod tibi grates rependamus.*

act to calibrate both churches' statements on the location of the Eucharist in their lives,[121] and also anything that is written, such as this book, about the Eucharist as a liturgical activity. But that means we need now to think anew about the practical activities of that activity of giving thanks; and so to this we now turn.

---

[121]For example, Vatican II's constitution on liturgy stated that 'the liturgy is the summit towards which the activity of the Church is directed; it is also the fount from which all her power flows' (*Sacrocanctum concilium*, 10) and 'the celebration of the Eucharist is the true centre of the whole Christian life . . . the summit of both the action by which God sanctifies the world in Christ, and the worship which men offer to Christ and which through him they offer to the Father in the Spirit (*Eucharisticum mysterium*, 1, B) – but both are understood christocentrically.

3

Locating our ritual: Food, community and prayer

'Most of the waking time of most of the men and women who have ever lived has been given to finding nourishment'.[1] Eating food is an inescapable fact of our existence. While we might question Ludwig Feuerbach's claim that 'man is what he eats', one can hardly question its inversion: if one does not eat, one soon ceases as a human being. Eating is a constant and central aspect of life. We in the modern developed world may have dissociated ourselves from virtually all the risks and toil of food production, have reduced the attention we need to give to our own sustenance to a minimum, and we can even talk of 'fast food'; but alimentation remains a vital constant several times each day. But even if we think of food as just another aspect of our busy lives, still food is central. Almost hidden from our view a host of people labour in supply chains and food-preparation facilities, while further from view policy-makers and strategists ponder future 'food security', all to make sure that when we wake up in the morning we can have our cereal, milk, orange juice and coffee – and having eaten can begin a new day. Being human and needing food are inseparable realities: and if God is creator of all, seen and unseen, then any serious religious engagement that takes account of the nature of the creation, and our human nature, must engage with food and with humans as food consuming animals. Food is basic.[2]

An equally basic observation about our humanity is that we are the *only* animals who cook our food. While we find ever more links between ourselves and our primate relatives – tool making, social organization, culture, basic language – we alone expend effort on cooking what nourishes us.

---

[1]Philip M. Wagner 1966, 63.
[2]Underlying this chapter – as an introduction to the place of eating together among our species – is Jones 2007. While many anthropologists and sociologists have written on the importance of food sharing, no one has located the evidence within the widest human frame as successfully and succinctly as Jones.

Cooking – and so elaborate food preparation and consequently the deliberate ways of eating required by prepared cooked food – is not only central to our humanity, but also uniquely human. Cooking presupposes our orientation to community/society and reinforces it. Cooking is a complex task, and an eminently social task, and supposes food sharing. Traditionally the task of cooking was shared, even having the fuel for cooking supposed shared work and a minimal social organization; and much cooking was planned around group eating. Cooking and community go together.

But cooking implies much more to us as beings of reflection, rationality and story: food is always more than taking nourishment. Food always involves meaning because it is a basic way we structure the world around us – in terms of people, the natural environment – and our aspirations about what constitutes a good life.[3] The simplest act of cooking – making a cup of tea to have a drink – implies a rich human cosmos of meaning. Food is more than food.

Cooking, moreover, is a fundamental bond within human society turning the hypothetical 'me' of my thoughts into the actual 'us' among whom I am a human being: human food presupposes society, it creates society, and it projects a vision of society. Not only must we work as a community to obtain food, but the preparation and cooking of food require community involvement. This was easily visible until just a few generations ago when everyone could see the range of skills collaborating; but if today we have the illusion of isolated cooking, one needs but a power cut to see how quickly we call on the assistance of the invisible others who make our cooking possible. Whether we see those who do the preparation and maintain the common fire or not, our manner of existing – eating cooked foods – depends on a larger society, and takes form in more intimate table-sized groups at which there is a meal. We do not simply eat food, or even eat food together, *we share meals*. The meal is as much a fundamental element of humanity as shared rationality or language. Again, this sense of solidarity can be obscured in contemporary western societies which can allow each person at a table to have their own specific food, while another carries on a virtual conversation apart from the table group on the phone; but while this behaviour may be the harbinger of a new phase of human social evolution, the fact remains that this individualistic behaviour take place in the common meal setting familiar to our ancestors.

Can one envisage human life without taking account of our meals together? It can be imagined but as a dystopia something like Aldous Huxley's

---

[3]Here lies the real answer to the medieval eucharistic conundrum of the mouse that ate the reserved sacrament: *quid mus sumit?* (see Macy 1992; and Mazza 1999, 220–2); while medieval theologians thought the question an ideal one to explore the nature of the presence of the Christ by asking if the mouse ate 'merely bread' or 'the body of Christ' or both or only one, they failed to appreciate that the mouse ate neither! Bread only has reality to us humans: the mouse ate what its senses indicated was nourishment.

Brave New World, while that solitary *factotum* Robinson Crusoe is an illusion. By contrast, one could write the history of our humanity as the history of our meals: from food left as grave goods in burials in prehistoric times, through the meal customs of every tribe and people, not forgetting the great mythic meals of story from Abraham's hospitality to Babette's feast,[4] and include all those memorable meals of our own lives. How appropriate that within our own Christian story it is having a place at a meal that is the image of God's eschatological welcome, the banquet of heaven[5]: 'I tell you, many will come from east and west and sit at table with Abraham, Isaac and Jacob in the kingdom of heaven' (Mt. 8.11).[6]

Every meal is an activity, an event, shared with a group that is bounded and bonded by that sharing. While, increasingly, many of us today eat our meals alone, treating this as a normal way to eat is a departure from our history. This may become even more accepted as a norm within some 'developed' societies, but while this may be of interest as a phenomenon to the sociologist, to anyone possessing this vision of community and communion that is inherent within gospel such solitary existence will remain exceptional. Moreover, in terms of our inherited meal culture it is somehow incomplete, and when we eat alone we may still employ some of the accepted meal-codes such as a particular sequence of foods: codes that have their origins in shared meals. Yet, despite seeming superfluous, even absurd, we may cling to them as memories and reminders that sharing food seems somehow more 'right'. In a modern urban setting the notion of sharing meals may be attenuated by comparison with a village society of extended families, but it is still the case that we imagine ourselves through meals as we can see in our fondness for 'eating out' or in the way meal-sharing is used in advertising where the shared meal is assumed as the norm.[7] Likewise, even in a modern urban situation 'the meal' is still imagined as an integral part of celebrations.

Our direct experiential encounter with meal sharing may be declining, as witness the number of modern household without a dining table, but that should not cause us to ignore the fact that human societies have evolved around the sharing of food, and that even when someone eats alone that act takes place in the context of many others working in sequence so that there is food there before that individual. Food sharing is and remains a key to who we are as humans. Given the complex links between our concerns over food,

---

[4]I am indebted to my colleague, Dr Simon Oliver, for drawing my attention to the possibility of a eucharistic reading of this film.

[5]See Priest 1992.

[6]Normally in this book I have cited scripture following the *NRSV*; however, here I have used the *RSV* because *anaklithésontai* is part of the formal vocabulary of banqueting, meaning literally to recline on a couch for a formal dinner (see the illustrations in Smith 2003, 16 and 17), and this is not reflected in the *NRSV*'s use of 'eat'.

[7]One of the tropes of detective films is that the police hero's dysfunctional social/family life is presented in terms of the breakdown of food/eating codes in his squalid food storage/kitchen area: the assumption underlying the trope is that we can decode it without thinking.

our collaboration to bring it to the table, and the tensions and possibilities of eating together, the meal is a primary locus of human ritual.[8] We eat our meals within patterned behaviour and so they enable us to communicate with each other, and become basic events in building, sustaining and celebrating our culture.[9] This was brought home to me many years ago when I attended the launch of a book promoting a Cartesian vision of rationality at which we had decent wine and excellent finger food: those organizing the event had a surer grasp on the unity of the human person and human solidarity than the subject of the book we were ostensibly celebrating.

These meal patterns express the assumptions shared by those eating the meal: the patterns both enact the community's structures – how is (are) the table(s) arranged, who carves, do all receive the same food, what is drunk, how much time is there . . . – and embody the group's vision of themselves.[10] And so deep are these rituals in our humanity that the way we share meals provides us with one of the few social activities allowing comparisons over cultures and periods.[11] In fact, we have never encountered a culture where meals were not fundamental!

From this flows an obvious, but easily ignored, truth. Because we invest such 'additional energy' in alimentation beyond that of simply obtaining food, there is no human eating that is devoid of 'additional significance'. Every time we eat, we are engaging in a common, indeed a ritual,[12] activity that tells us much about our nature and affirms our belonging within a society, restates our past and expresses our larger vision.[13] Meals enact for us in some way our ultimate concerns, and so all meals involve the fundamental issues of religion: even if only 'anonymously'. Meals are never simply meals.

To be a primate is to be a being who obtains food through group effort, to be a human being is to be one who participates in meals. Again, if we believe that we can see in our nature the *vestigia* of the Creator, then religion must take 'the human as meal-sharer' – *homo caenarius* – seriously. Indeed, if we believe that in the midst of this world, in the events of living, we encounter the mystery of the divine, then in our meal sharing we have a basic moment of encounter with the divine. Little wonder, then, that meals have played such

---

[8]This supposes an understanding of ritual as a basic set of games that are necessary for shared understandings, communication and society, and that 'formal' ritual is but a very visible case of fundamental human activity, see Rothenbuhler 1998.

[9]See Visser 1993, 4–37 for a survey.

[10]This has long been recognized by anthropologists, and it is now becoming a commonplace in studies of the early churches: see Smit 2011, 106–10.

[11]See Visser 1993.

[12]On this notion of humans engaging in ritual activity to a far greater extent than the way the word 'ritual' is used in some religious contexts, see Chapter 1.

[13]It is a matter of words whether one described this larger vision as 'religious' or not: many people today would reject any notion that they have a 'religious' vision – but the very fact that they claim there is no room for what they see as the formal elements of a 'religious' view is itself a religious statement. *Vocati atque vocati non, dii aderint!*

a variety of roles in the human religious search as seen in the feasts, fasts and food rules of so many religions, or in the place of meals in moments of high significance in our personal journeys. No meal is profane for those who know how to see![14] And, any talk about the *holy* Eucharist or the *sacred* meal needs to have as its starting point a recognition that all meals, because they are so centrally human, form a point of contact with the divine mystery that suffuses the creation, whether or not that mysterious aspect is invoked. This reality, that we are beings of food-as-meals, forms the bedrock of any theology of the Eucharist that locates the Eucharist not only within the community of the church, but also within human life and the way we travel as disciples. Equally, it must be the bedrock of any theology of the Eucharist which seeks to see the Eucharist as an essential element in Christian life viewed in terms of the incarnation of the Logos in the historical individual Jesus. The alternative is to see the Eucharist as simply the execution of a voluntaristic command placed in the mouth of Jesus.

Must we start with *homo cenarius?*

But why is the Eucharist so involved, and must it be viewed as so involved? Because even in its most extreme ritualized forms, whether as a Catholic *missa solemnis* with its operatic pageantry by clerics in fancy dress or with the deliberately 'anti-ritual' starkness and *ex tempore* informality of a Reformed 'Holy Communion' that might appear a brief appendix to a lecture with readings and singing, the Eucharist is a meal. In the practice of most churches this 'meal' is both atrophied and desiccated, but nonetheless (1) it involves humans sharing food (or in some churches potentially sharing food),[15] (2) it uses the language and gestures of a meal, (3) it self-consciously remembers a meal, (4) it claims to re-enact a meal and (5) it declares itself as an interim anticipation in a future banquet, the meal of all meals.[16] Far from being an arcane ritual almost outside normal human experience,[17] or a 'text'

---

[14]Readers will see that Rahner's approach to the mystery of God in the world informs my approach, and I am indebted to H. D. Egan's summary of that approach in the line: 'Nothing here below is profane for those who know how to see' (Egan 1985, 4).

[15]It is often forgotten that in the time before the reforms of the Second Vatican Council that it was common for there to be a large congregation at 'the later Mass' but for none 'to go to communion' (i.e. share in the food). While today in most Catholic celebrations, despite the fact that it is a meal of eating and drinking, there is only potential drinking by all but the president, while it is another indication why the notion of the 'private Mass' (without even a 'server') – forbidden by law but prevalent in practice – is absurd.

[16]See Priest 1992; Wolter 2009; and Marshall 2009.

[17]This is what it has happened, experientially, in many Orthodox churches and, likewise, what happened in the un-reformed Catholic liturgy (and this is the major problem facing those Catholics who do not internally support the reforms – though this is rarely acknowledged as a failing of the un-reformed rite).

in an esoteric 'sacral' language,[18] the Christian activity of Eucharist uses not only the coding of our basic human ritual, the meal, but is an activity belonging within the basic activities relating to food, cooking and meals that constitutes us as humans and as a society.

Nature – Grace

This groundedness of the Eucharist within humanity is more often than not forgotten; and when recalled is, for many Christians, an awkward fact. Therefore, to point to the Eucharist as a meal – so eminently human an event – invites immediate qualifications by specific differences. These, in turn, amount to denying the genus of meal as anything more than a necessary allegory or a linguistic analogy, a convenient didactic metaphor or simply an historical allusion to its 'moment of institution'. Indeed in this approach's extreme form, the meal can be swept away to be no more than a nominalist 'X' which can act as a sacramental vehicle for an encounter which is 'supernatural' – although that particular word may be avoided – and so not in any real sense a human meal.

A Catholic priest who spoke to his community of their coming together 'for the eucharistic meal' was challenged by some of his fellow celebrants that they had not come to a social event but to take part in the Holy Sacrifice: human event and divine event were taken to be mutually exclusive. With such a view on the relationship of the divine and the human, one wonders how they claimed to believe in the incarnation. In a similar vein, many popes – Gregory the Great is a fine example – have promoted the value of the Mass without ever mentioning it as a meal or seeing in it even analogies to other meals. Implicit in these approaches is a distinction between meals on the one hand and serious religious activities on the other, and, more profoundly, between their encounters in 'the natural order' and their religious encounters which belong in 'the supernatural order'. Presenting this attitude in its abstract form we glimpse a wholly nominalist perspective on Christian discipleship. The meal of 'the Last Supper' was merely as a result of a divine command that this sacrifice should take place in an 'unbloody' (*incruoris*) form, and so the meal has at best a catechetical function as an idea /image/ evocation. Thus the 'meal' elements of the physical practice of the liturgy is to the reality of the Mass as the word 'water' (which could

---

[18] As the liturgy tends to become not only among those churches who use or claim special value for dead languages (Orthodox who use Old Church Slavonic; Armenians who use classical Armenian; Catholics obsessed with preserving Latin), but also in those who cannot bear to part with received arcane language such as those Anglicans who insist on the *Book of Common Prayer* in reaction to *Common Worship* and its predecessors. On the implicit anti-incarnational tendency in these approaches, see O'Loughlin 2013e.

be substituted '*aqua*', '*wasser*', '*agua*', '*dwr*' or '*uisce*' without loss) to what flows in a river.[19]

The Presbyterian pastor who sought to invest Holy Communion with a deeper sense of a celebration around a real loaf and a shared cup of decent wine was challenged for his ritualism – by members of a community that had a wonderful tradition of pot-luck suppers and 'hunger lunches' together to express their Christian fellowship and witness. Again, there is an assumption that nature and grace must be experienced in opposition lest the latter be confused with traffic of the everyday or formalized ('ritualized') lest it be less than a formal conscious and named engagement with the divine. The Anglican organizers of the Alpha Course do not include a section about the Eucharist in their programme, yet eating together is a fixed, and significant, part of its curriculum – and considered one of the keys to its success. But could that meal be itself part of the ultimate encounter which the Alpha Course seeks to enable? They see the group meal as a very important element in the whole growing/learning process. And, of course, it requires a great deal of effort to organize it on a weekly basis, thus indicating the seriousness of their hospitality; while in eating this meal together, they are discovering that being a disciple is about being a member of a community and that faith cannot be viewed as an individualistic affair. The Alpha Course asserts its desire that faith come alive, and has discovered that meals are a valuable part of living and sharing discipleship. As such these meals can be viewed as an anonymous experience of Eucharist, and that which it is not focused on in the talks is experienced and enjoyed in what could seem to a casual observer as no more that than the wrappings and trappings of the course.[20]

Meals, we are happy to acknowledge, may work, and may indeed be crucial at the human level; but is this not distinct from the encounter with 'grace'? Grace in this context being virtually equivalent to that which is 'out of the ordinary', or 'the spiritual' in an oppositional relationship to 'the material' and 'the worldly'. Hence when 'meal' is mentioned, there is such an immediate use of adjectives to distance the Eucharist from the ordinary world of meals! Phrases such as 'a sacred meal' or 'a ritual meal' serve not so much to identify the Eucharist as a specific meal among our other meals, but to stress the differences, indeed the chasm, between it and everyday life (which is implicitly 'profane' and God-less). Put in this form, there is then a cry that 'we' do not see 'nature' and 'grace' in such distinct compartments: but the statement is made in attitudes, ritual, vesture and architecture long before this corrective piece of formal theological reflection. There is, indeed,

---

[19]On the ubiquity of a *de facto* nominalism (and so a voluntarism) in Catholic sacramental theology in the aftermath of Trent, see Moonan 1994 and Ball 2013.

[20]One of the 'discoveries' of many involved in training leaders for 'church planting' activities is the importance of eating breakfast and lunch together. While space does not allow me to do more than reference this phenomenon, and while to a sociologist of education this might seem no more than the obvious, this should be the subject of theological reflection for all involved.

a long tradition in Christian ritual of seeking to emphasize the discontinuity between the 'ordinary' and the divine: the iconostasis in Orthodoxy is the extreme example, but altar/communion rails,[21] or using of archaic languages make the same point. However, the most significant expression of this phenomenon is *the use of token amounts of specific ritual types of food*, for example unleavened wafers in the west, or the use of non-normal wine,[22] all of which (together with umpteen other signals) serve to stress the discontinuity between the eucharistic meal and the meals that sustain life. This desire for separation is a symptom of a particular theological vision whereby the divine and the created are seen as opposing poles, and where the divine drops into the creation as a visitor.

By contrast, the Eucharist has to be seen as another instance where grace really builds on nature. All meals partake somehow in the mystery of our being creatures within the creation. Every meal involves us as needy beings who are parts of creation's interlocking dependencies. Imagine all the steps and chains of causality and agents – including bees – that interact to bring you one spoonful of honey on a piece of bread in the morning; imagine the human complexities to ensure that everyone in the 'developed' world (with the money to pay for it) has what they want for breakfast. The 'facts' of this inter-dependency are acknowledged by all: it is the basis of food-commodities markets and economics of food; that this interdependence is another instance of our createdness, and so ultimately an expression of our dependence on the Creator which we can acknowledge with our thankfulness, is the insight and response of faith. From this perspective all the meals of the covenant peoples become encounters with the God who has spoken in history, while the meals of Christians can become an expression of the eucharistic dimension of their lives as disciples of Jesus. For his followers, all meals, including those that explicitly express his thanksgiving, become part of their calling and witness as disciples: can they feast while others starve (cf. Mt. 25.31-46)? Meanwhile, their community eucharistic meals can become through, with and in Jesus a foretaste of the divine table[23]; but is not the divine involved in the meal prepared from tins from the food bank? *Missarum solemnia*, simple breakfast, shared sandwiches, soup kitchens, formal dinners, famine relief, feasting and food banks: all belong to our

---

[21]The eastern iconostasis and the western rood-screens/altar rails share a common origin as a low barrier in the assembly needed for segregating the sacred persons (the clergy) from 'the others' in the liturgy as an enactment of [divine] imperial court; see Kitzinger 1954.

[22]In both east and west the wine now used is a kind of dessert wine/sherry – technically known as 'fortified wines' – rather than the wine now served at dinner. This is a legacy of earlier wine transportation habits when the stickier, higher in alcohol, wine travelled better in casks, and then was thinned out with water before drinking. This ancient practice is referred to in 2 Macc. 15.39 and can still be seen in the Roman rite's use of mixing the wine with water at the Preparation of the Gifts – now explained with a suitable medieval allegory which if taken 'seriously' or literally would be tantamount to a denial of Chalcedon's christology!

[23]Marshall 2009.

human world and the world of the Word made flesh forming a continuity we must not sunder as disciples.

It is now commonly asserted that our traditional christology has often been functionally docetic; and an analogous problem exists in our thinking on the Eucharist: we tend to be functionally gnostic and nominalist. We may use the language and forms of a meal, but we tend to consider our eucharistic activity as involved in something other than a meal. The Eucharist, in this view, is a sacred entity which appears in our world merely clothed in meal-related terms, perhaps simply because every 'sacrament' has to have some materially perceptible image. We see this in the language of many hymns that stress that the Eucharist (thought of as a food object rather than activity) is 'angelic food' belonging in itself to a realm outside that of human living. This 'food' (now envisaged of as an allegory) descends into the world of our consciousness using the external impressions (in scholastic terms: the '*species*') of bread, wine and meals, but its 'finality' is to allow us to engage with some transcendent reality that is 'naturally' beyond us.[24] While indeed, this approach argues, it is true that this supernatural event uses a rich set of human symbols, to be exploited in didactic and artistic allegory – or explored exegetically as part of a rich scriptural background, this still should not confuse us about 'what is really taking place' when the Eucharist is celebrated or when someone takes Communion. But the relationship to food and meals, within this view, belongs to the world of appearances, the world of the *species* and so official Catholic parlance, the actual foods capable of being eaten, bread and wine, only exist as 'appearances'. The Eucharist is (often emphasized by the quaint theological pleonasm: 'really is'), quite literally, substantially distinct. And, as such, it not part of 'this' world except as a supernatural 'visitor'. Furthermore, the hermeneutical result of thinking in scholastic categories (e.g., on the Catholic side, in terms of there being no substance of bread or wine, but merely 'species' for minds which depend on the senses for external impressions; or, on the Reformed side, arguing that the substance remains but the 'presence' is spiritual) is that for most Christians the meal has been reduced to the status of a dramatic presentation, and a token one at that. It can be decoded with value, it can recall the Last Supper, it can bring to mind any number of moments from the Christ-event as liturgical remembrance, but the form of the action sits nonetheless in a parallel, and inferior, position to 'reality' – the 'spiritual' purpose which drew a group together to celebrate a Eucharist. Indeed, this can be taken to such an extreme that any celebration becomes strictly speaking unnecessary

---

[24]By treating biblical metaphors as relating directly to the Eucharist – conceived as a 'thing' rather than activity – an inversion of meaning took place. From 'the bread of heaven' (see Jn 6.31-2) being a metaphor for relating to other realities, it became a poetic name relating directly to Eucharist, and the actual bread (or more precisely the 'species' of bread) became the metaphor. A full study of the use of texts such as Ps. 81.16; Wis. 16.20; 2 Esd. 1.18; and Jn 6.31-2 in medieval writings on the Eucharist is long overdue.

for those who have the assurance of grace (as some Reformed Christians would argue); for others it becomes the necessary means to renew the sacramental presence of Jesus and thus allows an encounter with him, or the fulfilment of the need to offer sacrifice; while for some its rationale lies in obedience to the carrying out of a dominical command: 'do ye this'. The meal is as extrinsic to the reality which engages Christian attention as the human person of Jesus was to his reality as the Logos: what we see is just what seems to be (*dokei moi*), mere *species*, appearances.

This book, beginning with this chapter, will argue in the very opposite direction. We are meal-sharing beings, and this is at the core of our lives and our human development: around the table, sharing a meal we affirm our nature, build society and present to ourselves our vision. There also we celebrate all that is important to us – and that is where we celebrate that which is truly good for us humans: love, community, collaboration, social bonds of respect and caring. There also we affirm the bonds of humanity and our need for reconciliation with one another.[25] For us who are baptized meal-sharing beings, these gatherings for food are moments of encounter with the Lord – having shared meals with disciples in Galilee and Judea he now is, for those who believe in his promise (Mt. 18.20), among all meal-sharers gathered in his name, and there we bless the Father from whom all comes. Our eucharistic activity is located in the midst of our ordinary existence as meal-sharers. There in the creation we engage simultaneously in a basic human activity (meal sharing which builds us into a community) as sisters and brothers, in Christ, and in the basic creaturely activity, acknowledging and praising God, as daughters and sons, in Christ, of the Father. Just as a rejection of a docetic christology commits us to seeing Jesus, another unique human being, within our world, so our eucharistic activity must be located firmly in the reality of living meal-sharing lives as disciples. In short, grace must be seen to build upon nature and bring it to perfection, rather than present itself as in opposition to nature.[26]

Food and religion

Before, however, we can move to looking at celebrating the eucharistic meal and its food, we need to step back and consider in more detail the relationship of food and religion. At first sight, food only figures peripherally in religion; and when it is mentioned directly in a religious context, it appears to carry, most obviously, negative connotations. We are familiar with the prohibitions

[25]See Diamond 2012, 84 who describes the need for 'a simple meal of sweet potato . . . and other vegetables' as part of a reconciliation meeting between two groups who were potentially murderous of one another. The act of eating, simply but formally, seems to have formed the seal on their agreement to be reconciled.
[26]Thomas Aquinas, *Summa theologiae* I, 1, 8, ad 2.

that religions make on the consumption of certain foods either because they are 'unclean' – as with pig meat among Jews and Muslims – or because they would involve the dangers of sacrilege – as in the eating of cows among Hindus.[27] While Christians claim that part of their revelation is that 'all foods are clean',[28] it is still a fact there is hardly a culture where there are not some potential foods that are rejected with a squirm or which it is simply unthinkable that one would eat them.[29] Thus we may affirm theologically that all comes from the Father and so is good, and that nothing edible is to be seen as belonging to the realm of 'the unclean', the profane, the unholy, yet food is so deeply located within our cultures that some of these gifts are simply unacceptable. Food, precisely because it is significant to us, is not simply 'the edible'.

Fasting

The other common place where food and religion impinge on one another is in the practice of fasting – avoiding food either as a means to promote religious consciousness or the chosen suffering of fasting which is seen as contribution to religious reparation.[30] Fasting is part of many religions, and has played, and continues to play, a significant part in the lives of Jews, Christians and Muslims. However, for Christians, at least, it is an ambiguous practice.[31]

While those who followed Jesus seem to have taken over and adapted fasting – the twice weekly fast that became a standard component of Christian practice is found in the *Didache* – without much hesitation, there was another tradition that Jesus took fasting practices lightly or indeed passed over them completely.[32] When challenged about fasting during an

---

[27]See Douglas 1966 for a context for such prohibitions.

[28]Mk 7.19 – this is a second-century gloss (i.e. because this is the only verse in the story in Mark not carried over into Matthew – it was not in the text of Mark at the time Matthew saw it) on a piece of teaching about defilement and eating (for the contrary opinion, that it was a comment of Mark's not suited to Matthew's views, see Smith 2010, 926 – against this view is that it does not fit well within Mark's story, but reads exactly as a gloss); in Acts 10.9-16 and 11.2-10 we are given a formal moment of the revelation – complete with *bat kol* – that Christians should regard all that the Father gives for food as clean.

[29]The ordinary garden snail is in my culture considered 'revolting' and can only be considered edible under special 'foreign' situation such as when one is in France – and it is then assumed that it is a special edible snail; meanwhile it is known that horseflesh is eaten by 'foreigners', but in my culture it is simply not on the food horizon.

[30]Part of the inheritance of Christians is the suspicion of food that can be found in Philo's *De vita contemplativa*, 34 where food is for the body (as distinct from the soul) and belongs to the world of 'night' rather than day; while the 'sacred meal' of the pure philosophers would be made impure if animal flesh were eaten (*De vita contemplativa*, 73).

[31]O'Loughlin 2000.

[32]O'Loughlin 2003.

encounter with a group called 'the scribes of the Pharisees' (Mk 2.16) who
compared him and his followers with 'John's disciples and the Pharisees'
(2.18), Jesus gives the cryptic answer that no one can fast at a wedding
while the bridegroom is there, 'but the days will come when the bridegroom
is taken away from them, and then they will fast on that day' (2.19-20).
This has usually been read as implying that while there was to be no fasting
while Jesus was alive, that fasting would be practiced during 'the time of
the Church' (as indeed happened). But this interpretation fails to do justice
to the text. One of the underlying tensions within the early churches was
between those who came to Jesus with significant baggage derived from
John the Baptist and other followers who did not share John's apocalyptic
outlook and who saw Jesus not as the harbinger of the 'great crunch' but of
the prodigal Father's gift of forgiveness and new life.[33] These views seem to
have taken on a food/fasting dimension whereby for some disciples, to use
a recently popular phrase, 'Jesus was a party animal' while for others Jesus
was seen as succeeding John and so should retain the latter's proclamation of
fasting and impending destruction. Mark replies to these tensions by putting
the question about John's practice (no doubt being followed and argued
over in churches he was visiting) into the mouth of an apparently innocent
'third party': the otherwise unknown 'scribes of the Pharisees'. Then Mark
gives an answer that lets them down gently, while firmly rejecting John's
practice: they can fast when the bridegroom is not with them – but this is
not 'the time of the church' as the kernel of the kerygma is that the risen
Jesus is still with them now. But if a future time should occur when Jesus is
not with them, then they could fast![34] This interpretation – that one cannot
fast in the presence of the risen Jesus *encountered in the eucharistic meal* –
is confirmed in a first-century agraphon where the risen Jesus goes to his
brother James, who has been fasting since the final supper, and:

> the Lord said: Bring a table and a loaf. And . . . he took the loaf, and
> blessed [God],[35] and broke [it] and gave [a portion] to James the Just, and
> said to him: 'My brother, eat your bread, for the Son of Man is risen from
> among those who sleep'.[36]

Moreover, when this piece of teaching was adopted by Matthew in his
narrative (9.14-5), the ploy of 'scribes of the Pharisees' was dropped, and
those posing the question are described simply as 'the disciples of John'.[37]
For Mark, fasting was an indication that individual disciples had not grasped

[33]Meier 1994, 439–50.
[34]See O'Loughlin 2010, 66–84.
[35]See Chapter 2 above; this word is merely inserted so as to correct the tendency to see Jesus as
'blessing the bread'; 'God' is used as it assumes less than 'Father' or 'Lord'.
[36]See O'Loughlin 2009b.
[37]Lk. (5.33-5) follows Mark without change.

the distinctiveness of Jesus, but were continuing within the apocalyptic cosmology of John the Baptist. Similarly, the *Gospel of Thomas* on two occasions rejects fasting,[38] and it is clear that it would not fit with its theology of Jesus letting humanity share in the perfect day of the Lord's rest.[39]

But if fasting was problematic within the Jesus movement, and we can see Jesus breaking with the religious culture around him, it soon became an important part of Christian praxis. The *Didache* presents the Christian week marked by 2 days of fasting – Wednesday and Friday – and this became the Church's norm, and later it would become an important part of the pursuit of Christian perfection in monasticism. By that time, in the fourth century, the celebration of the Eucharist had become a distinct, formally religious ritual, and fasting had become one of the boundaries marking off the Eucharist from other meals. So that one had meals at which 'grace' was said – on the profane side of the *profanum/sacrum* divide; and a wholly distinct 'meal', the Eucharist, at which there was some eating and drinking – set clearly and firmly within the *sacrum*, with fasting (the negation of the meal sharing) as the boundary action between the human activity of eating and formal praise of the Creator, while it also did duty as a boundary marker between ordinary food and the food at the Eucharist. Traces of other ways of thinking did survive, such as the monastic common meal[40] which may be a vestige of the times when Christians celebrated thanksgiving at a real meal, but, for the most part, fasting pushed the Eucharist to the periphery of ordinary human experience, and would continue to do so. Fasting is still a key part of practice of non-western churches; and for the largest western church, Roman Catholicism, it would remain so until the 1960s.[41] Moreover, the suspicion of celebration that was concomitant with fasting meant that many reform movements within monasticism became suspicious of mitigating fasting even on the great feasts[42]; while this fear of banquets (now disconnected from the 'work' of fasting)[43] continued in

---

[38]Sayings 14 and 104 (and note the reference to fasting in Saying 27).

[39]Davies 1992, 673.

[40]See De Vogüé 1985.

[41]In a private conversation in 1981, one of last of the great pre-Conciliar rubricians, Dr J. H. Murphy c.m., who had watched all the liturgical developments of the 1960s and 1970s with great attention, pointed out to me that the greatest shift in deepening the participation of ordinary Catholics in the Eucharist over that period arose not out of the change of the ritual, or even language, but from the virtual elimination of the link between fasting and the reception of the Holy Communion.

[42]The ninth-century Irish monastic reformers known as the *Celi Dé* ('the party of God') even extended fasts to the great feasts of the liturgical year: in their model of holiness, there was no room for a banquet!

[43]Fasting – as a cornerstone of medieval penance – became the very symbols of 'salvation by works' for the Reformation: as such it was both vain and an affront to God's grace, and incidentally was seen as an indicator of the beginnings of the corruption of the Church. For an example of this attitude, see the rationale given in Metzger 1975, 101, for the deletion of the references to fasting in Mk 9.29 and Mt. 17.21.

many Reformed churches as smacking of a less than serious attitude to religion, this fear that banquets, feasts and parties were frivolous – and so a distraction from fervent religion – was most famously exhibited when in England the Commonwealth (1649–60) banned Christmas. In short, despite the example of the Eucharist, Christianity has had an ambivalent attitude to food, meal sharing and the place of celebrations within its vision of holiness. Few Christians would express that ambivalence explicitly today, but the legacy of such attitudes is long lived and still, indirectly, informs our understanding: 'grace' and 'nature' still seem alien to one another.

Rituals relating to food

But if food – except as allegory for being sustained by divine grace – has been marginalized in our thinking about the Eucharist, then we need to begin by recalling the important place of food in human religious thinking more generally. Food production and the fertility of the land, has been for as long as we can see within the archaeological record an issue that involves the divine. The return of spring, the coming of suitable weather, the fruitfulness of the fields and the success of the harvest have been those primary concerns that took expression in prayers, offerings and rituals. In those same societies where agriculture and sedentary urban life arose, we find the female figurines that have been seen as tokens of fertility goddesses,[44] temples are linked with storehouses for the harvest,[45] the names of gods are linked with food production, and most offerings in temples are of foodstuffs testifying to the links between prayers and having sufficient to eat. In a subsistence economy where famine was often but one storm or one livestock disease away, food was always to some extent precarious – and this brought it into the heart of the religious realm. Food was fragile, and so was seen as a divine gift.

This concern was one of the great impulses in the liturgy. The fundamental shape of the Christian year has its origins in the agricultural year of Canaan: the festival of the first lambs and the various harvests[46]; and the Roman ritual agricultural year left its imprint on the Catholic liturgy until 1969.[47] While the rituals of ordinary Christians in their folk calendars – usually disparaged and never dignified with the name liturgy – are often linked to the annual tasks of obtaining food from the land. Until recently, August was replete with a variety of harvest festivals asking for a good harvest and offering thanks for it. The pre-Christian festival of 'Lughnasa' took on

---

[44]See Healey 1992.
[45]See Ward 1992; Robertson 1992; and Dever 1992.
[46]See Bokser 1992, 756.
[47]The former rituals of the 'Greater Litanies' on St Mark's Day (25 April) have their origin in the Roman festival of the Robigalia which was a procession and sacrifice to keep crops free from disease; see Blackburn and Holford-Strevens 1999, 171–4.

Christian forms in many places in western Europe.[48] While 1 August was 'Lammas Day' – literally 'Loaf Mass Day' – when loaves made with the new corn were blessed at a Mass offered in thanksgiving for the harvest[49] – a commemoration that survived into the *Book of Common Prayer*[50] and has now been given new prominence in *Common Worship*.[51] In an agrarian society food production and prayer went hand in hand: divine blessing was sought on crops and animals, and for weather for the harvest – as can be seen in the number of blessings for these concerns in the *Rituale Romanum*[52] or in the special prayers for Masses for these intentions that can even today be found in Roman Missal.[53] Prayer of petition relating to having enough to eat is a central aspect of all human prayer. As such, the first petition addressed to the Father in the prayer of Jesus' disciples, 'give us this day our daily bread',[54] can be seen as primary petition as well as the culmination of human prayerfulness. Correspondingly, food was invariably seen as indicative of divine blessing. We can recall that the promise of God to the people of the covenant was that he would give them 'a land flowing with milk and honey' (Exod. 3.17); and when famine stalked the land – note the apocalyptic imagery from Rev. 6.8 – many Christian theologians saw it as divine punishment.[55]

In prayer for the food we need – expressed in any number of symbols – we are as close as we can get to an immediate expression of our ontological situation. We are dependant beings created by a loving God in whose mystery we live, but who need both food and the grace of God for our existence. We are needy, we are aware of the fragility and contingency of our existence, and we express our need before God hopeful of God's care. Food has left its mark right through human religious experience, and this is exactly as it should be if prayer and worship is to be seen as a meaningful engagement with the seriousness of existence. Such prayers to have enough to eat are for most people in the developed world a rather remote matter: we may pray 'give us this day our daily bread' but if all the food we need is not just there, then it is probably but a temporary hitch. Food just happens. We do pray for famine relief and for rain and seasonal weather, but it somehow lacks the urgency of the woman bringing a sick animal for a blessing to the

---

[48]See MacNeill 1962, 12–25.
[49]See Blackburn and Holford-Strevens 1999, 315–16.
[50]The Calendar, with Table of Lessons, 26.
[51]In *Common Worship* its eucharistic parallels are brought out in that it is recommended that it be celebrated in 'the setting' of 'Holy Communion' and that 'the Lammas loaf or part of it, may be used as the bread of the Eucharist' (*Common Worship: Times and Seasons*, 619). This is a liturgy that deserves imitation by other churches.
[52]There are many blessings for foodstuffs – quite distinct from blessings at table – in the *Rituale* such as that for eggs and cereal crops.
[53]For example, the Masses 'for productive land', 'after the harvest' and 'in time of famine'.
[54]See Yamauchi 1964.
[55]Gildas so understood famine in the sixth century – and he is representative of a major strand of Christian theology; see O'Loughlin 2012d, 111–21.

local priest or the farmer sprinkling his fields with Holy Water to invoke protection and fruitfulness.[56]

If we are to be really in touch with creation – truly ecologically conscious – we have to appreciate our interdependence on food; and this appreciation is the real starting point for our being eucharistic. Conversely, if we engage in eucharistic ritual without this appreciation and engagement, we are behaving falsely, while discussions about 'validity' or 'orthodoxy' or 'admission to communion' are but games among hierophants.

Blessing God for food

One intersection between food and faith still does just get our attention: offering thanks to God for the food we eat. 'Saying grace' – the very term in English coming from *gratia*: 'thanks' – is now a peripheral activity: something usually confined to religious groups,[57] special occasions,[58] inherited customs[59] or the fervent.[60] For most, 'run of the mill', Christians, the 'blessing at the table' has disappeared! The historical situation, however, offers a complete contrast. We have already noted how Deut. 8.10 can be seen as being in the background of Jesus' meals in Mark's gospel: the invariable preliminary to every encounter of Jesus with food is that God is blessed.[61] In this Jesus was doing what we find prescribed or described in virtually every other mention of a meal in ancient Jewish literature.[62] When wisdom is imparted

---

[56]The Roman Ritual of 1614 provided two blessings for seriously sick animals, while the blessing for water spoke of its power to scatter evil and invoke divine aid.

[57]In religious groups where grace is still a normal part of a meal, it is often something that can take visitors by surprise: it is not part of their ordinary experience.

[58]A few decades ago it was taken for granted that at a wedding meal, the cleric present would be 'called on to say grace' – but this element of dining ritual is increasingly less common; and when said it is felt as an awkward religious interlude best 'got through' at speed.

[59]Historic corporations – such as universities – often have elaborate 'graces' (see, for example, Adams 1992), but these are now often upheld simply as cultural heritage or baggage. The crucial test is this: if someone were forming a new corporation, would they include a 'grace' or even see the value in a common table? Likewise, in Scottish circles, the celebration of Burn's Night (25 January) a grace is said which has become part of the tradition of this night:

Some hae meat and canna eat	Some have meat and cannot eat
And some would eat that want it	Some cannot eat that want it
But we hae meat and we can eat	But we have meat and we can eat
Sae let the Lord be thankit	So let the Lord be thank-ed

[60]There is a common perception – caricatured in *The Simpsons* – that any family which 'says grace' is 'very religious' – and there is always the phenomenon of the child who asks, when the local cleric is the guest and 'grace' is said, 'why are we saying these prayers today?'

[61]See Chapter 2.

[62]See Bokser 1981; and see Bahr 1970 who give the details of the rituals of blessing God at formal meals.

to the young man on how he should preside at a banquet – wisdom on wine, manners and speaking (and when not to speak) – the advice concludes: 'But above all bless your Maker, who fills you with his good gifts' (Sir. 32.13). The meals in Qumran were probably far less sumptuous than those imagined by Jesus Ben Sira, but it was a requirement that they ate in common, and blessed in common (1 QS 6.2-3).[63] And in the equally serious 'sacred banquet' of those 'disciples of Moses' – the Therapeutae – described by Philo, the leader stands and sings a hymn of thanksgiving to God, followed by the rest of the company, before they eat their meal of bread and water.[64] And ever since the publication of the *Didache,* it has been recognized with ever greater clarity that the origins of Christian Eucharistic Prayers lie in Jewish table prayers: the exact relationship may be argued about among scholars,[65] but the fundamental insight that it was blessing God for his gifts of food that lies at the origin of the Eucharist is not disputed.[66] Indeed, the prayer forms of the *Birkat Ha-Mazon* have even influenced the Catholic Church's attempts at liturgical reform in its 1969 rite.

Down the centuries, Christians have devised many forms of table blessing from elaborate texts with biblical readings to the simple '*Benedictus benedicat*', alongside many other food blessings: that for eggs lies behind our Easter Eggs, and these serve to demonstrate the constant links between food and religion. Indeed, the creation of formal texts for use at table continues today as witness, for example the work of D'Avila-Latourrette[67]; but it is well more than a millennium since there has been a direct link between these prayers and Eucharistic Prayers.

Prayer as acknowledgement and praise

Given what we have said about the prayer of petition for food being a fundamental expression of our creaturely response to the situation in which we find ourselves and our hope in the mystery of God, then this expression of

---

[63]See Weinfeld 1992.

[64]*De vita contemplativa,* 63, 66, 71, 73 and 80. Whether or not such a meal ever actually took place (see Engberg-Pedersen 1999) is irrelevant to my argument, indeed the point is made stronger if it is the case that when Philo imagined an ideal meal that there should be such an organized song of thanksgiving begun by the leader and then taken up in a formal pattern by everyone else present such that the place of the symposium is a place of praise (*De vita contemplativa,* 83) – it could be said that this reference (n. 80) is the first mention we have of a sung eucharistic prayer addressed to God as Father (n. 90).

[65]See, for example, Talley 1976a, or Stewart-Sykes 2004.

[66]Box 1902 was one of the first to note this; and then the work of Finkelstein 1929 made the conclusion inescapable to all but the most conservative of scholars (e.g. Middleton 1935, and, in effect, this became the common opinion (e.g. Mazza 1995, 12–41). On the modern, and to my mind perverse, tradition of trying to separate this 'grace at meals' in the *Didache* from the Eucharist, see O'Loughlin 2013a.

[67]D'Avila-Latourrette 1994.

thanksgiving – blessing God for our food – must be seen as the fundamental act of praise. The action of thanking God for food is even more expressive of our being within the universe – as we Christians conceive it – than even our expression of need. In thanking God for food, we are expressing our hope that where he has placed us is a good place, that his providence is with us, and that joyfulness, expressed in thanksgiving, is the basic note of our existence. In a nutshell: the vision of a life lived under the care of a loving God finds its simplest expression in being thankful for food.

Food as a human right

The other intersection between food and religion is in the Christian discourse on social justice. The right to food is as basic as the right to life, and a concern for justice must include a concern that the resources of life are as equitably distributed as possible, which means, as a minimum, that no one suffers unnecessarily for want of food. To feed the hungry is one of the marks of the righteous person (Mt. 25.44), and part of the joy of the Kingdom is that the poor shall no longer suffer hunger (Lk. 6.21). This challenge that no human being should go hungry has moved in recent decades within Christian thinking from being a moral consequence of Christian living to become one of the hallmarks of the presence of Christians in the world. The alleviation of hunger, the destruction of systems that would so deprive human beings of food, and the just and ecological use of the earth's food resources have been taken up as a part of Christian responsibility for development, as part of Liberation Theology and as part of the ethical dimension of discipleship.

But in addition to these complementary ways of looking at the duties of Christians towards the need of the just use of the world's food, it is worth recalling that this ethical demand has always had a connection to the theme of food and worship. 'Isaiah' reminded the people that fasting, as prayer, was useless unless linked to justice for the poor, the needy and the hungry:

> Such fasting as you do today will not make your voice heard on high. . . . Is not this the fast that I choose: to loose the bonds of injustice, to undo the thongs of the yoke, to let the oppressed go free, and to break every yoke? Is it not to share your bread with the hungry, and bring the homeless poor into your house. (Isa. 58.4-7)[68]

Righteousness in prayer involving food (whether that be fasting or sacrifice) and food-justice towards others (the poor and the hungry must have enough to eat) are inseparable. And this is a theme that can be followed through the prophets up to and including Jesus.

---

[68]This is a theme that could be followed in detail in the prophets and the in the use of these texts in the liturgy.

Similarly, today, several theologians have pointed out the incongruity of celebrating the Eucharist as the Lord's bountiful love while at the same time being complacent about injustice in the world – and this takes on a pointed significance when that injustice involves food. This is a dimension of the theology of the Eucharist that goes far beyond anything found in the older scholastic and devotional treatments, and represents an important re-grounding of the Eucharist in the actual reality of the creation and the on-going call of discipleship. And, as Christians have become more aware of how food, its just production and proper distribution are matters of concern, they have become more dissatisfied with liturgies where this dimension of Christian action is not acknowledged.[69]

Our concerns for the correct use of this primary human reality, food, must find expression in our celebrations, and in our reflection on that activity, or else our eucharistic eating can become as useless as the fasts criticized in Isaiah. It is significant that it was a failure in this social justice dimension of the eucharistic meals in Corinth that prompted Paul's most extended treatment of the Eucharist, while, a century later at the weekly Eucharists described by Justin, one of the fixed elements during the meal was a collection for the poor.

Cooking as the human 'specific difference'

If we need food to live, it is one of the curious aspects of human existence that we expend so much additional energy, effort and care on preparing food before we eat it. Cooking – taken as a term covering all that is done to food before we eat it which can range from preparing a complex banquet of many courses to arranging salad items on a plate before eating them – is very much part of us. In even the most limited circumstances we want to go the additional bother of having a fire in order to brew a hot drink, and except in extreme situations whatever we consume has been processed in some way before we eat it. This may seem so obvious as not requiring notice; and when noticed it is by anthropologists not theologians. However, given that, first, the Eucharist is always about 'eating and drinking' foods which have involved complex preparation, and, secondly, for much of Christian history we have been arguing about the significance of what we consume at a eucharistic celebration, it seems sensible to reflect first about the basic human significance of how we prepare what we eat.[70]

The preparation of food-materials into what is actually put into our mouths is one of the great bonds that hold societies together. We do not eat

---

[69]See the expression of 'pain' and 'disappointment' expressed on the last page of Méndes Montoya 2009, 160 when he compares what is of concern to him from his study of food production and its human significance with what he sees happening in contemporary Catholic liturgies.

[70]For the significance of the biblical phrase 'eating and drinking' – and the importance attached therefore to cooking – see Wenks 1992.

cereal crops just as they are found in nature (and even those vegetables that can be simply 'picked and eaten' are exceptional as food). Indeed, wheat as it is harvested is inedible for humans as are many other staple items of the human diet. Moreover, long before there was any mention of 'GM' technology, human groups had modified what was grown to be that which they wanted for cooking. Similar processes have occurred in animal husbandry: selective breeding has produced the beasts we tend until they are slaughtered for our consumption. In every instance this is the work of a society over time, and still that harvested produce needs yet more processing before it is eaten. Cereals require the organization of settled life: the harvested forms that can be made into bread took millennia of breeding to evolve the species used in milling, and then before there is a crop there is the cycle of planning, planting, maintaining and harvesting of the grain. Grain, as yet inedible, must be dried, stored securely in barns (itself a complex social achievement), and then be milled into flour – all labour-intensive operations requiring a range of technologies and skills. The preliminary process of obtaining the ingredients over, there must exist the domestic skills to turn it into dough and bake it. This, in turn, presupposes some cooking apparatus – another set of skills – and the availability of the fuel to bake it. By the time it appears as a hot loaf, those who will eat it are in the debt of almost the whole web of people in their society. Yet this bread – and virtually every society has some sort of cereal product equivalent to bread – is seen as a basic 'foodstuff' and, if the circumstance allow, we always want an even more elaborate diet than bread – quite apart from special times of celebration. 'One does not live by bread alone' (Deut. 8.3)[71] is, to say the least, an important anthropological truth!

Our diets, our lives are bound up with our interest in a variety of cooked foods, and our willingness to invest significant resources of energy, time, wealth and skill in transforming 'raw' foodstuffs into the 'cooked' food that we eat. Cooking is our constant daily practice – whether we ourselves or others do the preparation. Not only do we have this in common with every other human, but the practice links us into supply chains that under-gird our society and link us with other groups near and far. Long before we speak explicitly, in a religious context, about 'significance' we need to recognize that every cooked item is already much more than simply sustenance, and that it is as full of implicit significance for us as it is chemically full of proteins and carbohydrates.

Moreover, this process of cooking is very dear to us and to our identity. We know the difference between 'home cooking' and 'institutional food'; we can distinguish 'eating in' and 'eating out'; we distinguish between 'good food', 'rich food' and 'poor food' and – assuming that everyone has enough to eat – these judgements relate to the quality of cooking as much as to the

---

[71]Christians are more familiar with this from Mt. 4.4 and Lk. 4.4, but its significance as a statement of divine care for the people of the covenant as seen in Deut. 8 is often not appreciated.

'raw' materials such as a dietician would evaluate. We know how cooking makes the difference between 'grub', on the one hand, and 'a sumptuous feast' on the other. Food can stratify us, divide us, and show our relationships between one another. Do you sense the different social worlds conveyed in the notion of '*haute cuisine*' and a '*salade paysanne*' – or is '*nouvelle cuisine*' more 'your thing'? Are the people with whom you 'do lunch' the same ones you would offer a 'slap up meal'? There is a world of difference between giving a cup of water to the thirsty (a basic act of justice and religion as we see in Mt. 25.31-46), 'going for a pint' with friends, and a toast with glasses of champagne. Each action is much more than just shifts in the liquids imbibed.[72] Each constructs a world around us in a different way. We even have foods that are specifically and explicitly vehicles of meaning: the wedding cake and the birthday cake are good examples within our culture.[73] While each Christmas it is seen as essential to have, or at least invoke, the 'traditional fare' and to be without those specific cooked products is seen as a particular suffering.[74]

Moreover, each culture has its own cuisine: basic ingredients prepared in different ways become markers of group, national and religious identity. We know that in Italian cooking we will find pasta and polenta, while the mention of curry and poppadoms conjures up what we casually refer to as 'Indian' cooking. In a multicultural society a trip through a supermarket with its special shelves of food products for specific groups and times can tell the observer where the people in the locality have come from, their religious make-up, their festival calendar and the value they place on these identities.[75] What I choose to cook, when and how, says as much about me as the boxes I tick on a census form. Our prepared food is always wrapped up in meaning, tradition, culture and identity. As such cooking forms the boundary between being one more animal and the human world of significance. It is a basic way by which we create the universe we inhabit.

Cooking is also a gendered aspect of our lives. In most societies the task of obtaining the raw materials (hunting, pasturing, agriculture) and the basic processing (slaughtering, milling) is men's work, while food preparation and feeding is women's work.[76] This is a basic gendering that we inherit within

---

[72]This is the human basis for the sharing of the cup as a commitment to discipleship, which we will examine in detail in Chapter 6.

[73]See Charsley 1988.

[74]Hence each year there are special charity events to provide shelter and 'a Christmas dinner' (which is taken as a known) for the homeless: this is an act within the domain of human ritual; if it were simply alimentation at a time of particular need, then some of the emergency rations prepared by military for crises would be more appropriate.

[75]Some years ago when Pesach and Easter virtually coincided in one London supermarket, I found one aisle devoted to matzo and kosher wine, while another was decked out for Easter with chocolate eggs and bunnies. It would have astounded everyone (Christians included) to suggest that Easter too had a eucharistic dimension and so might include special loaves and, perhaps, better than usual wine.

[76]See Meyers 2002.

our cultures long before we look at matters such as gendering in liturgy.[77] Given that food involves gendering, are there basic aspects of that gendering that need to be considered when we think about eucharistic food, its preparation and the meals of the community? Is that gendering absolute – as some Christians would argue that some eucharistic roles are – or is it inherited and as such open to alteration: the 'cook', after all, tends to be a woman, but the 'chef' is a man? In many contemporary western societies, this gendering of cooking roles is now far less rigid than it would have been even a generation or two ago; and it is in those cultures that questioning the notion of only male presidents for the Eucharist has arisen.

It is curious that in the common artistic image for the Last Supper is invariably presented as an all-male affair. Yet the references to 'the disciples' and 'the twelve' in Mark's presentation do not allow for such certainty.[78] Likewise, we tend to think of two males going to prepare the room, the text merely says 'two disciples' (Mk 14.12). Why do we think of these events with only male characters, why do we forget the women who baked the bread, prepared the other foods, and in all likelihood would have served such a meal? We have no difficulty in hearing the references to women serving at other meals recalled by the early followers of Jesus.[79] Food, cooking, meals not only link us into a human web, but also invite us to become conscious of how details of real life can so easily slip out of our religious reflection; and, in the case of the Eucharist because it is a work of food and feeding, to reflect on how it reflects gender in our cultures, not simply as a matter of 'doctrine' which can be severed from culture.

It might seem that making much out of the religious significance of cooking is merely 'a new insight' or 'sidelight' being 'added' to the tradition of liturgical reflection, so it is worth considering these four cases. First, when avoiding pork became a marker of being Jewish is a disputed question.[80] However, it is noted as a part of Torah in Lev. 11.7 and Deut. 14.8, and had become a clear marker of religious identity by late second century BCE.[81] Refusing to eat it was not only a statement of identity, but indeed tantamount

---

[77]See Berger 2011, 67–94.

[78]The supper narrative in Mk (14.12-26) makes the assumption that it is a meal of disciples (see v. 12) with 'the twelve' present (v. 17), and when Jesus says that one of those present will betray him (v. 18) he then further specifies it as 'one of the twelve' (v. 20). This shows that in Mark's memory it was imagined as a larger affair than that of 'the twelve' – and his audience were expected to think about it in that way.

[79]For example: Mk 1.31 (and parallels), or Jn 12.2.

[80]Note that while we think of the prohibition on pork as the prohibition of an impure *foodstuff*, we should bear in mind that no one has ever thought of eating raw pig meat but only its cooked forms as in the great pork spit roasts of classical literature: it is only when foodstuff, such as a slaughtered pig, is cooked that it comes into the realm of significance.

[81]There is a difference between an activity being rejected by The Law, and that practice being, in effect, a badge of identity; of course, from the perspective of an insider's narrative this is not a distinction: it is a badge because it is forbidden (and may indeed have been forbidden so as to be a badge).

to a declaration of faith. We see this in the stories of Eleazar the Scribe and the Mother and Seven Brothers (2 Macc. 6.18-7.42). But that pork could carry meaning is also seen in it being a symbol of all that is suspect (Prov. 11.22), pagan (Isa. 65.4), repulsive (Isa. 66.17; and 1 Macc. 1.47) and inimical to the people (Ps. 80.13). While for Matthew, swine's flesh is linked to the presence of the demonic (Mt. 8.30-2).[82]

A second example of how cooking carries religious meaning can be seen in the image we are given of John the Baptist in the gospels. Mark tells us that 'he ate locusts and wild honey' (Mk 1.6).[83] While Luke presents the matter negatively by telling us that 'he has come eating no bread and drinking no wine' (7.33). The significance – and it was intended to be a significant statement – is that John has turned his back on cooking and the social world that cooking creates. Locusts are hunted insects – they fall into the category of 'wild' animals – rather than animals bred and cared for within the community[84]; equally, he was not even prepared to eat husbanded honey – the product of the social world of beekeepers – but only what he happened upon. John rejects the prepared foods of the society and, thereby, becomes someone who is outside society, a solitary hunter-gatherer, a precarious loner. This action had often been misunderstood as an act of asceticism (i.e. fasting writ large), rather than one of *kasruth* (i.e. refraining from polluting food).[85] The implications of *kasruth* then need to be drawn out: if one considers the cooking of the society around one to be that which makes one impure (because its cooking is a fundamental expression of all that a society is), then one must be prepared to live outside that society. The result is that one becomes as a hunter-gatherer implicitly affirming that common cooking is the door to common life.[86] Bread and wine are socially prepared foods par excellence. A rejection of bread and wine amounts to a complete rejection of a society and every practical link to that society. And such attitudes to cooked foods were appreciated in full by John's adversaries who saw it as evidence of his having a demon (Lk. 7.33). By contrast, in the resurrection appearances there is cooked fish and bread (Jn 21.9-14) or bread and wine on a laid table. Jesus, who engaged with society in scandalous meals in his lifetime, continues to endorse society after the resurrection.[87] Likewise, cooking must not set up barriers between Christians: the implication of 'all foods being clean' (Mk 7.19) is that one can be a follower of Jesus and share in the

---

[82]I am indebted to my colleague, Dr Holger Zellentin, for pointing out this aspect of how food carries meaning in the life of a group.

[83]Mt. 3.4 follows Mark, without adding any other detail.

[84]Locusts were considered food and were usually eaten roasted (see Davies 1983), the key difference between them and other animals (excluding those which were 'unclean') was that they were not farmed.

[85]See Davies 1983.

[86]This use of separating from a culture's food to separate oneself in purity from that culture had a paradigmatic form in the story of Daniel's refusal to eat Babylonian food (Dan. 1.5-17).

[87]See O'Loughlin 2009b.

cooking and tables of gentiles as well as Jews.[88] Cooking – and all it means to us humans – brings one into the presence of the demons and the divine.

The third example is the explicit significance given to all-but-avoiding prepared foods in Philo's *De vita contemplativa*. The purity and spiritual excellence of the Therapeutae is seen in their being willing to eat, both at their weekly meal and their once every 50 days' banquets, only bread sprinkled with salt and cold spring water – the only concessions being that some can have some additional hyssop flavouring or have their water warmed.[89] This is an expression of who they are – and they are minimally dependent on cooking – and Philo makes this abstinence stand out even more in that they explicitly reject wine and elaborately prepared meals.[90] Cooking is such a marker of society for Philo that he can describe all those whose lifestyles he wants to reject by giving details of what they choose to eat and how they prepare it!

Lastly, there is the concern of the early communities of Jesus-believers about eating food offered to idols such as we see in 1 Cor. 8.1-13. This, indeed, may have no absolute danger for believers for 'the idols are nothing' (1 Cor. 10.19), but still it was a matter of practical concern in communities – and remained so until much later.[91] What is important for our purpose is to observe that it was commonly recognized that food could be the bearer of significance quite apart from its 'practical' value as human nourishment. Even if one believes and knows that 'idols are nothing', food could not be cut off from its cultural 'baggage' by an act of will: somehow the food and the 'baggage' – its cultural significance – were bound together. These were foods with deep histories.

If our cooking expresses the rich variety of our humanity, then this has implications in many ways for our approach to the Eucharist. Foremost among these is the fact that, historically, the story of our theology of the Eucharist has been the tale of bitter divisions over what the food commodities – viewed in abstract terms, without cultural reference, as intellectually definable substances – on the plate and in the cup are. The assumption is that 'bread' (presuming, for now, this is what we should be referring to)[92] and 'wine'

---

[88]See O'Loughlin 2013c; the statement about food in Mk 7.19 is a gloss, probably dating from the second century, which reflects a definite rejection of cooking boundaries, while the eating events in Acts 10-11 represent Luke's formalized presentation of the 'decision' – so we can see the stories in Acts and the exegetical gloss in Mark as belonging to the same second century Christian development.

[89]The weekly diet is described in n. 37, and the fiftieth-day diet in virtually identical language in n. 73.

[90]The antagonism of the Therapeutae to wine is expressed on several occasions (e.g. n. 40) and the detail of the elaborate cooking they despise is found in nn. 53–6.

[91]As we can see from the references in Rev. 2.14 and 20; and the comments of Luke much later in Acts 15: 29, and again in 21.25.

[92]A careful study of the early practice shows that it was the *loaf* of bread that was the key bearer of meaning in the thanksgivings offered in union with Jesus; see O'Loughlin 2004.

(again presuming that this is what is at issue)[93] are simply physical materials (albeit with 'symbolic', i.e. subaltern allegorical value) to which we need give little attention. They are just there; and their only necessity is that they were chosen by Jesus – hence debates about their chemical composition such as does the bread contain gluten or the wine alcohol.[94] These materials, in this view, only become significant – that is they only enter the human world of meaning – in terms of their 'consecration' for use in an explicitly religious ritual – and at that point, for many Christians, they explicitly cease being what they are as foodstuffs! But even for those who do not take this extreme view, for most Christians it is only at that point of use in the formal ritual that they begin to see them having importance, significance, meaning and religious value. We see this arrival of a moment of religious value in, for example, the Catholic test for when children can 'receive first holy communion': it is when they can 'distinguish' consuming a consecrated wafer from 'ordinary bread'. But this notion that ritual use imposes a theological identity on foodstuffs implies that our eucharistic activity is not located from the created realm and in the domain of our human histories and, equally, does not do justice to 'God in the creation' in Jesus.

Meals and liturgy

No area of research connected with the Eucharist, the history of liturgy, or early Christianity has seen such an explosion of interest in recent decades as that involving the place of meals and phenomenon of commensality.[95] This is matched by interest from classicists into the structure and significance of *symposia* and the meals of various associations.[96] To this we might add the results of research by anthropologists and the historians of food, and still the list of contributing disciplines would not be complete. No one has yet brought all this material together as a comprehensive study of meals in Christianity, but the work of Dennis E. Smith and Hal Taussig comes close.[97]

---

[93]The use of water in many communities indicates that it was the single cup from which many could drink, not the nature of the liquid drunk, that was central; see McGowan 1999a.

[94]For nearly 30 years there has been a running argument among Catholics about 'gluten-free' wafers for use at the liturgy: the official position is that if the wheat is gluten-free (and therefore suitable for coeliacs) it would not be proper matter, and therefore could not be 'consecrated' and therefore there would be no Eucharist. One cannot engage with this sort of argument without, thereby, giving credence to the sort of theology that could imagine such a problem. Meanwhile, many Protestant churches who believe that total abstinence from alcohol is a fundamental demand of discipleship seek complex solutions to avoid the problem of using wine at the Eucharist. Again, these arguments only make sense from within the world of the problem.

[95]See Smit 2011 for a glimpse at the range of material.

[96]See Ascough 2008 for a survey.

[97]Smith 2003 is a key text; Taussig 2009 likewise; while their combined earlier work (Smith and Taussig 1990) is a beacon to other scholars of how historical theology is a creative discipline for the life of Christians today.

The effect of this work has been to see the gathering for a meal as being a basic element in the formation and maintenance of the early communities of disciples; indeed, one can go so far as to describe 'primitive Christianity as a feast'.[98] Moreover, while studies of the Eucharist in 'the scriptures' was formerly confined to 'the eucharistic words' or attempts to find 'warrants' for later theology, now through the focus on the meal as that which brought disciples together, how it expressed their relationships to one another, how it related to meal sharing in Judaism and in the wider society, and how the meal events shaped those early communities' memories, the meal is firmly close to the centre of early Christian studies. Indeed, even studies of Jesus now invariably have detailed treatments of what we can know about his behaviour at table.[99]

However, rather than attempt a survey of contemporary research about meals in the world of Jesus and his early followers, it is simpler to note that all this research demonstrates that societies express and define themselves by their meal practices. Indeed, in the small-sized groups that most human beings have lived their lives down the millennia – the group meal not only gave form to the society, but also enabled the society to express its structure, perform its vision of the universe and maintain the internal bonds that held it together. We can talk about communities, societies and churches, but if these are anything more than collective names, then in some shape or other sharing meals comes into play: meal sharing within our social group – whether it is a formal banquet at the time of some rite of passage or a summer afternoon's barbeque – is a datum within our humanity. And whenever this meal sharing takes place, it expresses and shapes our identity quite apart from any practical purpose that might be invoked as the basis of meal sharing.[100]

Commensality is not an optional aspect of human existence that we can study for insight into some specific topic: to study commensality is to study ourselves as who we are. Until recently it was possible to write on the practice of the Eucharist as if it was only accidentally a meal as a function of its need to mime in a token way the 'Last Supper'[101] or as a need to link it typologically to its earlier 'anticipations' in the Passover meal,[102] or to suggest that it was a 'ritual meal' simply because of the need to have some human form, a 'sacramental' basis that would be rich in allegory for a reality that was fundamentally other than a meal. But as we learn more about meals within human societies, it becomes clearer that such relegation of the meal to the periphery of Christian activity, and the Eucharist as a ritual

---

[98]Wolter 2009 makes this point.
[99]For example, Crossan 1991, 332–53 and 360–7 – and similar discussions of commensality can be found in virtually every other modern study of Jesus.
[100]See Grignon 2001.
[101]This is a common tendency in 'Protestant' explanations of the presence of meal forms.
[102]This was a common tendency in 'Catholic' explanations of the presence of meal forms, see for example Aquinas's hymn: *Pange lingua*.

wholly separate from an actual community meal, is itself a most erratic development for those who believe in creation and incarnation, as well as being a deviation from the practice the earliest communities saw as being in continuity with the practice of Jesus. Examining this break in continuity is as worthy of historical research as the continuities within the tradition that have driven liturgical studies since the time of Martène (1654–1739).

Meals are very obviously a bonding between us in society, but that comes with a darker side:

> Commensality can approve and express discontinuities that separate human groups as well as negotiate those discontinuities by temporarily and symbolically bringing together separated groups, even by confirming and reinforcing their opposition in the end.[103]

The Kingdom announced by Jesus both broke the boundaries that kept humans apart and proclaimed a new community of welcome, forgiveness and a restoration to a state of innocence. This was expressed around the shared table in that within a society of honour-based stratification, rich and poor were called to share the same food, men and women were to see themselves as of equal worth,[104] and master and slave were to drink from the one cup. But while it is easy to affirm in words such a vision, when it had to take actual shape at the community meal, itself the believers' principal activity, then the act of eucharistic behaviour itself became part of the price of discipleship.

Paul in the fifties already knew of the divisions caused by commensality in Corinth, and that was but a foretaste of what was to come. Complaints about the good order of the communities' meals,[105] disputes about who has precedence at these gatherings,[106] and fears that people will take advantage of the hospitality[107] become the concerns of successive generations who

---

[103]Grignon 2001, 28.

[104]See Gal. 3.28 for the nature of the new community and Taylor 2004 on how the notion of men and women being equal in sacred meals was already known in Philo's vision of the Therapeutae/Therapeutrides.

[105]Jude 1.12 and 2 Pet. 2.14-5 deal with 'disorder' at meals; but what is desired as 'order' is unclear.

[106]The letter of James supposes that these disputes concern the ranking of members of the community at their meals: see Smit 2011 for a full analysis; and we need to recall it is the segregation at meals where there should be unity and equality that is part of the problems Paul responds to in Corinth: see Hollander 2009 on this problem; while the teachings of Jesus on the places of honour at feasts have to be seen in the light of these teachings being preached by evangelists at eucharistic gatherings which give them added significance, see especially the 'parable' in Lk. 14.7-15 (see Marshall 2009) where the ideal feast is (a) free from competition that would destroy the equality and unity of the ideal Christian banquet and (b) marked by commensality with the poor and the outcast; and also the parallel saying Mk 12.39; Mt. 23.6 and Lk. 20.46 where 'they' must not be like those who compete for 'places of honour' at feasts.

[107]The various fears of the *Didache* 11.4-12.5 (see Milavec 1994) and that of 2 Thess. 3.10 are examples.

became more concerned with the fact of the churches' customs and less •
with the new ethos of the Kingdom that was to animate these assemblies.
In a nutshell, while someone might be prepared to drink the common cup
of destiny with the crucified Jesus,[108] it was a step too far to drink it with
one's own slave. Eventually, ease and social convenience reduced the meal to
a token affair, with the implicit implication that there was sufficient natural
material to carry the supernatural form of the specifically religious action,
now with its own special name, of 'the Eucharist', administered by that same
group of cultic specialists in whose hands other aspects of public Christian
activity were being concentrated – a group that by the later third century
would see themselves as a *sacerdotium* socially analogous to the various
priesthoods of the Roman empire.[109]

It would take over a century for this formalization to take place, but the
important point for anyone seeking a theology of the Eucharist is that when
this development is seen (1) against our nature as meal-sharing animals
and (2) the meal practice of Jesus, which (3) we declare that we remember
as significant, then it has to be seen as a contraction from the reality of
discipleship. While celebrating 'the Eucharist' was now a less fraught activity
it also became an action that ignored – perhaps we should say 'forgot' – the
nature of what Christian communities were called to become. Moreover,
now, 'the Eucharist' isolated from its original setting needed to find other
justifications for its continuing prominence within community practice.
The act of giving thanks having lost its connection with a community's real
celebration, Jesus-fashion, of the Father's goodness, was now a piece of
religious ritual in search of a theology which would justify its inherited sense
of importance. And in it being the mystery of the encounter with Christ for
his church, it found such a theology which could be explored as a liturgical
enactment of the dominical command (as we see in the introduction of the
institution narrative in the Eucharistic Prayer)[110] and as a preached moment
of intimate revelation (as we see in patristic homilies such as that of Gregory
of Nyssa).[111]

---

[108]The notion of sharing a common cup is found most explicitly in Mk 10.38 (and parallel
in Mt. 20.22), but it can also be seen in Jn 18.11; and it is implicit 1 Cor. 10.21 and 11.26.
The notion of the shared common cup as the cup of common destiny does not appear in the
Didache. This will be explored in Chapter 6; and see O'Loughlin 2014b.

[109]See Laeuchli 1972; it is not my concern here to show how this development of a notion
of 'priests' (*sacerdotes*) was accommodated to the notion found in Hebrews that the Christ
was a unique priest. The significant point to note is that such theological justification was
generated *post eventum* when *episkopoi* and *presbuteroi* had already taken on the social
functions and self-understanding of being the Christian equivalents of the various priesthoods
they saw around them in society, and which they could also historicize as being themselves
the 'new covenant' version of the Levitical priesthood – again this historicization is part of a
post eventum quest for justification.

[110]See Ligier 1973.

[111]See Chapter 2, above.

Forgetting and remembering other meals

The new interest today in the meal as a human phenomenon and in shared meals among various groups, both Jews and gentiles, in the Greco-Roman world has another implication for those seeking to build a theology of the Eucharist: we must look to *all* the meals that were remembered concerning Jesus – not just 'the last Supper' or 'the eucharistic words' (along with some passages in John such as 6.48-58) – to see what his followers understood about the meals they were sharing and during which they engaged in the activity of eucharist. While many would without hesitation extend this interest to those meals where 'the breaking of the loaf' is mentioned (such as the Emmaus story in Lk. 24.13-25), that is not enough. The information on other meals without any of the expected pointers to 'the Eucharist' need be examined for the light they throw on the early communities' self-understanding of their meal sharing. So the Lukan story of the meal with the outcast Zacchaeus (Lk. 19.1-10) is as valuable in this quest as the Emmaus story, and along with the other memories involving the sharing of food or instructions on table fellowship.[112]

Once one has stated this position – that all meals remembered as important by a community throw light on their own meal practice and the values they attached to that practice – it seems so obvious as not to need any further justification. But it should be borne in mind that this is not readily recognized. Some exegetes writing from within communities with very developed theologies of the Eucharist feel they can adopt this approach only after a self-justifying section on the 'eucharistic words'.[113] Many more theologians writing on the Eucharist still only cite the standard passages as directly relevant to their topic, and leave issues like commensality out of account. While the teaching documents produced by churches, or church organizations, today are invariably tied to the inherited approach.[114] Yet the historical evidence continues to beckon us to recall what we have forgotten. The effect of broadening the evidence base from that small handful of passages to material that comes from every part of the narrative memory of the early churches as found in the gospels, and then being able to see that many other early texts have a bearing on Christian commensality (some such as the Letter of James were never even noticed in earlier studies), enables us to see the community meal as a basic element in all of the churches' lives to such an extent that such practice was seen as a basic form of continuity with Jesus and his activity in relationship to the Father. As Jesus was a person who valued meals, who took part in them, and used them as models of the

---

[112]See Smith 1987; and O'Loughlin 2013b.
[113]An example would be LaVerdiere 1996.
[114]The document from the World Council of Churches in 1982, *Baptism, Eucharist and Ministry*, is an example. To see that document, so remarkable in many ways, in perspective, refer to Lathrop 1996 and Wainwright 2007.

renewed Israel, the Kingdom, and the eschaton, so his followers build their communities around these meals and made them central to their identity.

If considering the whole extent of the meal practice of the early churches is of value, there are two specific implications of that approach, already touched upon, that need explicit attention. The first of these concerns 'the words of institution' with their echoes of 'the Last Supper'. If someone were to take part in any celebration of the Eucharist today, in any church that has fixed liturgical forms, one would quickly come to the observation that the key ritual texts of the Eucharist are the expressions, recalled as the *ipsissima verba Christi* within the liturgy, from the Last Supper: 'This is my body' and 'This is the cup of my blood'.[115] Indeed, so much attention has been given to these phrases as 'words of consecration' that their study has in the past often been seen as the study of the biblical basis of the Eucharist. Moreover, this view persists in a modern form whenever it is asserted that here the biblical text is itself a reflection of early practice/liturgy such that these words were being used by the communities in their meals/Eucharists; this ecclesial *Sitz im Leben* then presented them in the kerygma within the paradigm dominical meal.[116] While this seems a plausible, methodologically sound, explanation of the early situation, it is actually without historical foundation. The use of these 'dominical formulae' does not belong to the earliest strand of the church practice, but belonged as the pinnacle of all the meal stories *within the narrative kerygma* expressing the value attached in the memory of the church to Jesus' attention to their community meals. Their use as liturgical formulae only *developed at a later period* when our gospels were already being used as sacral texts to furnish a basis for the institution narrative – in effect, miming the Last Supper – within a Eucharistic Prayer.[117]

So, despite a long tradition of vociferous assertion of 'unbroken continuity' with 'the time of the apostles' on this very point, in the early centuries there were, to use the popular phrase, 'Masses without consecrations'![118] Hence, for the early period, it is quite useless to strain every drop of exegetical juice from those formulae in the hope of seeing what value those Christians placed on the Eucharist: those texts need to be viewed as part of the larger picture of practice and memory that have survived. For those key ritual texts of that practice we have to look to the formulae of blessing the Father such as those found in the *Didache*, which themselves can be shown to stand in the larger tradition of Jewish table prayers (to the extent that we can re-construct that

---

[115]The actual forms used in the liturgy vary in minor ways between the churches, and these, in turn, are harmonizations of the various forms found in the scriptural texts.
[116]This approach is criticized in detail in McGowan 1999b.
[117]See Ligier 1973; and see Talley 1976a and 1976b.
[118]See Taft 2003; the complex appeals to theories of 'development' in some of the Vatican's declarations on the 'validity' of the *Anaphora of Addai and Mari* (which in antiquity did not share in the development of 'a consecration') to assert that it had such a formula in an 'implicit way' can be seen as headline example of the differences in assumptions and method between 'apologetics using history' and historical investigation.

practice from a variety of sources) such as that of the *Birkat ha-Mazon*.[119] In these prayers we glimpse the anaphoric moments of the early meals[120]; if any formulae are going to carry the weight historically given to the 'words of institution', then it is these formulae. Clearly, such formulae were used widely in the meals of the disciples of Jesus, and indeed continued in use at meals even after the formalized and ritualized 'Eucharist' had evolved out of a real community meal.

So if the 'words of institution' were not the key ritual words used and valued as sacral formulae committed to memory as the prayers of the *Didache* were, what role did they play? The answer lies in the role the narratives we refer to as 'gospels' (and this also applies to Paul's act of remembering the final meal) played in relation to the kerygma and practice of the churches: they were interpretative texts that located the communities' present activity in its meals with the time of Jesus and his meals. These texts were narratives of what the meal meant to Jesus and the significance he attached to the blessing of the Father, and so were statements of how they too should view the meal, their sharing and the food. It is in this way that Paul appeals to the memory of the meal on the 'night when he was betrayed' (1 Cor. 11.23-6) as a guide for when the Corinthians gather for the Lord's supper (1 Cor. 11.20); so too the supper narratives in Mark, Matthew and Luke are interpretations of the actual event at which the narratives were being performed[121]; and this can be seen obliquely in the way Luke uses meal-memories to promote the evolution of the church's understanding of itself in Acts.[122] Therefore, we should use the now famous formulae to help us to understand the meal and its significance, rather than seeking to understand these texts as if they could reveal to us 'the meaning of the meal'. Put another way, if we consider liturgy/community practice as '*theologia prima*' which is followed by interpretation, then the actual prayers of the *Didache*, taken as typical, relate to the category of primary theology for the Eucharist, while the 'institution narratives' must be considered as secondary aetiological interpretations.[123]

---

[119]See Finkelstein 1929; and Bahr 1970; on the significance of Finkelstein's article, and how it was sometimes deliberately ignored by Christian scholars, see O'Loughlin 2013a.

[120]There is a tendency to refer to these prayers as the 'ritual component/element/words/moment' of the communities' meals, but this ignores the reality that it was the whole of the meal that was their ritual; hence my use of 'anaphoric moments'.

[121]The best exploration of this issue is McGowan 1999b.

[122]For example: Acts 2.46 or the various meals of Peter in Acts 10-11 and their subsequent 'exegesis' by Luke (see O'Loughlin 2013c).

[123]For many Catholic theologians who have inherited much from the scholastic mode of theology when dealing with 'the sacraments' this may seem shocking because the theology of 'real presence' assumes that the '*est*' is a metaphysical statement; while for many Protestants inheriting much from the tradition of placing the scriptures in a category apart from the churches' practice as the *norma normans non normata* or who seek locations for 'the sacraments' in dominical warrants (if not the *ipsissima verba*), this may seem to leave the Eucharist in the lurch; but it is no more than applying to these words the hermeneutic we apply to other statements in the gospel narratives.

The second point is to note that in early practice the eucharistic dimension was *inseparable* from the meal. Again this may be obvious from what has already been said, but there is a well-developed tradition (dating back to the nineteenth century when historians first noticed the role of the meal among early Christian groups) which has sought to sidestep this fact as part of an apologetic for inherited doctrine; and this apologetic is more pervasive than many would care to admit. This apologetic takes several similar forms such as 'the Eucharist took place *in the course* [my emphasis] of a meal' which suggests that 'the Eucharist' was a distinct entity that merely had an historical location at something that was formally distinct from it: 'a community meal'. We therefore do not have the meal of the Christians where they offered thanks to the Father, but a bundle of two substantially distinct realities merely combined in an accidental fashion. In this view, the meal gathering was the occasion for the celebration of the Eucharist. Then 'development' accounts for a growing intellectual clarity that allowed these two entities to be distinguished and separated: the religiously essential ritual (of which Jesus spoke when he commanded its repetition) was then preserved on its own (a formal Eucharist) while the common meal (a non-essential) became 'simply' a fraternal meal which gradually disappeared. This apologetic fantasy does not take account of the historical facts, is tenable only on the assumption that there is a perfect 'theology' at a later period which can judge the earlier, and, most importantly, it fails to account for the actual problems which led to the meal being abandoned in favour of the token affair that continues as an intrinsic part formal eucharistic liturgy.

This apologetic sought linguistic evidence in its support by treating 'the Eucharist' as a well-formed concept, which must then be distinct from all other terms such as 'the *Agape*' or even 'the Breaking of the Loaf'. So it was assumed that there were two distinct events, 'the Eucharist' and 'the Agape', which sometimes were (perhaps for convenience) conjoined! This 'solution' had its most famous exponent in the work of Gregory Dix[124] – and continues to crop up with depressing regularity among theologians who 'dip into history' for background. Imposing such partitioning on the past to accommodate and support later doctrinal certainties cannot be maintained once it is clear that one should look to the whole range of early meal events as a foundation for eucharistic theology. Meanwhile, historically, we should note what Andrew McGowan says of the long-standing practice:

> Dix consigned the meal of the *Didache* to the obscure category of the *agape*, understood to be another form of ritual meal whose very vagueness has often made it a convenient dumping ground for the unwanted meal evidence of the first few centuries.[125]

---

[124]Dix 1945, 19–23 (and in many other places besides).
[125]McGowan 1999a, 21–2; and see also McGowan 1997 which examines the problem more extensively.

In short, the emergence of the formal Eucharist must not be seen as a case of development if that is being imagined as a positive affair by which greater clarity and insight emerged out of some primordial confusion; rather the development must be seen as a failure in practice by communities who found the demands too great. Because the meal, given its place in practice and memory, could not be abandoned altogether, so it was curtailed until it had reached a minimal point and which was then re-validated by theological narrative. The meal, therefore, should be understood within 'the myth of monastic reform' – original insights become blurred, made quotidian, and reduced to tokens over time and need to be re-invigorated by reform[126]; rather than be seen within 'the myth of development' whereby a clear and sharp image emerges as the photograph gradually develops.[127] Those who seek the justification of the *status quo* in a quest for origins should perhaps note that they are invariably disappointed![128]

The event of significance

I appreciate that this chapter which began with noting how food is part of human culture has come by a series of steps into looking at the details of how theologians have assembled evidence for and against particular church practices and that this may seem a tortuous road! However, I do not see it as a road where every step follows logically on that before it, but rather as the series of pylons upon which rest a viaduct that can help us bridge the chasm between the insights into the creation which we can obtain from anthropology and history, on the one hand, and these discourses on the origins and theology of the Eucharist on the other. And as with crossing any viaduct on a motorway, I hope it has presented startling vistas coupled with that frisson of seeing from a distinct, perhaps precarious, viewpoint.

In a glimpse we could summarize this chapter in this way. We have seen that food is never mere alimentation because all connected with it is deeply significant to us – as is demonstrated with our constant concern with cooking. Moreover, we never simply eat food; rather, we share meals, and so in some way celebrate our basic human concerns and communion. The meal is as much a fundamental element of humanity as shared rationality or language: this is the basis of meals as religious events and a key to all liturgy. On a different note, food is crucial to our survival, its production and availability is central to economic, ecological and social systems – and so it is an ethical matter for humans. Every time we eat a meal we have to be conscious of the poverty that may mean someone close to us is suffering and

---

[126]See Ladner 1959.
[127]See O'Loughlin 1998b.
[128]See O'Loughlin 2012a.

undernourished, while famine is still common in many parts of the world despite our culture's unparalleled abilities to transport food around the planet. Believers in a Creator, much less the followers of Jesus, cannot hear these facts without acknowledging the duties of discipleship. Thankfulness to God and caring for the poor are inseparable activities that have their basic focus in food.

If any group of Christians then wishes to claim that the Eucharist is at the centre of the Christian life – and so presumably, believing in the incarnation, at the centre of human life – then both their practice and its explication as story, explanation and doctrine must be centred in our reality as *homines cenarii*. To the task of so locating the Eucharist we must now turn.

4

Locating the Eucharist

When we set about any theological investigation, we run up against the question of how our viewing of the world affects what we see; as Pierre Bourdieu has written: 'A vision of the world is a division of the world, based on a fundamental principle of division which distributes all the things in the world into two complementary classes. To bring order is to bring division, to divide the world into opposing entities'.[1] With this warning in mind, it is clear from the level of very early concern expressed by the disciples of Jesus regarding their common meals – Paul in I Corinthians, Mark in his narrative and James in his letter: all three sources being datable to before the destruction of the Jerusalem temple – that it was a matter of importance.

The meal and its conduct were more than just a matter of table manners and customs, however important they may be, but involved imitating the example of Jesus at his meals, and acting in and through him in the ultimate relationship with the Father. This imitation was, moreover, not merely a matter of historical mimesis of Jesus' actions in the past, but of modelling in the present the Kingdom inaugurated in Jesus.[2] As such, its importance was so implanted in the life, customs and the memories of the communities that despite all the changes in their circumstances, new influences, cultures and pressures, along with the sheer build-up of its own corpus of habit and reflection, that this practice remained central, and consequently would continually seek new explanations of its evolving roles within the communities.[3]

---

[1] Pierre Bourdieu 1990, 210.

[2] On this importance in liturgy of this distinction between mimesis and modelling, see O'Loughlin 2013f.

[3] We can see this by contrast with another practice that was seen as building the community desired by Jesus, and imitating him, but which became peripheral in practice: the washing of each other's feet. This practice, imagined by John as coming from a command of Jesus (Jn 13.14-5), did not embed itself in such as way in the churches' practice that as situations changed it needed to be re-invented rather than abandoned.

In this tradition of memory and community custom,[4] the accumulating body of explanation was the result of the need to answer simultaneously two practical questions. First, why were they bothering with this meal gathering at all; and so the question became one about what they were doing when they met? Second, if they were so bothered about this meal, then why was participation of importance, in what did participation consist, and how did they benefit from it? The first question evolved into the question of the nature of the Eucharist: what is it (with the dangers of reifying the action) or what does it mean (with the dangers of seeing the actual gathering as a practical/visible expression of a concept/spiritual reality). The second question became that of significance: what was its role in relation to the rest of Christian belief (which runs the danger of all such systematic building that the distinctiveness of the original custom becomes but a 'part' in newly constructed 'whole') and how much value can be placed on the practice (which runs the danger that 'purpose' or intended 'outcome' displaces the value that belongs to doing and living in a group). When something is done as the means to an end, it tends, imperceptibly but surely, to become 'but a means' towards that end – and when this happened to a human celebration such as a banquet, then activity is denatured at that very moment. A feast may have an occasion, but is its own justification (we party to party!); when a meal is used for some other purpose, it may still be perceived by some as a banquet, but its 'purpose' now means that the actual meal is changed into being an instrument producing or facilitating that outcome.[5] The activity stops being itself 'an end' and becomes but a vehicle towards something other than itself – and eventually concern resides in whether the instrument 'works': such concerns as 'is it valid?' and 'are all its parts valid?' become the crucial issues. How could one ask if a meal gathering at which, in Christ, the Father is blessed is 'valid' or 'invalid'? Until one instrumentalizes the action of the disciples' meal such questions do not even arise!

However, if the early meal-sharing practice was to continue in the communities – and we are thinking of groups of less than a hundred people,[6] it had to have a clear and important value that could be expressed in terms meaningful to those who posed the question. And this need has remained a constant down the centuries: indeed, the need that generated the question is more constant that the particular forms the question has taken, and far more constant than the range of answers that have been supplied to it. In any question relating to the importance of a practice, the simplest strategy

---

[4]The clearest evidence that that was the case is the fact that it was part of 'the *didachē*': as we see from the *Didache*.

[5]An example is the practice of net-working dinners whose purpose is to provide a forum where influence can be discreetly exerted; the table community thus is not merely utilitarian but exploitative, and such a cynical use of humans' eating together should be a warning to seeing the Eucharist as a meal with an ulterior motive.

[6]Except in most unusual situations, gatherings larger than a hundred people are virtually unknown before modern times, see Audet 1967, 167–70.

in providing an answer is via the way of opposition: dividing the world into parts that fit the existing understanding of the questioners.[7] The 'Eucharist' – here used as shorthand for the meal – is presented as *not* an ordinary meal in this reckoning and is distanced as far as possible from ordinary meals. Likewise, because it involves eating and drinking, this eating and drinking is viewed as *not* ordinary eating; it involves food, but this food *is not* ordinary food; and, its preparation is *not* ordinary cooking. Eventually, it becomes so distinct that it is not even perceived as a meal except that meals provide it with an allegorical vocabulary of emotions, images and words.

This way of opposition fitted the inherited divisions between the Levites and the other tribes, the temple and the rest of the land, the holy and the unholy; while it also made sense within the gentile context of the *fanum* – 'the other' – and the *profanum*. The classic modern statement of this position is that by Rudolf Otto where 'the holy' is the *ganz andere*[8]; there is no 'room' for the incarnation except as a token of itself. As such 'the actual incarnation' – a man called Jesus – becomes 'the means' of knowing an aspect of the mystery of God: and it is forgotten that instrumentalizing a human being is a contradiction of what it is claimed 'incarnation' means. Just so also with the Eucharist when it becomes so sacramentalized in its focus on what is not there in the meal, it contradicts the basic claim about God's closeness that can be celebrated in a human meal!

Moreover, the notion that the employment of such divisions in Christian explanation might not accord with either the memory of Jesus or an acceptance of the incarnation does not appear to have left any trace in the historical record. So the Eucharist was re-packaged within a set of *a priori* divisions that made it the point of encounter between the holy and the rest of life; and that point of encounter was itself otherworldly: an explicitly religious event whose very appearance reinforced this distinctiveness. The path became a well-worn one, and it ended in a total separation of eucharistic activity from the rest of Christian practice in either an iconostasis where the mystery was encountered beyond earthly sight, in a 'tabernacle' where the divine presence became physically located in food whose function was that of 'being there' and offering the real presence of Jesus for adoration distinct from its being there for eating, or in a rejection of these approaches such that the Eucharist became one more memory-producing ritual that could prompt minds to think of the truths of revelation but where the encounter with the divine had only a mnemonic origin in something actually done by Christians. In each case, there was a severing of the event of the Eucharist and Christians' normal course of living; and this fissure took practical expression in that

---

[7]This strategy was employed by Philo in *De vita contemplativa* to distinguish the pure God-centred symposia of the Therapeutae/Therapeutrides from the drunken symposia of the larger society, including philosophical meals described by Plato and Xenophon.
[8]Otto 1950.

'taking communion' became in most churches a rare event for 'the ordinary people' and this was not seen as problematic by pastors or theologians.

The complementary strategy in providing explanations was that of analogy with that which was more familiar, which had the additional benefit of making the whole event more comprehensible to on-lookers. While the first Latin apologist Minucius Felix (early third century) might point out that the Christians had neither 'altars nor shrines' thereby testifying to the unique nature of the worship inaugurated by the Christ[9]; for most Christian writers, however, Ignatius of Antioch being the most famous,[10] it was simpler to press Christian liturgical forms into the familiar shapes of Greco-Roman religion. Just as that society was familiar with altars – both domestic and communal – and sacrifices in every form and for every occasion from the libation of a drop of wine to the gods of the household to the most elaborate civic events, so too the Christians had a ritual which made sacrifices possible. Sacrifices were, after all, a key part of Greco-Roman cosmology by which life was kept going on an even keel and were viewed as one more, necessary, element in life. Just as the rituals of the society found physical focal points in altars – which are anything but table-like – so too the Christians had their focal points such that their common tables could be presented as their 'altars'.[11] This had ceased being a metaphorical identification by the mid-second century in some places[12] and was to become such a dominant idea that for many churches today the table on which they celebrate is simply referred to as 'the altar' (as if that were a proper descriptive noun without any trace of metaphor).[13]

---

[9]*Octavius*, 10, 2 or 32, 1 where he makes the same point – and 'altars' are representative of the whole network of pagan cult in the *Octavius*; Minucius knew that altars and repeated sacrifices upon them were the cultural heart of the experience of Greco-Roman religion, and because he knew what they actually looked like, there was no danger of his confusing them with the tables from which the communities ate their meals.

[10]The issue of Ignatius is complex for many Christian theologians in that he is often still dated to c. 100–110, whereas he should be dated to c. 150–160 at the earliest (see Barnes 2008), and as such an early writer seen as the best witness to the notion of three-tier ministry (i.e. for many this is seen as equivalent to a demonstration of the authenticity of a Christian priesthood *qua tale*) and so it is presumed that his views on the Eucharist are therefore above reproach (and, of course, they do fit with what later emerged!); but if one studies his views on the Eucharist in contrast to that of earlier writers or indeed his contemporaries, then it is clear that he has absorbed many assumptions from Hellenistic religion without question (see Brent 2006) and, in particular, has come to present the purpose of eucharistic activity as a direct counterpart to the role of sacrifices in those cults (see Lathrop 1990).

[11]In the final pages of Pocknee 1963, the author tells us that we can now see that there is no basis for not using the word 'altar' or preferring instead some formula such as 'the Lord's table'; but despite his conclusion which was intended as an apologetic of the then current 'High Church' style of Anglican liturgy, one can find there what is still the most convenient account of the evolution of the altar from the table.

[12]For example, in the environment in which Ignatius worked, see Lathrop 1990.

[13]Just as the hand-tool that inserts nails is a 'hammer', so the oblong box-shape in a church-building is called an 'altar'; the demonstration of this lack of metaphor can be seen obliquely in that the object known as the 'war stone' intended to recall the 'sacrifice' of British soldiers in World War I could not be called an 'altar' but took over the familiar ecclesial shape to convey the same intent.

In this scenario, the activity of the Eucharist became effectively the prescribed formula that had to be used in order to achieve the sacrificial intention. So as the spilling of a token amount of liquid constituted fulfilling the required Hellenistic sacrifice, an interrupting but necessary religious moment in the course of one's life, so too the Christian sacrifice answered a similar need for Christians, save that, as Christian writers were swift to point out, their sacrifice was genuine and true: directed to the true God from the altar of the, now known, true God.[14] But the Eucharist was now something done, distinct from the gathered activity of the community. It was now also formally distinct from the reality of living in dependence on God (acknowledging their ontological location) and thanking him (the ethical response to that awareness) in Christ (the source of their identity).

Such 'explanations' of the Eucharist as a particular, and indeed 'true', version of a virtually universal religious phenomenon were so attractive in their power of communication and comprehension that it is little wonder that there is almost no trace of any awareness of how it was betraying so much that was basic to the Christian eucharistic activity.[15] This failure is all the more understandable if we remember that at the same time these explanations were produced, actual practices at the community gathering were changing because of the practical and social problems that a real meal-gathering – except in self-selecting groups – was causing within the stratified confines of Greco-Roman urban society. Indeed, these social problems may have been the primary driver of the need for new explanations being developed. However, once these separations had taken place, we can see it was but a small step from seeing the Eucharist as something that 'we' as the community do together to it being a religious action that is done by the ritual specialists, the clergy, for us and on our behalf. This not only fitted with the notion of the way the civic priesthoods offered sacrifices for and on behalf of the communities (and so was eminently comprehensible), but also explained the value of attendance at the ritual (and so served as a justification of actual continuing practice) as well as fitting with what was increasingly the self-understanding of the church-leadership. The bishops who assembled at Elvira in Spain in 306 had gone sufficiently down this road that they saw no problem in perceiving their place within the Church as being the Christian equivalents of the *flamines* and *pontifices* – language that has in part survived down to today – and as sacral cultic figures

---

[14]The adequacy of this as a form of apologetics (and indeed possibly its value as catechesis) is not in question; what is in question is its adequacy as a witness to the tradition of early Christian thanksgiving to the Father of the Christ.

[15]The only possible trace is Minucius: if one sees apologetic as directed to one's fellow believers to sustain them in their discipleship using the form of a dialogue with 'the other', then his concern to distance a cult of altars and sacrifices from Christian worship could be seen as an attempt to correct what he saw as a confusion within Christian thinking. If that was his aim, however, it appears to have been a failure.

whose lifestyle and status (*ordo*) distinguished them from the Christian populous.[16]

Centre and summit?

The outcome of such approaches is that the Eucharist might be declared to be 'the centre and summit' of the Christian life, but actually it was an event that a Christian non-cleric 'went to', to which one had as minimal exposure as was compatible with fulfilling laws (which needed the added 'force' that they bound under pain of sin such was the experienced irrelevance/unattractiveness of the practice), and then one resumed life with all its demands afterwards. One may take one's appropriate part in the ritual, but it belonged to a separate sphere of life identified specifically as the cultic domain. Moreover, such encounters only made sense in so far as they answered an individual's need: 'why need I bother' is answered by 'because you will get this as a result for your bothering'. So there was a further division between the claims of ecclesiology and the imagery of the Lord's banquet, on the hand, and the actual narrative surrounding the liturgy, the paraliturgy of practices came to become indistinguishable from the Eucharist in practice. In short, it became a temple-based activity, from which an individual could obtain a variety of religious benefits.[17]

There might be attempts to bridge this separation by the adoption of a specific spirituality, but this was always something belonging to the interpretative consciousness of the few, while most Christians either considered the eucharistic event as but a variant on a worship service fulfilling a religious duty or an almost magical encounter with Jesus or a complex of many such notions. Meanwhile, there was never a shortage of new, informal explanations as to why that which was important in the tradition of worship was deemed to be so valuable to people in the course of the lives. Such explanations ranged from the pragmatic (hearing Mass before a battle or an examination to invoke divine mercy or aid)[18] through notions of a divine commerce (as

---

[16]See Laeuchli 1972. The Synod of Elvira – although just one local gathering of bishops – has a special place in the history of Christian practice. For some Roman Catholics, it is prized as the earliest 'conciliar' sources for clerical celibacy (see Denzinger-Bannwart 1922, nn. 3001–2); however, its real importance lies in its providing the clearest evidence – as shown by Laeuchli – of the extent to which Greco-Roman notions of sacral personages, and so 'clericalism', gradually replaced earlier notions of ministry where all the baptized shared the same theological standing – and with no *living* person have a distinct sacral intercessory role (see O'Loughlin 2013i).

[17]One could read the *miracula* relating to the Eucharist in hagiography to see the full range of these benefits; for anyone unfamiliar with such material can do no better than read the *Dialogi* by Gregory the Great.

[18]The most famous example is that of the English army 'hearing Mass' on the morning of the Battle of Agincourt (25 October 1415); see Keegan 1976, 82.

in Gregory the Great's popular catechesis)[19] through the ascetical[20] to the eschatological (for instance, the practice of the 'Nine First Fridays').[21] Having divided the Lord's meal from meals, the 'Christian altar' from real tables, and made the leader distinct as one enrolled in a Christian *sacerdotium*, one then had either to abandon the practice altogether, and this from the nature of ritual as repetition was not possible (nor would it even have been imaginable as an option until the sixteenth century), or to discover new theologies to justify it.

Paradigm dissonance

In so far as the Eucharist gained its special status through being distinct from the rest of our constant engagement with food, we Christians found ourselves distanced from the paradigm of our memories (all those meals where Jesus ate with his followers and whose recollection in the early churches has been perceived as the basis of the Eucharist), while still in need of surrogate experiences as communities which very often took meal forms because we are *homines caenarii* (the earlier analogues to the contemporary 'coffee after church' so that people can speak to one another),[22] and special 'graces' for meals (for we still had to be thankful and in the precariousness of food we recognized the divine goodness) without linking such practices to the pattern set by Jesus. Likewise, we not only declared a belief in the incarnation, but also espoused an 'incarnational theology' – God is present in the whole of his creation and most especially in our humanity – but then,

---

[19]See the presentation of the effects of multiple regular celebrations on those suffering *post mortem* for their sins in his *Dialogi*; the impact of this catechesis is explored in O'Loughlin 2009a; for the reception and development of these views of the Eucharist by Bede, see O'Loughlin 2014.

[20]A major theme in writing on the Eucharist and the religious life was that 'hearing Mass' was part of the perfect day; and so 'daily Mass' (and later would be added 'and communion') became an ascetical ideal. The various admonitions to devotions to the Blessed Sacrament such as 'visits' and 'holy hours' are another form of this trend: see Mitchell 1982, 129–95.

[21]A devotion that became very popular in Catholic countries in the twentieth century: it was pursued because in a 'private revelation' to St Margaret Mary Alacoque (1649–90), it was announced that anyone who went to Mass, and received Communion [imagined as separate events], on the first Friday of nine consecutive months would be certain to have a priest present at the time of their death who could both absolve them of their sins and grant them a plenary indulgence for the punishment due to their sins. As a boy I remember a priest who promoted it in the 1960s each month as 'the best special offer in town!'

[22]While 'coffee after the service' is a practice linked clearly to the cult and those who take part in the cult; traditionally communities have found occasions when they ate and celebrated together – but they did not link that celebration with the Eucharist; although in the case of the community's feast day – *fiesta* – a celebration of the Eucharist might be one of the events on the programme.

somewhat discordantly, imagined the eucharistic meal *by its distinction from* that most human of our characteristics: our meal sharing.

Remedying this discord, removing the cognitive dissonance, and avoiding the path of world division are the challenges we must face as theologians if we are to be true to our eucharistic memory, our human integrity both as creatures and as *homines caenarii*, and to act incarnationally. So, can we relate all our meals in a continuum in such a way that the eucharistic meal is the summit of our human meal sharing? Put another way, can food, eating and drinking, and sharing meals really be a vehicle of that which is most important and significant in our relationship with God?

We should begin any answer to this question on a realistic note. If we were to try to quantify Christian experience (i.e. what most Christians have thought most of the time), then the answer would be a firm negative. Meals that provide physical sustenance, even those taken together in an avowedly Christian group such as the shared meal of some Mennonite communities[23] or the formal community meals in a monastery, are one thing; gathering for the Lord's Supper or Mass is quite another.

Let us now pose this question obliquely. If one suggested that there is need to engage in personal prayer as part of the Christian life – being alone in one's own room in the sight of the Father (Mt. 6.6) – then most Christians would agree this was a 'religious act' and a Christian activity. Likewise, recalling how the core memories of Christian faith – as found in the canonical scriptures – had been part of worship activities since the beginning, few would now doubt that the activity of engaging with them is both religious and Christian. Moreover, this practice would be the basis for many other reflective activities such as individual scripture study, *lectio divina* or various forms of meditation. More controversially, one could look at the widespread practice of lighting a candle before an icon or statue as a prayer. Even those who would reject this action as not appropriate to themselves would acknowledge that it was an act that belonged within the sphere of religion. Likewise, the act of burning a few grains of incense, while rejected by many Christians today, can be seen as having a long history as an act of prayer in Christianity, in the Roman world, and in the world of the Jerusalem temple. It is part of our religious memory (e.g., Mt. 2.11), and is seen as, fundamentally, a religious act. Similarly, there are actions beyond the cultic sphere which are seen as demanded by Christian faith – and, thereby, intrinsic to living a religious life – such as care for the needy, providing for the poor, seeking liberty for the oppressed and caring for the sick (to employ for convenience one early list of such actions as found in Matthew's gospel). To engage in any of these actions is to engage simultaneously in a human action that can be perceived

---

[23]The place of the Eucharist in Mennonite tradition was explored in a special issue of their journal *Vision: Journal for Church and Theology* 2/1 (2001) entitled: 'Holy Communion'; the papers by Finger 2001; Boers 2001 and Steiner 2001 are particularly important in terms of my argument here.

as good, and in a religious action belonging to the arrival of the Kingdom (see, for example, Mt. 25.31-46). Likewise, there are actions such as bearing witness to the good news, or acting as teachers or prophets within the church, which, if not perceived as cultic, are perceived as actions that are essential to discipleship.[24]

Could it be that eating and drinking together by Christians, sharing food with one another or preparing food for one another is just as much a religious, cultic and Christian activity as those just mentioned? Could having a common meal not simply be liturgy in the sense of 'public service', but in the specific Christian sense of liturgy as 'common worship of God'? If we can answer this question, then the task of locating the Eucharist, that is Christian eucharistic activity, within Christian living might become a more manageable issue.

Levels of added significance

To answer this question, one must develop some way of thinking about food, its preparation and its sharing in a meal as activities that can be seen within the sphere of specifically Christian action, because, even more fundamentally, they are in-built into our humanity and our history. We might begin by re-imagining the Eucharist in terms of an analysis of our relationship, both now and in the past, to our sustenance. This proceeds by noting how in every human encounter with food, whether of individuals or groups, there is a specifically human 'added significance' lying alongside the practicalities of the task; and that this added significance embraces a religious dimension. In turn, this allows us to imagine that in every food memory we, as disciples of Jesus, possess there is an opening to the divine and the possibility of acting in continuity with Jesus in the relationship he established between us and the Father and which is enabled for us by the Spirit. If that can be shown, then in our engaging with food, celebrating it in continuity with our basic Christian memories, we are acting truly and properly in a religious manner.

From another perspective, because we never have 'mere matter', 'just sustenance' in terms of food/eating/sharing meals, while, likewise, we never have at the Eucharist 'simply the spiritual' or only 'the divine' for there are always the liturgical vestiges of the meal,[25] we can but conclude that this 'added significance' is a graduated phenomenon, and we can see its

---

[24]See, for example, 1 Cor. 12.28; Eph. 4.11; or the various ministries mentioned in the *Didache*.

[25]Even in the most rarefied scholastic analyses of the Eucharist, there is the token eating of the wafer; and even if that eating is not considered essential to 'the confection' of the Eucharist, then there is still the wafer held in the presider's fingers which forms the 'this' for consecration. Trent insisted that no substance of 'bread' or 'wine' remained, but had to face empirical reality and note that a '*species*' of each remained.

religious dimensions as building-up incrementally within our nature.[26] Such a perspective can highlight how eucharistic action is grounded in the reality of what we are and what we do as humans in living life. Such a vision would be a genuinely incarnational theology of the Eucharist.

We might recall also that this notion that the Eucharist must be located in the world of lived discipleship and be in continuity with the created order is a Christian *desideratum*. This is emphasized, for instance, in the basic blessing formulae that can be found in many modern liturgies. Here is an example:

> Blessed are you, Lord, God of all creation. Through your goodness we have this bread to offer, which earth has given and human hands have made. It will become for us the bread of life.[27]

This prayer implies that we locate eucharistic activity in a continuum from encountering the life-sustaining earth, through human work, common skill and ingenuity, through to the explicit memory that the food being held on a plate for the community to share and eat will also become for them 'the bread of life'.[28] This simple action assumes that the act of blessing God is intrinsically linked to the whole that is the human situation as food-dependent creatures.

So could we proceed – giving priority to practice – through a set of ascending binary relationships that would both identify what is unique in the Eucharist, while refusing to isolate such moments of our activity from the rest of life? Such an approach would then be genuinely rooted in the creation where the divine is not an 'addition' to the creation but works in and through it. While acknowledging our dependence on the Father which is the basis for our action of blessing/thanking, we would then be celebrating the richness of our memories of God-with-us in the historical individual, Jesus, whose distinctive manner of blessing the Father we have made our own. In this sense also this would be an incarnational eucharistic theology.

Moreover, just as it is a set of binary divisions that have been used to remove the Eucharist from the centre of 'ordinary' life to a pious periphery, so too we can use another set of binaries – in this case additive binaries – to

---

[26]Thomas Aquinas, *Summa theologiae* I, 1, 8, ad 2.

[27]This prayer is taken from the 1969 Catholic ritual; it has inspired similar prayers among other western churches (e.g. in *Common Worship*) who have reformed their liturgies in recent decades, while itself showing the inspiration of early *Berakah* forms such as those in the *Didache*.

[28]The content and meaning of a liturgical text is not simply that of its verbal statement; the text comprises that verbal element, who makes the statement, the actions that always accompany it [at the very least that is what the person who uses the words is doing when the words are uttered], the material elements that are involved and its location in the whole liturgical event.

show how eucharistic activity is both unique and wholly within life's process for the community of the baptized.[29]

Level 1: Biological matter to foodstuff

An obvious starting point is the human situation in the natural environment. Through ever more complex involvement with the environment, we humans moved from supporting ourselves by hunting and gathering into the new cultural situation of farming and agriculture. This process did not merely change what we ate, but transformed those foodstuffs themselves, and, in the process, we were transformed as a society and as individuals within it. Our food production processes made us the societies we are. Moreover, while the foodstuffs were gradually transformed, so too was their significance in our societies: some were staples, others were seasonal, while others became rare and luxurious. The new foods not only allowed the growth of more complex social networks, but they also became a central part of culture because society was formed around their production and expressed its identity in relationship to that production. Still today we use categories such as 'hunter-gatherers', 'pastoralists' and 'farmers' as basic descriptions of societies. So we have a given – the raw materials of food such as the various grains – and something else, the community's skills and labour network that can transform such biological materials into actual food, alongside the web of culture that enables that transformation to take place. Here is the first binary: raw materials and a culture which can transform them into foodstuffs. In this process these foodstuffs become imbued with meaning and become the vehicles of meaning for us. Food does not grow, it is plants and animals that grow: it is human work, situated within a society, that turns plants and beasts into what can become our foods.

Because we turn plants and animals into foodstuffs, even the apparently simplest foodstuff, such as a handful of grain, is a bearer of human memory and meaning.[30] It is a product that retains within itself both what grows and the fruit of human agency – and it is that agency that is the cause of its being a foodstuff rather than biological matter. As such, it embodies the significance inherent in that human processing. As the work of art has

---

[29]For an example of how such a set of additive binaries can be used to gain a fuller appreciation of the meals imagined by Philo, see Engberg-Pedersen 1999.

[30]Many years ago I made this point after giving a paper in Ireland, and was challenged that this simply was not the case: food was food and related to the biological order, memory related the intellectual order (and so the level at which issues of eucharistic theology should studied). At that point, to my great amusement, I could see through the lecture hall's window the illuminated logo of the Bank of Ireland: the stylized head of a stalk of wheat! While my theological opponent wished to limit the domain of human memory, the advertising genius who devised this logo in the late 1960s knew that actual memory is far richer in its power of association.

meaning in that it embodies the genius of its creator and is significant to its perceiver, so a foodstuff is a primary work of human art and meaning.

For those who sow, reap, thresh, dry, transport and mill, the flour that results from grain is already invested with various layers of human value. It is their contribution to the network, by which we sustain ourselves as human beings, that makes possible the survival of the society. Moreover, it is the means by which we celebrate our existence. Already at this fundamental stage in our sustenance and survival human beings are aware of the mystery of the universe around them: the order of the seasons, the fertility of the earth, the wonder of the first green shoots or of the new eggs or lambs and of the fragility of the whole sequence – a sudden storm in spring or a disease can spell famine later in the year. At this stage there is also a complex set of human relationships, expertise and creativity. Furthermore, all these require collaboration, exchange and the sharing of skills; hence it enters the ethical sphere with the need for prudence (and today this would express itself as ecological concern), justice, honesty and peace. Collaboration in food production cannot be imagined apart from the ethical dimension of our existence, nor our existence apart from food production.

There is an implicit awareness of the divine in the appreciation of the goodness of the earth or the precariousness of existence, and an explicit invocation of the divine in human prayers for the harvest – be that a fertility figurine from the Ancient Near East or any of the blessings relating to the production of foodstuffs in the 1614 *Rituale Romanum* or the section on 'The Agricultural Year' that is an intrinsic element of *Common Worship* – whereby we invoke God as the creator and sustainer of our lives. Looking at this from another perspective, to assert that one could imagine food production holistically without some reference to the divine is tantamount to a declaration of atheism.

The human, indeed religious, awareness that is inherent at this level is probably that which is most alien to most of us in the developed world today. Most of us have very little contact with those primary transformations or with the precariousness of the link between food and life. We may hear of food shortages (perhaps as fluctuations in the 'futures' market' of the stock exchange) or famines in distant places, but we have the luxury of being able to think of such news in terms of problems to be fixed: we read the nature of food production in a radically secular way. Likewise, we might engage in a little home baking or buy some vegetables from a farmers' market or even have a small vegetable plot, but these are incidental activities even for those who take part in them. This experiential distance produces a lack of sensitivity to the place of food production in our humanity: it just happens! So likewise, while we may profess faith in God as creator, we may not be aware of this dependence or indeed even of our own skills, 'the work of human hands', that transform biological materials into foodstuffs. It is worth recalling that the origins of blessing God at a meal – the eucharistic activity in which we see Jesus engaged – belongs to a world that was close both to agriculture and the basic food production processes. We see this in the naturalness with which the Yahwist storyteller in Genesis imagines the first people as agriculturalists – from his perspective what else could they be![31] Likewise, the incidental awareness of the seasons in the evangelists' stories,[32] or the ubiquity in archaeological sites of that primary piece of food-processing technology: the quern.[33]

This first level has also direct implications for our eucharistic appreciation. If a community gathers to praise the Father for his goodness, then they must seek to stand in his presence with integrity as human beings as well as with integrity as disciples. This integrity has all too often been seen in individualist terms of private sinfulness or in terms of the cultic problem of purity[34]; but it is the community's integrity that is at issue in the Eucharist for it is an ecclesial action. In what would such ecclesial integrity consist? Just as consciousness of our own relationship to food is supposed in making thanksgiving over food our basic eucharistic action – we must be aware of God's goodness in giving us the food before we can be genuinely thankful for it – we can only act with integrity if we are aware of other communities' needs with regard to food and their rights within the creation as children of God who are as loved in the creation as we are ourselves. So can we simply rejoice in a banquet when there is a failure of food elsewhere? If there is famine or food poverty somewhere else is that not a call to help our sisters and brothers – precisely because we are aware of our debt to God's goodness that allows us to gather and thank him. To bask in a liturgical banquet thanking the Father while others starve without it impinging on us is the liturgical expression *de facto* of self-satisfaction. Our verbal language may say one thing; our real communication is the declaration: 'I'm all right Jack!' In a similar vein come the ongoing issues of social justice and corporate human responsibility: a community that declares itself in dependence on God's mercy for its sustenance must act in a sustainable way itself.[35] So integrity in blessing the Father in prayer demands corporate concern for the ecosystem that sustains life. Likewise, because we can only have our food through a complex of human interchanges we must be aware of what makes a just exchange that does not exploit another child of God, along with the corresponding awareness of the respect we owe to others and their skills. Indeed, in asserting our dependence on God for food, because food is also 'the work of human hands', we must be aware of our dependence upon, duties towards and thankfulness to God for the whole human network.[36]

---

[31]Gen. 3.19 – Adam must labour for his bread by tilling the land; and 4.2 – 'Abel was a keeper of sheep, and Cain a tiller of the ground'; and being food producers their first action must be to thank God, here lies the sanctity of Abel and the wickedness of Cain (4.3-7).

[32]Jn 4.35; or, for example, the imagery of harvesting in Mk 4.26-9.

[33]See Kuijt and Finlayson 2009.

[34]See Meens 1996; Elliott 1999, 14–34 and 61–80; and Berger 2011, 107–25.

[35]This is the interplay of the human and divine that underlies the prayer 'forgive us our trespasses as we forgive those who trespass against us'; and can be seen in narrative form in Mt. 18.23-35.

[36]The work of Méndes Montoya 2009 brings this out in detail.

This level also has direct implications for our liturgical behaviour. In times past the agricultural year was apt to make its presence felt in a variety of special devotions, but these were seen as paraliturgical, popular affairs rather than being linked directly to the Eucharist. At best, the Eucharist became the key presbyterally dominated devotion among others. This disjunction was due, for the most part, to viewing the Eucharist as an action done because of its consequences, the *opus operatum*, rather than seeing it as the mode by which Christians uniquely thank the Father. In a similar fashion many churches in the nineteenth century developed new liturgies of thanksgiving of which the 'Harvest Festival' is the most famous.[37] Many have decried this as some sort of debased artificial liturgy that makes little sense in an industrial world where few if any in the gathering are involved in food production. However, to simply accept such a 'disconnect' between nature and sustenance is to undermine the very consciousness that must characterize the vocation of Christians to have a real engagement with nature as God's creation. However, in those churches where this is one of the 'big events' of the year – with tangible and action-based involvement by many groups within a community – this festival is sometimes not seen as intrinsically eucharistic. The Eucharist – seen perhaps as the possibility of 'taking communion' – is not celebrated that Sunday, when the focus is upon 'thanking God for his bounty'.[38] While for Catholics the cycles of the weekly Eucharist is determined as part of an overall scheme for the year, which does not include a harvest festival, there is, usually, no formal moment in the year when the relationship of human beings to food production is celebrated.[39] These various disconnects go a long way towards explaining why there can be such a gap between official eucharistic rhetoric, formal theology, liturgical practice and what is *actually experienced* by those whose actions, ordinary Christians 'in the pews', create liturgy. Yet the drama of God and humanity has its 'first act' in the production of foodstuffs.

Level 2: Foodstuffs to food

The second step is that foodstuffs, once produced, need again human involvements so that they become the food we eat. The farmer, the miller, the commodity trader, the lorry driver, the shopkeeper deal in foodstuffs; it

[37]In some hill communities in Wales, there are still today Church in Wales services held in the springtime in thanksgiving for the lambing season. Alas these are rarely perceived as eucharistic, but arguably they are in their inspiration in continuity with the origins of the Passover.

[38]However, in what is the most serious attempt to overcome this disjunction – 'The Agricultural Year' section of *Common Worship* – there is a presumption that a celebration of the Eucharist is the most fitting context.

[39]Expressions of dependence on God's goodness for food often took forms that had minimal formal links with the Eucharist such as rogation processions around the fields.

is cooking that produces food.[40] So foodstuffs, already bearing one layer of meaning, become the bearers of additional values, of culture, a yet richer expression of human skill and artistry, and, most importantly, witnesses to the love and care of those bonds that are closest to us. Not only does food become a bearer of meaning within the community where the cooking takes place, but it also becomes a bearer of the distinctiveness and individuality of those who prepare it. It is *our* cooking, it is *our* culture, and it speaks of *our* community and *our* family. It carries our history, our present values and, indeed, our images of perfection. More intimately, the interplay of the work needed in preparing food binds society at the domestic level and is constitutive of the relationships that matter most in life. Because food preparation affects us at all these levels, when we ignore its place in our lives we become blind to an essential element in making us who we are. This may seem an extravagant claim, but imagine a couple or a family professing love for one another where no one even made a cup of tea for another!

How food preparation relates to memory and understanding is most easily seen at the community level. Every human group has its distinctive foodstuffs (as can be seen by the 'ethnic shelves' in any supermarket with a culturally diverse clientele), along with its own styles and values in cooking. A stroll in any large town will show the range of different cuisines available. My daily walk to my office might be taken as typical: I pass a Greek restaurant, a Thai (two of these), an Indian (two of these), an Italian, a Chinese (three of these), a chipper, a pizza place and three fast-food outlets – these latter are as laden with cultural memories and values as any 'ethnic' restaurant one could visit. This medley is a direct index to the cultures that live side by side in a Nottingham suburb, and indirectly a guide to the different histories of those groups. What, for example, is the difference between Greek and Turkish coffee? No one seems to know, but one will never be served Turkish coffee in a Greek restaurant! In most societies (but not in modern urban societies), the *local* cuisine is as distinctive as the landmarks, and so the local variant of stew carries the ethnic name: 'Irish stew', 'Scotch broth' or 'Poté Asturiano'. How we react to this diversity of cooking styles also carries our cultural memories: in Britain there are umpteen 'Indian' restaurants but they are invariably staffed by people of Pakistani origin, meanwhile modern India and Pakistan are often on the brink of war. There is no Vietnamese nor north African restaurant on my walk to work; but were I living in France, I would probably meet one of each! Cooking is deeply connected with our view of the world around us and who we are in that world!

---

[40]These activities do not form a simple continuum: 'food production' is a diffused and lengthy process with only the general aim of producing human foodstuffs; cooking tends to be local and immediate (or virtually immediate in the case of making a special cake or pudding that is to be eaten on a definite timescale or where it is done vicariously as in 'ready to eat' meals or by using a freezer to distribute the work of cooking over a longer time span) and is directly linked to the actual moment of eating.

Cooking not only carries cultural memories: it is the locus of far more personal memories. The hearth (where cooking took place for most people over most of human history) or more recently the kitchen is often thought of as the *focus* – in all senses – of the domestic unit. Here basic society is created and our closest relationships maintained. Cooking, indeed, is a key part of family tradition, and even in an age of celebrity cookbooks there are recipes handed down in families often bearing the name of their originator such as 'grandma's stew' or 'Aunt Mary's cake'. Likewise, there is 'the taste of home' which even if it is simply a romantic illusion of 'the good old days' still exercises a powerful draw on our emotions: as we can observe in the way it is exploited in food advertising. Cooking is central to the domestic rituals that are still to be found in modern families: menus carry memory.[41]

This relationship of cooking to memory and perception can be illustrated by the diversity of our reactions to some stock phrases: What image does the term 'fast food' conjure for us – and is it more than simply a style of food? Have you heard of the 'slow food' movement which is as much a philosophy of life as a set of recipes? We all know what we expect from 'pub food'; surely you would recognize 'institutional food' and in deploring the lack of care in its preparation indirectly affirm that cooking can be a vehicle/sacrament of love between people. We are never far from some engagement with cooking. In the refectory of a theological college in Bangalore (in India), I saw this plaque: 'Food shared; power released'.

Cooking is also a gendered affair. The butcher and the baker may be men, but most of the cooking at home is done by women – and historically it is this essential contribution that is forgotten. People remember the food as an object and the event at which the food is eaten, but those who prepared it are rarely mentioned. The most studied meal in human history, 'the Last Supper', has had almost endless studies devoted to its food, yet we skip over the preparations as little more than arranging the room, and wholly ignore the fact that all that food had to be cooked! But those who cooked the food were most probably women, and the bread was baked, almost certainly, by women[42] – and the food carried the stamp of their labour. The history of cooking is now a significant part of cultural history; a development that is seen as taking the equality of men and women seriously; and if our eucharistic activity ignores cooking, then it fails to acknowledge the historical contribution of women to our ecclesial endeavour.

Hence, when we appreciate food, we must appreciate the memory, skills, creativity and love that had brought the food there and of which it is an

---

[41]Some people imagine that domestic rituals have disappeared with the rise of modernity, but ritual as a feature of human life is far more resilient. We may not make a particular plum pudding at Christmas like our parents did, but we may have an equally sacrosanct ritual such that on a child's birthday we go for a pizza. And pizza chains, in response, foster such ritual adherence.

[42]See Chapter 3; the point is repeated here as we are so apt to ignore it.

ontological expression. Today when an informal 'grace' is offered before a meal, it is commonplace to recall 'those who prepared it for us'; but, significantly, if one looks back at the 'classic' shape of western blessings,[43] the food is thought of simply as a product of divine action and nature: all the loving energy of those close to the table who made it possible is simply ignored – the prayer becomes part of the veil of women's invisibility. Likewise, formal theologies of the Eucharist that speak of the actual 'food' as 'elements' whose substance ceases 'save for the *species*' forget that this is equivalent to declaring that all that labour is nugatory, merely incidental to later events when this 'food' becomes 'significant'. The fact that it is already rich with human significance is devalued to virtually zero. By contrast, if we take human reality seriously, this fundamental significance must be valued and celebrated no matter what else is celebrated and remembered with that food.

At this point we see one of those telling disjunctions, and anamnetic dissonances, that are part and parcel of most medieval and modern eucharistic practice. The anamnetic dissonance takes this form: when we recall the food of the Eucharist we recall the very best foods mentioned in the scriptures[44]; yet the actual bread used by most western Christians, commonly referred to as 'altar bread', is not only tasteless, but one would be hard pressed to eat more than a few particles without a sense of disgust. Practically, the disjunction takes this shape: most cultures value their own bread as an expression of who they are, and the more elegant the table the less likely one is going to see mechanically produced 'sliced bread' or bland 'bread rolls'. Appreciating a local or distinctive bread is a part of culinary refinement – and we are prepared to pay for a share in that refinement when we eat out! But the bread of our eucharistic celebration – too often pre-cut standardized wafers – is the original industrialized food commodity! At a moderately festive meal, we might be offered a choice of half a dozen types of bread – all carefully baked and skilfully presented; for the anticipation of the Heavenly Banquet, we have a mass-produced paste of flour and water piled in a heap!

By the time we come to the table where we eat, what is before us is not merely an assemblage of foodstuffs but a share in a cultural experience, a set of values, a product of skill, creativity, an expression of caring and a web of memories. The more we can appreciate this, the more we can appreciate the nature of who we are, and where we stand in the larger drama of God-given life.

---

[43]The prayer '*Benedic, Domine, nos*': 'Bless us, O Lord, and these thy gifts which from thy bounty we are about to receive, through Christ our Lord. Amen'.

[44]See Ps. 81.16: 'I would feed you with the finest of the wheat, and with honey from the rock I would satisfy you'. This verse as the antiphon/motet *Cibavit eos* became an important textual image in the cult of Corpus Christi in the thirteenth century.

Level 3: From food to shared meals

While it is conceivably possible to live on raw foodstuffs such as berries and fruits, for most people this would be seen as a serious privation. Likewise, it is possible to imagine someone who cooks all his/her own food and also always eats alone, but such images do not convey a human ideal nor portray a scene of human flourishing. Humans do not simply consume food in proximity to one another; we *share* meals. While we may often eat alone, the meal is at the heart of human culture – this is a primary location of communion between us; and in the shared meal, the food consumed takes on the function of establishing all that we are around a table. The table, indeed, has been seen as transforming us from individuals into a community.[45]

This may seem such a commonplace as to be hardly worth stating, but I have been taken aback over the years by the number of times I have heard meal sharing debunked as little more than a utilitarian convention. Just as Adam Smith expounded his vision of 'the division of labour' by an appeal to the manufacture of pins, so meal sharing can be 'explained' in terms of one having the skill of the hunter, another those of the cook, while a common fire divided the effort of fuel gathering, and so 'sharing' was merely the occasion for each individual in the enterprise to make sure he/she got a fair portion! While this may explain sharing as an economic transaction, it is ridiculous in terms of observing the complexities of human beings. It might also be observed that such a manner of 'explaining' food sharing is functionally atheistic in that it gives no role to the desire for community and the fundamental role of the human search for meaning: for theists both desires are *vestigia* of the Creator. However, before going on the offensive in this matter, we should recall that many Christian groups down the centuries have become so fearful of levity, gluttony or 'time wasting' in their meal practices that they have all but written out the value of sharing meals and the sharing of conversation that accompanies it.[46] We have the ironical situation that in Christian memory sharing food is praised as an historical memory, as a liturgical expression, and as an eschatological hope, while in Christian practice it is ignored, viewed functionally or even minimalized as a distraction from serious discipleship.

In claiming that the sharing of food in a meal is a deep value within our humanity, we should be careful not to imagine that there is an ideal kind of sharing, a paradigm meal, or to present this as something that belongs only to certain sections of society. It does not matter whether it is a

---

[45]See Bahr 1970: when Jews in the ancient world met to eat, they each blessed God for what they were about to put in their mouths before the group came to the table; but once they were at table, they now formed a unity and so only one said the blessing for the group.

[46]Silence or the substitution of reading for commensal conversation in monastic settings – a practice that we can see already in Philo – fails to value the human importance of conversation. When I heard a defence of this as a form of Christian ideal from group of monastic sisters some time ago, I could not but reflect that it is as well that Jesus preferred talking to reading at table or we would have even less of his thoughts than are preserved.

home-cooked organic meal of a family around a table or a takeaway from fast food restaurant: while one may be better for your health, both express the place of food sharing among us. Equally, while we may affirm some particular food philosophy or a specific culinary aesthetic, such assertions are secondary to the more basic involvement in sharing meals. The fact that every society has a code of 'manners' for eating together is sufficient demonstration that we share food as a unity,[47] and behaviour that does not respect this unity is seen as reprehensible individualism.[48]

If food sharing is accepted as part of being human, it is surely significant that there is no traditional 'grace' from either a Jewish or a Christian source[49] that does not assume that the food is being shared by several people, that those at table form a unity, and that the food is there as a common possession to be shared. This fact does not depend on the quality or even the quantity of food, or whether the meal is considered as some sort of 'feast': it applies to all shared/communal eating. This can be brought out more clearly by recalling that the sort of meals we, in the developed world, take for granted as 'ordinary food' would have been seen in times past as 'a feast'; yet even in those past conditions the shared meal, that feast, was seen as an ideal of human happiness. Likewise, what we sometimes airily dismiss as mere formalities, table manners, are an expression of the basic grammar that links us as people. There are right and wrong ways of behaving at table which reflect in miniature the values of our society!

Food sharing, identity and belonging are closely related realities. We see this in the part played by meals in those celebrations which build our personal memory, to the extent that often the meal celebrating an event and the event itself become one. While if one were to imagine any significant human event without a meal (be it a wedding or a funeral or any other event between these emotional extremes), we would consider it a jejune (literally: fasting) affair! A shared meal not only celebrates events, but also becomes part of the event just as the event cannot be remembered apart of the meal: could one have a wedding feast without a wedding cake?[50]

Shared meals both establish and maintain fellowship: I am one with those, to a greater or lesser extent, with whom I share a table – hence the horror in some cultures of sharing food yet plotting warfare against those with whom one has eaten.[51] In any meal of a group, however transient, I can say that I belong to that group because I share that table. Food sharing generates the

---

[47]See Visser 1993.

[48]We have an example of this in Paul (1 Cor. 11.20-22) where the failure in table manners is that which destroys the unity of the meal and so causes disunity in the church.

[49]The minimalist form '*Benedictus benedicat*' is so distant in form from both Jewish and Christian table prayers as not to have any force as a counter-indicator!

[50]The role of the wedding cake in the contemporary wedding feast is a case in point (see Charsley1988) which still employs the notion of having a share in a single food object that is basic to eucharistic ritual.

[51]This horror is the expected response to the presence of Judas Iscariot at the Last Supper in Mk 14.18 (followed by Mt. 26.21-3) and Jn 13.21 with 21.20.

belonging that makes us a community – and this community might exist only for few moments, it may be episodic as when a group meets periodically, or it may be the communities with which I most identify and in which I can say 'here I belong' and 'here I exist'. We have all these variations as part of our formal memory: the groups that shared food at the feeding miracles, the table of the tax collector or Zacchaeus; communities that lasted for just the time of the meal; regularly gathering communities such as those who ate together in Corinth; and the long-term stability assumed in communities such as the Essenes/Qumran and Therapeutae and Therapeutrides with their necessarily elaborate rules for meals. Moreover, it is because it is a community and a place of belonging that mutual behaviour there – the everyday rituals of table manners – is so important. So the table is not only the *locus* of our historical identity-forming memory, but of our ethical, social and personal memory.[52] Every tray brought to a shared meal is as laden with strands of human significance as it is with varieties of food. No meal is 'just a meal'.

Is it surprising, therefore, that from around the shared table have evolved so many rituals which are indistinguishable from those we usually think about under the heading of 'religion'? For example, for a formal meal we will dress specially, engage in special forms of communication such as toasting each other, invoke idealized paradigms in behaviour,[53] perhaps sign a 'dinner book' or a menu to mark our 'being there' and even take away relics – menus or name cards – to remind us of the event, while tokens of the banquet may be sent to those whose physical presence was impossible. Indeed, the rituals/grammar of table sharing and the rituals/grammar have evolved together, illuminate and constantly borrow from each other, and cannot be understood separately from one another. This overlap of table manners and religious wisdom is also deep within our memory as we see from the inclusion of a summary of behaviour at the banquet table in the Wisdom of Jesus Ben Sira (31.12-32.33); and this leads us to the next level.

Level 4: Shared meals and religion

As we have gone through these three levels, you have probably reflected that they merge imperceptibly into one another. There is a continuum between the producers of foodstuffs, cooks and food preparers, and the final diners – these levels merely draw attention to moments in a process allowing us to see how the final morsel in the mouth or sip from the cup comes to us as much more than the biological material we chew or swallow. Similarly, there is a continuum between the simplest shared meal (people eating out of individual lunch boxes and perhaps swapping an apple for a banana) and the most formal dinner (the wedding meal which formally brings together and bonds

---

[52]This was recognized by Philo in the attention he gave to presenting the meal practices of the Therapeutae and Therapeutrides in *De vita contemplativa*.
[53]'Saying grace' in a formal manner is another example of the special discourse of meals.

two clans): we are complex animals and are linked to one another in all sorts of ways and to many different degrees. Likewise, there is a continuum between the most unobtrusive of rituals when we eat and those of the most formal banquet. Ritual begins in the way we tend to sit facing one another and how we place common food, for instance, a plate with some biscuits, as close to mid-way between those at table as possible. Ritual reaches its apogee when there are many special pieces of cutlery, glasses and formal speeches; but in between are the social rituals such as knowing how one orders food in various countries, the complexities of getting one's food in a burger restaurant, or whether or not to tip. So too when it comes to 'religion' there is a continuum between the simple grace and the invocation of memory implicit in a toast to absent friends and the most developed religious expressions in what some would call 'ritual meals' or 'religious meals'.

The celebration of the annual Seder meal in a Jewish household at Pesach is a case in point: it shares a similarity with all the other meals with an explicitly 'religious dimension' such as Shabbat meals; they in turn share a similarity with every meal at which God is blessed; and these in turn share a similarity with every other act of eating and cooking. The Pesach meal may be a most memorable event in the year, but, as such, it is a pinnacle distinct *within* a group's meal experience rather than something distinct *from* that experience. This might seem obvious: we must eat and we share meals everyday – so any special meal such as a party for a birthday, Christmas lunch, a Seder meal, a Valentine's Day supper or formal mess dinner – will be seen as 'high points' (which they are consciously designed to be) but also continuous with 'ordinary' meals. This is of the nature of human ritual: it is the stressed moments that give form to ordinary time; it is the ordinariness of ordinary time that makes a special day and its meal stand out.

However, this view has not had many supporters among those who have studied what are referred to as 'ritual meals'. According to most approaches there are meals which are formally religiously significant in such a way that they must be classed apart from all other meals. This classification is such that if this 'religious dimension' can be asserted to be present, then the actual meal is reduced to being simply an occasion, a language, or (at best) as auxiliary metaphor to the real business of gathering. Those who adopt this approach – usually calling these gatherings either 'cultic meals' or 'sacral meals' – then need to define these meals in such a way that they stand apart. So, according to one influential definition such 'meals' would include (1) meals in which holy food is eaten, (2) covenant meals, (3) the meal of the sacrifice of communion and (4) the meal offered exclusively to a god.[54]

---

[54]This definition has a long history in German scholarship, but it enters the world of early Christian meals with van der Ploeg 1957, 164–6; and it has exercised a major influence on the study of meals at Qumran (e.g. Schiffman 1979, 50–1). This tradition of scholarship simply does not take human ritual tendencies into account. It should be noted that more recent scholarship is far more at ease with the notion that the meal practice of Qumran is part of their distinctive identity within Judaism, see Weinfeld 1992; Pfann 2006; and Hempel 2012.

Using such a starting point, any link between the Christians having a meal and a celebration of the Eucharist is made secondary or accidental from the outset, and one need look no further. However, not only is the definition of such 'sacral meals' defective, but it is of such limited value within the framework of Christian memory as to be positively misleading.

How does one define 'holy food' or a 'covenant meal' or a 'sacrifice of communion' or the exclusivity of any meal offering because, in a meal, there is the benefit of the food eaten? In fact, when we look at these criteria it seems that what has happened is that someone familiar with modern rituals for the Eucharist has seen this as so utterly distinct from ordinary meals, yet having the form of a meal in that a sacrament of 'communion' is eaten and drunk, that it has created in the mind a wholly distinct category – 'the sacral meal' – which, now existing as an anthropological phenomenon, can be used as the basis for searching out parallels in other religions. It is certain that the Eucharist – whether imagined against a background of Lutheran or Tridentine practice and explanation – is the only 'meal' that would fit these criteria without Procrustean surgery of the phenomena. That being the case, the 'sacral meal' approach is little more than arguing in a circle, and begs the question of whether or not the Christian meal should be such a distinct affair. Suffice to conclude that the 'sacral meal' approach's greatest benefit when employed in eucharistic theology is to rationalize the ecclesial *status quo*; and then make that the gauge for all other religious contexts.

There are other dangers lurking in the invocation of this notion of a distinctive 'religious meal' that lacks continuity with, or which is studied in contrast to, other meals. The tradition of Christianity is that God is wholly other, uncreated, and that the relationship of dependence of the creation upon God is not a mutual one. But all that is created – religion included – stands over against God. The notion that *religion* (i.e. the cult of the deity rather than God) is 'other worldly' – as a category – is, however, a product of the Enlightenment whereby religion becomes 'the other' to the real. As such, 'religion' is a real category within experience into which one can place, or dump, that which does not make sense in terms of the world as we rationally construct it from the senses. Whether or not one accepts this view of religion – and I would argue that no Christian could give it assent – is one thing; that it was not part of the epistemological make-up of people in earlier times is, however, beyond dispute. The notion that any group – for example a group of Pharisees in Galilee, some Greek speaking Jews in Alexandria, or a group of Essenes on the shore of the Dead Sea – would have operated with such a separating category is risible. If one were to invoke the category of 'religious' one would have to extend it to the whole of life's business – and so it would be useless as a category. Likewise, the farmer who offered prayers as he sowed, blessed God for the harvest, rejoiced when there was enough to eat, and all the while took part in the liturgical routine of the church did not separate the mechanisms of this world as 'real' from those of some other 'religious world' – if anything the world imagined in faith's narrative was more 'real' in that it was immune to the vagaries of weather, pests and luck.

Those who advocate the existence of a distinctly 'sacral meal' also fail to take account of the way we experience life. We rarely do anything from a single 'pure' motive: purity of purpose is more usually a matter of reflection by which we separate the significant motive of an action from all 'the accidental factors' which go to make up the manifold experience of life. Thus a Seder meal – which Christians sometimes imagine as a completely formalized ritual such as they experience from their liturgical books in church buildings – is a real family meal with all that entails; it varies between families; and it is experienced in much the same way as other family meals in terms of preparation, the tensions that crop up whenever a family meets, the problems of different expectations about what is a 'good' Seder meal, and the inevitable tensions that appear, for all but the most indulgent, when there are several generations at the same table. Interestingly, Ben Sira gave advice on such inter-generational problems at banquets almost two centuries before the Common Era![55] Likewise, at a wedding feast today there will be much going on apart from celebrating 'the happy couple'. For some it will be mainly a time to catch up with rarely seen relatives – and the wedding will be praised for making such opportunities. Some will be there simply because they enjoy parties, 'big events' and 'dressing up', and, incidentally, many other exchanges will take place from the analysis of football to the little moments of business 'networking'. We do not divide our lives into neat boxes, nor simply re-act to the stated purposes of events. Therefore, it is wholly unreasonable to imagine that we can divide our meals into such compartments, especially a category so distinctive as 'the religious'.

If, conversely, modern Christians have a 'meal' – the standard form of contemporary Eucharist with their token eating and drinking – that can be easily isolated from all their other meals (as indeed they have), then this should give them pause for reflection on (1) how it came to be so distinct and (2) the way it characterizes a division of faith and life. Moreover, while the distinction between 'ordinary food' and the sacred event of the Eucharist may be insisted upon by many Christians, that does not mean that the sacral gathering is not viewed by its participants in terms of any number of its accidental or secular benefits. 'Paris' as Henry IV reputedly remarked 'is worth a Mass'; but it is just as true that for many people the importance in their lives of 'attending church' was to be found in the contact and cohesion it gave them with their society rather than in the event's rationale in theological treatises. We are complex beings who invariably act from a wide variety of motives, and that is a variety even wider than those which we can identify or name.

---

[55]Sir. 32.3-9; Smit 2011, 118 views this section of Ben Sira as background to early Christian meals.

But are there more profoundly Christian reasons for the rejection of the category of 'the sacral meal' as a distinct category? First, we are not presented with any evidence for their existence in the earliest strata of our memory.[56] Jesus is recalled as present at meals both before (Lk. 10.38-42) and after his death (Lk. 24.41-3), and this continuity was emphasized in teaching (Acts 10.41). Was he considered more present in one meal than another, or more present in the time remembered than in the time of the remembering? This too was not the case: the presence of the risen Jesus in the communities as they remembered is the basis for the stories remembered which, in turn, give narrative shape to that presence. The Sunday appearances of Jesus in the original conclusion to John's gospel (Jn 20) present us with a notable example of this.[57] This understanding of the continuity of the meal in the presence of the risen Lord with the other meals of the disciples is confirmed by the way that theme is developed in Jn 21.9-14[58] and the other accounts of post resurrection meals.[59]

The inappropriateness of a special 'sacral meal' category also clashes with a belief in the incarnation: if the Lord has come among us and shared in the ordinariness of our humanity, then every table must be capable of being a *locus* of divine encounter, and to designate the Lord's table or the Lord's supper as being in a wholly distinct class (however it might be perceived phenomenally by someone attending a Christian liturgy) is tantamount to adopting a functional docetism.[60]

Taken together these four levels allow us not only to appreciate the continuity of all meal sharing, the manifold links that bind these to our humanity, but also to see how meals can be distinctive within that continuity such that a meal, the meal of the Christians, could stand out with the significance that has been given to it in the practice of discipleship since the earliest churches.

The centrality of memory

By the time a group of Christians sit down to share their eucharistic meal, both the food that they eat and the meal at which they eat it is expressive of them, their identity and their history both collectively and individually. The answer to the question of what is distinctive about that meal is to be

---

[56]This is also stated by van der Ploeg and in this statement he is correct: there is no evidence for the sort of 'sacred meal' as he defines this (on the basis of later Christian liturgical meals) in early Christianity. Where I fault this approach is that it assumes a dichotomy between 'religion/ritual' and meals/community events.

[57]See Koester 2007, 142–4.

[58]Assuming that the appendix to John's gospel is later than the gospel itself.

[59]See O'Loughlin 2009b; this story was in circulation in the churches before the larger narratives, such as Mark's, came to popularity.

[60]See Chapter 3.

found in the explicit practices that take place during it – blessing the Father in the manner which Jesus showed his disciples – and in the nature of the memory and awareness it summons from its participants. 'Memory' and remembering are the keys to the whole process.[61]

By 'memory' we do not mean simply 'tales from long ago' or even 'our story' but that profound awareness of reality which appreciates its origins and its ends. This awareness is the realization, in this moment as we eat, that we have an actual connection to a much larger reality. At the simplest level this awareness is the memory of where the food comes from and our dependence within the creation, and so the awareness of the need to be thankful to the Creator for that fruitfulness, and, in turn, to act responsibly with the earth. At the next level, it is the awareness of the line of people that has brought this foodstuff to us, and so our interdependence as human beings. This awareness should provoke thankfulness to others for their ingenuity and for the society, and its peace, that allows this to happen. In turn, this should produce awareness of those in food poverty and our responsibility to all who are hungry, thirsty and in need. Eucharistic people need to be thankful not only to the Father but also to one another, and this cannot take place without social awareness of hunger, poverty and oppression. At the next level, it is awareness of our own culture and the domestic web which gives us our identity and brings us joy in life. It is at this level that memory makes us most individually aware of God's goodness for which we have to be thankful, and, in turn, we must be aware of our obligations to those who make up our local and domestic societies. Then there is the level of the feast when we are aware of the web of life in which we exist – and we formally invoke memory to help locate ourselves – and for which again we should be thankful. Eating with awareness involves memory, and for Christians should lead to thanksgiving: thus eucharistic action should flow from common eating. This festal recollection is not just the past we hold in our consciousness, it exists in the cooking/meal sharing styles that belong to the cultural memory of each human society, large or small, and if this cultural memory is not involved in a group's eucharistic memory, then it cannot be the case that the Eucharist can make a claim to be at the centre of their – that specific group's – Christian life.[62] Once again, eucharistic action will be real to the extent that it flows out of this communal experience and memorial awareness.

---

[61]On the recurring eucharistic meal as a fixed element in forming the community memory in the early churches, and providing the cognitive occasion for the integration early Christian memory, see Keightley 2005; and two papers by Czachesz 2007 and 2010.

[62]Hence the notion that there can be an *editio typica* of the eucharistic liturgy – a mainstay of Roman Catholic practice since the advent of printing and which has made a resurgence in recent years under the influence of Pope Benedict XVI whereby liturgy is judged by conformity and uniformity to a given text – is inherently at odds with the notion of the centrality of the Eucharist in Christian life. Each culture's Eucharist must reflect its unique cultural situation and memory.

Lastly, there is that level of memory and awareness when in the midst of gathering bonded by discipleship we are conscious of the kinship that gathers us, we recall the memory that constitutes our identity, and give thanks for all of Father's goodness in union with the Christ. And at this level we can name the Spirit as the one who gathers us, gives us awareness and memory and enables us to act as the People of God called into being by the Christ. At this point we can echo one of the blessings from the *Didache*: 'We give thanks to you, our Father, for the life and knowledge which you have made known to us. Through Jesus, your servant, to you be glory forever' (9.3).

This level of remembering is bound up with knowing that our meal takes place in the presence of the risen One and that, through him, we are present to the Father in our meal sharing; and, as such, this shared meal is the Christian sacrifice. This remembering and awareness is both an act of imagination – as a human action – and a possession of a share, in that time of sharing the actual meal with sisters and brothers, of the larger reality which includes all the banquets of Jesus, all those of his disciples over time, and it is a recollection of the banquet he promised. This has traditionally been expressed in terms of the sacramental nature of the table/altar at which the Eucharist is celebrated, and appropriately so because the table becomes the physical focal point of our meal sharing. Seen in this light, the table is at once in union with our own tables in our homes – for a table is a reality of the ordinary world – and in union with the table of the heavenly banquet. The table transcends the dichotomy, which is a false dichotomy for Christians, of the sacred and the profane: the domestic is the *locus* of the sacred. The Lord has come to our table; we gather as a priestly people, at his.[63] Then, through, with and in the Anointed, we can bless the Father of all for all.

But if this is a fruitful way of viewing the Eucharist, then we should also investigate whether the experience of the early disciples whose eucharistic activity took place at actual community meals and which forms the basic treasury of Christian memory can help us see how such a meal could be simultaneously both a 'sacral event' and a 'community activity'. Put another way, have we any glimpses that when early communities ate together a common meal that they imagined themselves engaging in an activity at which they were specifically placing themselves in the presence and service of God? To modern Christians where the Eucharist is 'one thing' and a community meal (for all its pastoral value) is 'something else', this seems strange and, to many, preposterous. Moreover, any questioning of this separation of the Eucharist from real community meals is bound to be seen as undermining more than 1,700 years of practice – and it is part of our ritual nature to assume that what one inherits is assumed as co-extensive with 'the tradition'. But even a glance at the early evidence shows that this should not be seen

---

[63]See O'Loughlin 2012e and 2013g.

as preposterous. Luke, writing in Acts in the early second century, sought to imagine the ideal community[64] in its first days and presented this image:

> All who believed were together and had all things in common; they would sell their possessions and goods and distribute the proceeds to all, as any had need. Day by day, as they spent much time together in the temple, they broke the loaf at home and ate their food with glad and generous hearts, praising God and having the goodwill of all the people. And day by day the Lord added to their number those who were being saved. (2.44-7)

This ideal not only places 'the Breaking of the Loaf' firmly within the pattern of meal sharing as an intrinsic part of Christian life, but also places it in the context of spending time together in the temple. The clear implication is that for Luke time together sharing meals in homes, at which the Breaking of the Loaf took place, is as much a sacral activity as time in the temple. Both activities have God, now addressed as Father, as their finality. Once this is accepted, then the study of the place and significance of the banquet in early Christian community life is transformed. From being the study of a social institution and the study of a stage in the evolution of the formal liturgy, it can become a study of how they imagined that they were placing themselves in the presence of Jesus, whose meals they were recalling in continuing his meal practices, and of what they were saying about their relationship to the Father in their eating and drinking together. To the extent we can enter into those early understandings, we can say that we are looking at aspects of the first eucharistic theologies of Jesus' followers.

---

[64]This is the passage known as the First Major Summary; and it needs to be read as an ecclesiological ideal presented as 'history' for imitation in Luke's own environment rather than as a reflection of what had happened in the period before the destruction of the temple in Jerusalem.

5

Meals and Christian memories

'First, collective memory is a model *of* society – a reflection of its needs, problems, fears, mentality, and aspirations. Second, collective memory is a model *for* society – a program that defines its experience, articulates its values and goals, and provides cognitive, affective, and moral orientation for realizing them'.[1] The issue of memory has been a constant part of theologies of the Eucharist based in the traditional statement found in Paul and Luke: 'do this in memory of me'.[2] In turn, the nature of this *anamnesis*, and how the liturgical celebration gives it effect, has been a concern in detailed discussions about the presence of the Christ in the celebration or in the elements. However, if the primary location of the Eucharist is the meal of the gathered disciples, then the context of all *anamnesis* should be the place of meals in the collective memory of those who experienced the meal as a primary element in their discipleship.

This question, which is at the heart of this study, can be put another way: what might have been the significance of eating meals together for the first generations of disciples? The answer to this lies in the significance they attached to the meals of Jesus, their own meals, and their inherited understanding of the religious value of meals within Second Temple period. This body of memories, remembered meals of their own or of others with whom they identified, constituted a storehouse upon which they drew in imagining their actual dining as his disciples, making memorial of Jesus in their blessing of the Father. We today can estimate how they used those meals in imagining their actual gathering through the memories they transmitted within their own tradition. However, while memory and imagination form for the modern historian this benign circle, we must always recall these crude facts. First, we have, in absolute terms, very little information about early Christian eating (all the evidence could be easily read in the course of an hour). Second, much of the evidence is fragmentary (e.g. material from

---

[1]Barry Schwartz 1996, 910.
[2]This command, later perceived as 'the dominical mandate' for the Eucharist, is found only in 1 Cor. 11.24 and 25, and in Lk. 22.19.

Qumran) and we know that we have only that which survived the sieve
of time. That said, we possess more data today, due to discoveries such as
Qumran, than at any time in our history; and, we have more sophisticated
methods for interrogating that data than ever before. Third, even where
we have overlapping evidence we know that the variety was greater than
what has survived. For example, the command to 'do this in remembrance'
appears to have been part of the explanatory teaching for Paul and Luke,
and even between these two strands there are differences. So we must
positively acknowledge the partiality of evidence rather than seeking to
harmonize the accounts into a single narrative which implies a greater level
of knowledge than we actually possess. Fourth, the materials we study were
not intended to convey answers to our questions about a highly contested
ritual institution, but were produced incidentally as part of the ongoing life
of those communities dealing with the problems they encountered in eating
together[3] while proclaiming to themselves who they were and what they
were about. The ancient evidence, the content of our memory, was intended
for their society and its problems, not for us or our concerns but we tend to
ignore this gulf due to the repeated recitation of those memories in events
that are truly ours: our liturgies.[4]

How then should one look at those early meals? One approach would
be to make a list of the meals that are remembered whether they be actual
meals (e.g. the meal in Capernaum when Jesus sat with 'many tax collectors
and sinners'),[5] stories involving meals (e.g. the banquet in the parable of
'the prodigal son'),[6] or guidance about meals (e.g. advice not to sit in the place
of honour at a banquet and on welcoming the poor),[7] and then list all the
references to eating whether direct (e.g. disciples not waiting for one another
at their meals),[8] miraculous (e.g. the feeding of the five thousand men),[9]
narrative (e.g. on giving food to the hungry and the day of judgement)[10] or
incidental (e.g. the saying 'My food is to do the will of him who sent me, . . .').[11]
Then from such a database seek to build a composite picture of 'the meal for

---

[3]Without such community arguments we would not have the earliest account from 1
Corinthians; nor probably the material in the letters of James and Jude.
[4]We are not the ideal audience – yet it is the assumption of the use of these memories in the
liturgy that we within our rituals are the ideal audience; and this is an assumption that is
shared by many formal church statements using these texts which are made with primary
reference to the liturgical practice of the churches.
[5]Mk 2.15-17; and Mt. 9.10-4 and Lk. 5.29-33; in this case the addition by Mt. (9.13) of Hos.
6.6 ('I desire mercy not sacrifice') is surely significant as pointing to the notion that the meal
achieves that which sacrifices were intended to achieve, and, as such, that the sharing in the
meal is their sacrifice. Clearly, this is an issue upon which Matthew has reflected having heard
Mark's story.
[6]Lk. 15.11-32.
[7]Lk. 14.7-14
[8]1 Cor. 11.21.
[9]Mk 6.37-44.
[10]Mt. 25.35 and 37; and 42 and 44.
[11]Jn 4.34.

early Christians'. In such a process one could draw assistance from research on the classical and early Christian banquets where a similar approach has allowed us to reconstruct some of the practices of early Christian meals and to throw light on otherwise obscure details in the text (e.g. reading the letter of James in terms of *symposia*).[12] However, such a procedure limits the meal-events that can be compared – can one, for instance, compare a miraculous feeding with instructions from 1 Corinthians or with the practical guidance found in the *Didache*, or can one treat the account of a meal of Jesus with a story attributed to Jesus about a meal, or can one consider a story of a meal in the life of Jesus alongside an account of a meal among the apostles in Acts[13] – because what is meant by 'history' is different in each case? There is also the issue of events that have 'multiple attestation': does one privilege one account or deal with a conflated account thereby ignoring the evangelists' differing theologies?[14] Likewise, while no mainstream theologian today would jump from a quotation attributed to Jesus in a gospel to asserting that Jesus of Nazareth actually made such a statement without painstaking analysis (and most scholars would consider the very question an ill-posed one), one must be equally cautious in moving from an account of an action to the conclusion that Jesus of Nazareth did something.

By contrast, if one approaches all references to meals and food from their status as *memories transmitted and preserved in early communities* one has a basis for asserting that these memories tell us of their own understanding of the significance of their actions. The task is to seek out the significant themes that recur in those memories and see how they frame their own understanding. Such themes are, in effect, a formalization of the theology implicit in the memories. These are not to be thought of in terms of 'aspects' or parts of the meal, much less as theological notions that the meal was harnessed to celebrate; rather they should be seen as permeating each and every meal that the communities shared for it was with this collective mind-set that they gathered, ate, drank, prayed, talked and listened. Thus each meal, Sunday after Sunday, can be seen as incorporating these themes or else being so lacking in one or other of them that some teacher, such as Paul, sought to recall them to that aspect of their meal sharing. Moreover, whatever memories the sharing of a meal evoked in the process of making sense of the *kerygma*, it was the actual sharing of a meal with the specific blessings and actions of Jesus that constituted their liturgy and their *kerygma*.

However, we should note at the outset that not only are these themes overlapping, as they must be because memory is always making links, connections and new scenarios,[15] but they are not well-defined formulae: what

---

[12]See Smit 2011.
[13]For example, the meals in Acts 10-11.18.
[14]See the case of Mk 2.15-7 just noted.
[15]This fact is amply demonstrated in the way that the gospel traditions evolved as we can see in just the ways that Matthew and Luke reinterpreted Mark.

'sacrifice' or 'thanksgiving' meant in one source and context can differ from what it meant in another. Rather they are unsystematic themes in that they group memories with common elements, and as is the way with such memories in a practical environment of repetition, what they meant was undergoing constant evolution.

The feast of thankfulness

That there was a formal action of blessing/thanking God at meals is not the issue here,[16] but that the actual meal itself was an expression of thankfulness. There are some definite indications of this perception of meal sharing in the early communities. In Paul's warning to the Corinthians, we find this expression: 'So, whether you eat or drink, or whatever you do, do everything for the glory of God' (1 Cor. 10.31). This implies that it is the actual eating and drinking which Paul has in mind as the service of God: in their manner of eating and drinking, there is the potential of giving glory to God, and therefore this is a mode of eating and drinking that they should adopt.

This theme of celebration as an expression of thankfulness is seen most clearly in the way that Luke presents rejoicing over the lost becoming found in a series of three parables.[17] The man who finds his lost sheep does not simply rejoice alone, but 'calls together his friends and his neighbours, saying to them, 'Rejoice with me, for I have found my sheep which was lost'. Likewise, the woman who finds the lost coin 'calls together her friends and neighbours, saying to them, 'Rejoice with me, for I have found the coin which I have lost'. While there is no explicit mention that this gathering and rejoicing – rejoicing in thanksgiving for the lost being found – included a meal, the supposition that the original audience would have imagined that such rejoicing would have included a meal is not too far fetched. Luke presents his version of these traditional parables of gathering to share in rejoicing in just such a meal context: in a situation where they answer an accusation against Jesus that he 'welcomes sinners and eats with them' (15.2). It seems clear that for Luke's audience the rejoicing imagined in the case of the shepherd and the woman are seen as similar to that which Jesus feels when he eats with those who were lost but now are found. Indeed, the demonstration of their being found is that they are sharing a meal with Jesus. Moreover, if we imagine Luke preaching his gospel at a meal gathering in a church, the audience who are already invited to see in Jesus' meals a reflection of their own eating together may also see in the narrative gatherings of the shepherd and the woman a

---

[16]See Bahr 1970.

[17]Lk. 15.1-32. While parts of the first two parables (that of the Lost Sheep and the Lost Coin) are also found in Mt. (18.12-4), Matthew has only the individual who finds the sheep/coin rejoice, while Luke has that person gather the community for a communal expression of gratitude and rejoicing.

reflection of their own gathering and rejoicing at a meal. In both parables what is imagined is, in Michael Goulder's words, 'a further Lucan party' (for men in the case of the shepherd) and 'a feminine Lucan party' (in the case of the woman).[18] Together, both parties are an image of the Church – listening as they eat with one another: sinner with saint, Jew with Gentile – as a community of forgiven sinners.[19]

However, the clearest indication that the rejoicing with thanks among the 'friends and neighbours' would have included some shared eating comes from the third element in Luke's story replying to the Pharisees' and the scribes' accusation: the parable of 'the Prodigal Son'/'the Two Sons'. This parable's two key points – forgiveness by the father and the need for the loyal son to forego resentment – are so clearly drawn out in the traditional reception of the story that we often fail to see the place of food and meals running through it, and that it is one of the clearest examples of 'the gospel' of forgiveness being manifested in a banquet/party. The wayward son returned home from a condition of famine, yet in this famine-stricken country there is enough for the pigs to eat (for he herds them and would be glad to eat their food), but 'no one will give him anything' (15.16): if he eats, he must eat alone or accept swine as his mensal companions. In that country, food is not for sharing or he, at least, has no share in the table. To reinforce this point about food and a place at table, the son's condition of famine is a contrasted with that of the father's servants: they have bread enough 'and to spare' (15.18); while in the father's country there is the possibility of shared food. Then when the event of finding occurs, it leads directly to the fatted calf being killed and the wish 'let us eat and make merry' which provokes a feast for the whole household (15.24-5). This detail of the 'fatted calf' was already an image redolent of welcome, festivity and the ideal meal – and demonstrates that memories of meals were important for those who heard Luke's story.[20] With the lost son's return, gratitude for the event is assumed to take, as its most obvious expression, the form of a sharing of food and a party. Likewise, the resentful son objects to such unlimited sharing – for he too would like a party (15.30) – but this simply draws out the fact that if there is something out of the ordinary (the gospel's offers of repentance and salvation) for which one is thankful, this results in a meal and party for the community. It is the whole feast – abundant festival food shared, dancing and music (15.25) – that make up the action of thanksgiving. Luke, and his audience, simply assume that in that meal of thanksgiving for salvation, the father would actually utter a blessing to God for the event.

---

[18]Goulder 1989, 605 and 607; Goulder sees having 'parties' – and these are so common that they must, in most cases, be seen as involving that *sine qua non* of a party: food and drink – as a special Lucan theme which he explores on 95–6.

[19]Goulder 1989, 607; and see O'Loughlin 2013c.

[20]The story echoes Jer. 46.21; and carried the imagery of 1 Sam. 28.24, Prov. 15.17 and Amos 5.22.

In their eating together the community was celebrating and thanking the Father for the life they had through Jesus, and in the actual word of blessing they were giving particular expression to their purpose in gathering. In the light of later developments we need to note that it was the actual celebratory event that was primarily the thanking, which then would include the actual verbal blessing, rather than the blessing *qua tale* which simply had the event as its surrounding context.[21]

The celebration of unity

That the shared meal is an expression of unity is probably the best attested aspect of the early Christian understanding of their common meals. For Paul the action of sharing the common cup and loaf is an expression of unity in Christ:

> The cup of blessing that we bless, is it not a sharing in the blood of Christ? The bread that we break, is it not a sharing in the body of Christ? Because there is one bread, we who are many are one body, for we all partake of the one bread. (1 Cor. 10.16-7)

This takes on a particular force when we recall that the letter is prompted by divisions and quarrels in the community (1.10-11 and 11.18-22), and that these become manifest in the way they eat their common meals when they will not wait for one another (11.33-4). Indeed, Paul is so concerned that he goes so far as to say that if the meal is not an expression of unity it is not the Lord's Supper (11.20). But because their eating together is an expression of who they are in Christ and how they are to behave towards one another he repeats for them the tradition he has received about the meal (11.23-6) and they are to be careful that they, in their manner of eating, are capable of 'discerning the body', namely their unity in Christ, or their eating and drinking is a judgement on themselves (11.28-9).[22] These admonitions in Paul allow us to appreciate the similar situation implied in the reference to the 'agape' in Jude 12. It also witnesses to the theme that eating together is a celebration of unity, in that these meals are 'blemished' when people feed themselves rather than recognizing the unity of the whole group.

---

[21]Mitchell 1982, 5, wrote 'For the eucharist, as both "holy meal" and "sacred food," rather quickly gained independence from its original setting in a *full* meal where other foods were shared in common'. However, this falls into the trap of seeing 'the Eucharist' as an independent entity that just had the meal as its occasion; but as such stories as that told by Luke make clear, it is the meal that is the thanksgiving celebration and the formal, recognizably 'eucharistic', elements are but elements of that meal.

[22]This theme of the meal as an expression of unity is studied in most commentaries on the letter, but see, especially, Theissen 1982, 145–74.

While Paul makes the explicit link between the unity of those eating a shared meal and the unity of the community in the Christ, this is a much larger theme that can be found in many early texts. To eat together is to be united with those with whom one eats: thus they should not eat with those who reject the life of discipleship (1 Cor. 5.11), while eating food with sinners and gentiles in Luke's writings is seen as establishing a unity with them. It is the willingness of Jesus, and subsequently the willingness of the apostles/disciples, to established unities across divides by sharing a table that becomes a mark of the universality of the gospel – and that breaking of bounds only makes sense if it is a fundamental assumption that eating meals together established a unity.[23] This assumption can also be seen to underlie the story of the Samaritan woman at the well in Jn (4.4-43) where it is made explicit that Jesus will drink with her, but the author notes for his audience's sake that 'Jews do not share things in common with Samaritans' (4.9). When we consider these texts together we see that to share a meal is as clear a declaration of identity with others – and so unity among those who eat – as to recite common credal formula. Moreover, as we shall see in the next chapter, the significance of a shared loaf and a shared cup when the words of blessing are uttered at the meal is closely tied up with the unity of those sharing the meal with one another and with the Christ.

The meal of sacrifice

Few issues relating to the Eucharist have been more contentious over recent centuries than the issue of sacrifice and the Eucharist.[24] One common strand linking those who wish to affirm that the Eucharist is a sacrifice has been to emphasize that it is the sacramental encounter with sacrifice of the Cross, and this is seen as a distinct aspect of the eucharistic liturgy – which has often been simply addressed as the *sacrificium*[25] – from anything connected with the Eucharist as a meal.[26] Indeed, there has been a tendency to juxtapose viewing 'the Eucharist as a meal' (and so emphasizing its origins in a community meal and the relevance of a study of meals to understanding it)

---

[23]See O'Loughlin 2013c.
[24]For a survey of the matter, see Daly 2009, 14–22.
[25]See, for example, Columbanus, *Regula Coenobialis*, 4, and this is but a token of the practice which can be found in many of the Latin fathers.
[26]So, for example, Daly 2009, in what is one of the most all embracing accounts of what 'sacrifice' in a Christian context means (and who examines in detail the links in Christian tradition between sacrifice and the Eucharist), does not address the issue of the Eucharist's origins in a meal (despite addressing every issue that has arisen with regard to the Eucharist and theological concerns about 'sacrifice' *qua tale*); the nearest he comes to it is when he notes that 'historically, the Passover began as a family sacrifice feast' (p. 42), but then the focus moves to the sacrificed Passover lamb 'and the elaborate rite of *tossing* or *throwing* the blood at the altar. . . .'

and viewing 'the Eucharist as a sacrifice' (and thereby seemingly taking a 'high' view of its importance in the Christian life, while also viewing it as of great theological significance); with the implication that an emphasis on 'the meal aspect' is tantamount to some sort of theological reductionism. While there is probably no conclusive response one can make to those who so locate 'meal' and 'sacrifice' in opposition to one another, usually with the added qualifier that while meals belong to the practicalities of historical existence, sacrifice is pre-eminently a numinous act usually involving the destruction of a victim; one can, at least, show that such a juxtaposition is an anachronism. While at the same time it is important to recall that for early Christians who lived in a world of actual sacrifices, the notion was one used by them by way of explanatory analogy, and it was later that 'sacrifice' came to be used as a direct description of an aspect of Christian worship.[27]

The world of the first disciples was one where there were blurred boundaries between meals and sacrifices. Hence, the task here is not to enter the lists on whether or how 'the Eucharist is a sacrifice' or what might be meant by such a statement, but the more modest aim of showing that actually eating a meal or holding a banquet could be seen, by all those who saw themselves as servants of God in the first century of the Common Era, as being a sacrificial event.

Philo's views on sacrifice are usually described in terms of what he wrote with reference to the temple or altars,[28] but he also viewed the meal which the Therapeutae/Therapeutrides held every 50 days as a sacrifice. That banquet (although we should imagine it without any hint of the fatted calves and opulence such as Luke wishes us to imagine the father's feast for his returned son) begins with prayer that it be acceptable to God,[29] and declares that the table – described as a 'sacred holy table' – was seen as being part of the temple.[30] This sacrificial dimension – the meal being their equivalent of the actions linked to the temple in Jerusalem – is made more explicit in that the meal involved the ministry of the priests who, therefore, were entitled to have a reward for their service.[31] Indeed, the roles assigned to the whole group in this meal amounts to them seeing their activities at this banquet as a matter of sacerdotal work involving both men and woman.[32] While there is always the difficulty with Philo, especially when he is describing groups of Jewish 'philosophers' that he simply provides his own ideal in historical dress,[33] this is not a problem for this chapter: the mere fact that he can

---

[27]See Lathrop 1990.

[28]Daly 2009, 85–7 contains a summary; but this does not mention *De vita contemplativa*.

[29]*De vita contemplativa*, 66.

[30]*De vita contemplativa*, 81.

[31]*De vita contemplativa*, 82.

[32]For a full discussion, see Taylor 2004.

[33]See Engberg-Pedersen 1999; a similar charge could be brought against his description of the Essenes in *Quod omnis probus liber sit*, 75–91.

describe such a meal in the explicit terms of altars, priests and the temple serves to illustrate the point (whether or not such a meal ever took place). Moreover, we can see that Philo was not alone in making this link between meals and sacrifices in that the same linkage is taken for granted by his slightly younger contemporary Josephus.

When we read Josephus, despite his apologetical motives, we find passing mentions of various parts of Jewish life that can be taken as typical of first century Jewish attitudes, and the connection he makes between meals and sacrifice is one such instance. What he assumes about historical situations taken from the history of Israel is implicit witness to the assumptions he makes of his own readers. In his retelling of Jewish history Josephus has many references to sacrifices that were made in the past and which pleased God. This in itself is not remarkable in any way: details and regulations for sacrifice were laid out in 'the books of Moses' and were seen as a central institution of Jewish life. What is remarkable is the frequency with which Josephus imagines a sacrifice in the past being linked with the celebration of a feast by the people. Moses, after the defeat of the Amalekites, offers sacrifices of thanksgiving, and then entertains the soldiers with a feast.[34] And when Moses tells this to 'Raguel', he 'offered a sacrifice and made a feast for the people' and 'the whole people, arranged in family groups, took part in the banquet'.[35] Now of the first meal there is no mention in his scriptural sources, but there is mention of a sacrifice (Exod. 17.15); while of the banquet for the whole people there is likewise no mention, but only that 'Aaron and all the elders came to eat bread with Moses' father-in-law in the presence of God' (Exod. 18.12).

Later in Josephus's retelling of history the preparations for setting up the tabernacle include Moses ordering 'a feast and sacrifices according to each man's ability'; so we have yet another feast on which Exodus is silent.[36] That these references to feasts are not some accidental slip of memory becomes clear when Josephus seeks to explain two different kinds of Jewish sacrifices:

> There are two kinds of sacrifice which take two distinct forms: the first is offered by individuals and the other by the people (*demos*). In the first case, the whole of the sacrificial victim is completely burnt (*holokauteitai*) whence its name [: a holocaust]; the other kind [by the people as a collectivity] has the nature of being an offering of thanks (*charistérios*) and it is done in such a way that those who have made the sacrifice can have a banquet (*euóchia*).[37]

---

[34] *The Antiquities of the Jews*, 3, 60.
[35] *The Antiquities of the Jews*, 3, 63–4.
[36] *The Antiquities of the Jews*, 3, 108 (and compare Exod. 40.17).
[37] *The Antiquities of the Jews*, 3, 224–6; this is the introduction to a section of the work (224–57) which is as close as Josephus came to a formal treatise on sacrifice – a topic on which he intended to write an entire treatise (see 3, 223).

Having thus made the link between the people offering a sacrifice of thanksgiving to God for his deliverance and then the people having a banquet at which they consume the sacrifice, they can look back on many such sacrifices/banquets over the course of their history.[38] For Josephus, when a community offers thanks – which he sees as an occasion for the sacrifice of an animal – it shares in a banquet.

This insight from Josephus is invaluable when we come to the only first-century Christian source that mentions sacrifice as an activity of the followers of Jesus: the *Didache*.[39] The passage deserves to be quoted in full, not only in view of the frequency of later Christian discussions about sacrifice and Eucharist, but because it is explicit evidence that the early communities thought of their meals in some way or other as their 'sacrifices'.[40]

> On the day which is the Day of the Lord gather together for the breaking of the loaf and giving thanks. However, you should first confess your sins so that your sacrifice may be a pure one; and do not let anyone who is having a dispute with a neighbour join until they are reconciled so that your sacrifice may not be impure. For this is the sacrifice about which the Lord has said: 'In every place and time let a pure sacrifice be offered to me, for I am the great king, says the Lord, and my name is feared among the nations'. (14.1-3)

The 'pure sacrifice' (*kathara thusia*) is not linked in any way with the sacrifice of Jesus, but has reference to their own sacrifice; and this takes place when they gather for their weekly meal. Hence, before eating this meal they must ensure that the divisions between them have been resolved and they have sought forgiveness for sins that would mean they were taking part with less than the wholehearted discipleship of the 'Way of Life' which is demanded of those who take part in the meal which bonds them as a community. Moreover, this meal – which is for them a sacrifice – allows them to take part not just in any sacrifice but in the new universal sacrifice prophesied in Mal. 1.11.

---

[38]Here are just a few examples: *The Antiquities of the Jews*, 4, 101; 5, 343; 6, 15; 6, 158.

[39]The references in Rom. 12.1 and Phil. 4.18 are metaphorical uses of the term; the same is true of the references to sacrifice in *1 Clement*. Much attention has been given over the years (e.g. Brilioth 1930, 44) to the significance of Ignatius' use of *thusiasterion* which not only is inherently problematic (see Brent 2006), but represents a confused reification of a metaphor (see Lathrop 1990). We should note that the significance attached in the past to Ignatius' use of the term is based on dating his letters to the first decade of the second century – a date that is now known to be impossible (see Barnes 2008).

[40]Daly 2009, 75–6 makes some brief comments on the *Didache* seeing it as of only peripheral value, and then concludes with the remark that 'However, apart from the obvious implication that "sacrifice" is something that Christians do in their weekly gathering, there is no further indication of what is meant by this' (p. 76). This comment fails to notice that because sacrifice is an act, the fact that they do it weekly in their 'gathering' – he makes no reference to the fact that this is a meal – is of profound importance for what is meant by it.

We have seen that in Josephus there are two kinds of 'sacrifice' one of which he says was called a 'holocaust' and the other, offered by a group, to which he gave no specific name but which is based on a shared meal. Milavec, on the basis of Old Testament evidence, has drawn attention to this distinction with regard to the *Didache* by arguing that the world of the Second Temple knew the holocaust – where there was no eating involved – and then thought of other sacrifices in terms of meals. Therefore, because the *Didache* does not use the word 'holocaust', that the link between a sharing meal and an offering sacrifice would have been entirely obvious within Jewish culture.[41] He also extends the argument in terms of Hellenistic culture to the effect that the *Didache* had no need to define 'sacrifice' because 'sacrifice permeated the ancient world, and it was a fact of life' and, in that world it was 'commonly associated with a fellowship meal'.[42]

This ubiquity of the connection between sharing a meal and the activity of sacrifice is also to be found in Paul where it underpins, as an assumption, his argument with regard to contact with pagan religion:

> No, I imply that what pagans sacrifice they offer to demons and not to God. I do not want you to be partners with demons. You cannot drink the cup of the Lord and the cup of demons. You cannot partake of the table of the Lord and the table of demons. . . . (But if some one says to you, 'This has been offered in sacrifice,' then out of consideration for the man who informed you, and for conscience' sake – I mean his conscience, not yours – do not eat it). (1 Cor. 10.20-1, 28-9)

Sacrifice involves shared cups and shared food; and it implies the same dynamic for formation of connections beyond the meal (in this case with demons) as their sharing of the cup of the Lord. However, the fact that a meal and a sacrifice are intimately linked is so widely accepted that it can be taken for granted by both Paul, his immediate audience [whom he flatters as having strong minds], and those whom they will encounter at their gathering [whose 'consciences' might be weak] for the community meal.

Having explored how sharing meals within a group and group sacrifices were seen as inter-related activities, we are in a better position to appreciate how, in a later generation, Luke can imagine an ideal time in Jerusalem and comfortably place the temple-activity [the place of prayer, sacrifices and holocausts] and domestic-activity in direct parallel: 'And day by day, attending the temple together and breaking bread in their homes, they partook of food with glad and generous hearts' (Acts 2.46).

This is not intended to be a summary of 'sacrifice: early Christian evidence', rather it is a demonstration that for anyone sharing in a common meal at

---

[41]Milavec 2003a, 66–7.
[42]Milavec 2003, 66: on the first point, Milavec quotes Stevenson 1986, 11, and on the latter point, he cites Sered 1994, 136–7.

the time, it could be understood, quite easily and naturally, that they were simultaneously engaged in sacrifice. The mere fact that, among the followers of Jesus, God's name was invoked and his goodness remembered at the meal would probably have been sufficient for many of them to think of the shared meal as 'a sacrifice' or 'a sacrifice of thanksgiving'.[43]

There is a curious, if silent confirmation of this linkage of meal sharing and 'sacrifice' in the evidence of early Christian iconography. Even when communities were using the term *thusiasterion* – in the later second century as we see its use in Ignatius – they did not invoke the imagery of such an altar but presented themselves at their common meal. Being at a meal and taking part in a sacrifice were not seen as being visually distinct.

The ecumenical meal

Meals establish boundaries and, conversely, eating with 'outsiders' breaks down existing boundaries while establishing new table-based communities. In the memory of the early communities, this sense of the meal as both an excluding and an embracing boundary can be observed. Recurrent common meals are, therefore, expressive of the collective memory providing 'a model *of* society – a reflection of its needs, problems, fears, mentality, and aspirations' and 'a model *for* society – a program that defines its experience, articulates its values and goals, and provides cognitive, affective, and moral orientation'.[44]

Jesus was recalled as deliberately practicing an embracing meal – as in his choice to invite himself to dinner with Zacchaeus (Lk. 19.5),[45] being aware that this was being observed and criticized in that he is presented as answering criticism (Mt. 9.10-13 and parallels), and being remembered as being willing to continue in that practice (Mt. 11.19 and parallels). In hearing the evangelists, presumably at a community meal, Jesus would have been heard as welcoming sinners and others who were considered outcasts at his table.

Likewise, it is clear from story of Peter's trip to the centurion Cornelius in Acts that their expanding of meal boundaries was seen as God's will, in that the appeal to the vision of the table-cloth coming down from heaven and the divine voice is made repeatedly (10-11.18). This 'historical meal' is set before the diners in Luke's audience not simply as a statement of divine approval of extending the boundaries of the meal, but the formal acknowledgement

---

[43]These actions would have been heard as echoes of Ps. 107.22 ('And let them offer sacrifices of thanksgiving, and tell of his deeds in songs of joy!') when they heard their stories; and of Ps. 116.17 ('I will offer to thee the sacrifice of thanksgiving and call on the name of the Lord') when they heard God blessed in the course of the meal.
[44]Schwartz 1996, 910.
[45]See Smith 1987.

that other meals – of 'the Jews' – are bounded restrictively and that some followers of Jesus accept those bounds but are wrong to do so.[46] Indeed, in the light of this story of Peter, welcoming people to the meal is part of the mission of the churches.

This piece of preaching in Acts that the Christian meal should be welcoming to all who believe in the gospel irrespective of background, combined with the background knowledge it challenges, is sufficient evidence that in the early communities meals were understood as statements of belonging. Moreover, they were sufficiently conscious of the issue of belonging signified by meals that they were aware this was a matter which they must take seriously and, ideally, one where they would be willing to challenge any false imposition of boundaries through meals. For Luke in Acts this openness is part of his mission strategy, for while the immediate force of the vision is about boundaries regarding food and the rebuttal of those who would restrict food to that which is 'clean', the force of his argument is found in its direct corollary that other people are to be seen as clean, and so potentially dining partners.[47] This is, indeed, the assumption underlying the instructions of the Lord about who should be invited to a 'luncheon or a dinner' (*ariston é deipnon*) – so any meal whatsoever – and which then evokes the response, as from an ideal voice in the audience, that 'Blessed is anyone who will eat bread in the kingdom of God' (Lk. 14.12-5).[48] Meals are assumed to define not only groupings in this world, but to define eschatological boundaries. Meanwhile, the commensality that is promised by Jesus was part of the new order within the creation, albeit one that was far more challenging as a practice than we can appreciate for those who were already believers.[49]

The gathering of Israel

Shared meals as an expression of common hopes, or indeed of hopes fulfilled, is one of the aspects of meals that today we encounter more often in advertising that is directed to us as consumers than something we experience directly as diners. That said the birthday parties of ageing relatives are still the great moments for 'catching up' and implicitly celebrating the ties that bind us although we are scattered and 'out of touch' for most of our lives. This human experience of our own is paralleled in the hope that scattered Israel

---

[46]See O'Loughlin 2013c.

[47]This theme – that they were aware of the table as a boundary – could be extended almost without end: the gloss in Mk 7.19; the reference to 'the children' and 'the dogs' in Mk 7.27-8; the reference to 'the dogs' in the *Didache*, 9, 5; Philo's statements about the common meals that characterize the Essenes (*Quod omnis probus liber sit* 86 and 91), or Josephus's comments about their meals (*Jewish War* 2, 130–2 and 143).

[48]On this last verse, see Marshall 2009.

[49]See Crossan 1991, 341–4 who illustrates the theme with a much wider sweep of examples as part of the *kerygma*.

would be gathered back in the time of the messiah which was frequently expressed in terms of shared meals.[50]

The image used in Isa. 25.6-8 can be taken as representative of a rich web of texts[51]:

> On this mountain the Lord of hosts will make for all peoples a feast of rich food, a feast of well-aged wines, of rich food filled with marrow, of well-aged wines strained clear. And he will destroy on this mountain the shroud that is cast over all peoples, the sheet that is spread over all nations; he will swallow up death forever. Then the Lord God will wipe away the tears from all faces, and the disgrace of his people he will take away from all the earth, for the Lord has spoken.

That this was something that could be imagined as being experienced in the table practice of the first churches can be seen both in their images of an ideal Christian meal[52] – especially the story preserved of the Great Wedding Banquet,[53] and in their specific meal practices as disciples of Jesus. In the *Didache* the gathering is asked to recall formally in the very words of blessing that:

> For as the broken loaf was once scattered over the mountains and then was gathered in and became one, so may your church be gathered together into your kingdom from the very ends of the earth. Yours [, Father,] is the glory and the power through Jesus Christ forever. (9.4)

The reality of a loaf which is a unity out of umpteen grains of wheat is explicitly invoked as being like their meal gathering: scattered people gathered into one in the Lord and so able to bless the Father.[54] But the key point for our argument is that eating together was being consciously recalled as being part of the divine plan of history. A shared meal was a moment in the history of God's people: gathered at the table they now can imagine themselves as the new re-gathered Israel who are rejoicing in being cared for by God.

The themes of the ecumenical meal and of the re-gathered Israel are, at one level, opposites: the first declares that the boundaries of Israel are to be considered porous, while the other builds on the assumption that Israel is the group with the perfect unity whose boundaries are intact. This difference

---

[50]See Priest 1992 who surveys the biblical evidence; while it is a case that many ancient hopes and fears are not common in our own experience, this notion of the meal as the moment of regathering is common – possibly as a function of being *homines coenarii* – and so a key to eucharistic preaching today.

[51]See, for example, Isa. 55.1-2; Joel 2.24-6, 3.18; 1 Enoch 62.14; 1 QSa 2.11-22; or 2 Baruch 29: see Smith 1992.

[52]Mt. 8.11-2; Lk. 13.28-9; 14.16-24; 16.19-31; and 22.28-30: see Jeremias 1958, 59–63.

[53]Mt. 22.1-10; Lk. 14.16-24; and the *Gospel of Thomas*, 64.

[54]We shall return to this theme as part of a larger suite of eucharistic images in the next chapter.

in perspective is usually interpreted in terms of the differing perspectives of 'Jewish Christianity' and 'Gentile Christianity' with regard to Israel. However, while that may be an explanation of the origins of these differing perspectives, the fact that both of them were recalled together within the Christian *oikoumene*[55] points to another significance of these memories relevant to this study. Both memories overlap to produce an image of the meal as embracing new members to the table, either those who are scattered (and so can be re-gathered) or those who are encountered between Jerusalem and 'the ends of the earth'[56] and who therefore can be included. The meal was, therefore, to be one which was ever more inclusive, but this has to be seen in tension with the ever-present human impulse to define by exclusion – a phenomenon whose existence is amply demonstrated by the tendency found in churches, right down to our own time, of being more concerned about who must be excluded (certain sinners, those who do not share our ecclesial bonds, those with whose 'theology' we disagree) than who can be included. This opposition between our pristine collective memory and our actual community practices is the source of one of the ongoing tensions in practical theology relating to the Eucharist.[57]

The supper of reconciliation

If we seek to imagine the difficulties in Corinth that gave rise to Paul's instruction to them with regard to eating 'at the Lord's Banquet' (1 Cor. 11.20), sharing in the 'communion' (1 Cor. 10.16), participating in 'the eucharist' (cf. 1 Cor. 11.24) we must assume that the difficulties arose mainly because of different social and cultural backgrounds. Divisions already existing in society were becoming manifest in what was intended to be a meal exhibiting the new participants' new identity in Christ. The community may have 'put on Christ' (cf. Rom. 13.14), but they were having great difficulty putting off the social values that underpinned and permeated their highly stratified society.[58] In response to this we normally note how

---

[55]See the studies in Bauckham 1998.

[56]See O'Loughlin 1998c.

[57]This issue of 'admission to the Eucharist' is an ongoing debate within many churches – for instance: it is rarely far from the letters' page of *The Tablet* – but few recognize that the whole debate is framed within model of divine–human interaction that is akin to that used in power transactions (for instance: checking a competency to drive a car); such a view destroys the logic of the incarnation as located in the absolute generosity of God. That this is a problem within some churches has even been acknowledged in a recent papal document: 'Frequently, we act as arbiters of grace rather than its facilitators. But the Church is not a tollhouse; it is the house of the Father, where there is a place for everyone, with all their problems' (*Evangelii gaudium*, n. 47). The task facing churches is that their practice, and the law underlying that practice, reflect their theology and not *vice versa*.

[58]See Theissen 1982 and especially Chapter 4: 'Social Integration and Sacramental Activity: An Analysis of 1 Cor. 11.17-34' (pp. 145–74); on stratification and the problems it produced in Pauline communities, see Meeks 2003, 51–73.

it afforded Paul the opportunity to develop his understanding of what is meant by Christian community and unity in Christ.[59] But the inverse of this emphasis is that they were being reminded that this meal was to be one of reconciling opposed groups and strata in society, individuals who were in disagreement with one another, and indeed (as we see in the teaching on sharing meals in Acts 10-11.18) where ethnic groups were to be reconciled to one another.

It might be argued that this was not an important consideration for the early communities or else the meal would never have been marginalized such that 'the Eucharist' became a matter of a token eating and drinking in a formalized religious ritual. But that argument is flawed in that it confuses an historical outcome with a deliberate intentional action. The meal was to be a supper where reconciliation was practiced as a reality.[60] But that having proven too difficult to maintain, the problematic practice gradually gave way to one that was less challenging. However, the development was a departure from that which was originally seen to be central to the meal. Paul – indeed Jesus himself on the basis that his 'eating with sinners' is so widely attested that it must have a basis in his actions – intended the meal to act as an event which overcame factions. We see this in that he tells us what a meal should be in reaction to an early appearance of divisions.[61] It is against this awkwardness of sharing the meal in such a way that it effects actual reconciliation between members and sub-groups within a community that we have to hear the meal – reconciliation stories that were preserved. Likewise, it is against the background of the meal as, ideally, a celebration of reconciliation achieved that we see why these stories had such a currency among them.

The most extensive range of such memories can be found in Luke's gospel where a succession of eating events involving Jesus and stories by Jesus involving meals form a recurring theme that the meal of the Christians, at which these recollections were performed, was to be an enactment of their own reconciliation with one another and with God. This set of stories begins with Jesus at table with a Pharisee for a Sabbath meal (Lk. 14.1), and this is a key linking event in that several items of Luke's teaching follow

---

[59]See, for example, Murphy-O'Connor 1976 and 1977.

[60]It survived, in vestigial form, in the liturgical kiss of peace.

[61]While social stratification is studied as a phenomenon of the Mediterranean society into which Christianity spread; we should not forget that socially stratified societies – using the notion of 'class' – are within living memory. Within living memory 'the first Mass' early on a Sunday morning – where all was done with dispatch and without a sermon – was referred to as the 'maids' Mass'; likewise, the level of solemnity in liturgy was seen as being class related; while it was frequently the case that the classes were physically separated in the building (separate doors, side aisles, galleries for 'servants' were common; it is still possible to see special places kept for those who have specific status in society and who are to be present at a eucharistic celebration) despite the fact that such 'respecting of persons' is incompatible with the nature of a common table.

directly from this meal setting. At the table there is jostling for position – and occasion for places at table to be a modelling of humility and wisdom (14.7-11). This is also the occasion for the instruction about welcoming the poor and crippled to one's table when one is organizing 'a lunch or dinner' (14.12-4). This then forms the setting for the parable of Great Banquet.[62] While this might not appear as evidence for a meal of reconciliation, we must remember that the audience is expected to identify with those who actually sit down at table for the banquet and so 'the poor and maimed and blind and lame' are now brought into communion while the busy, rich, 'normal', people are passed over. The banquet is, therefore, an instance of the reconciliation of the outcasts, the rejected and the despised with the very symbol of belonging: a meal.

This notion of the meal as the place where sinners are reconciled is then invoked again by Luke in 15.2 where in the context of Jesus 'eating with sinners' and welcoming them we have the parables of the parties for the lost sheep (15.3-7) and coin (15.8-10), but the actual party is the one at the table at which Jesus sits with the sinner who was once lost but is now found. Being at table with Jesus is the end of being a sinner and the arrival of reconciliation. That this is not a fanciful exegesis can be shown in the fact the Jesus' own table practice is then explained by Luke using of the parable of the Prodigal Son (15.11-32) where the feast is the evidence of forgiveness and the reestablishment of the right order between actors that is reconciliation. And this message is then repeated in the event of Jesus with Zacchaeus (19.2-10) where he explicitly chooses to go and eat with a sinner (19.7) – thus putting the sinner and the Pharisee on the same plane – and we see then that the conversion of Zacchaeus occurs at the meal (19.8) and have a formal declaration that in the shared meal reconciliation has occurred: 'salvation has come to this house' (19.9).

We get one other glimpse of the relationship of the meal to reconciliation in this statement in the *Didache*:

On the day which is the Day of the Lord gather together for the breaking of the loaf and giving thanks. However, you should first confess your sins so that your sacrifice may be a pure one; and do not let anyone who is having a dispute with a neighbour join until they are reconciled so that your sacrifice may not be impure. For this is the sacrifice about which the Lord has said: 'In every place and time let a pure sacrifice be offered to me, for I am the great king, says the Lord, and my name is feared among the nations'. (14.1-3)

This compact passage, with two instructions and a theological explanation, presents us with the meal both as that which should be seen as the rationale

---

[62]That this meal story was important in the early communities can be judged from its presence also in Mt. 22.1-10 and in the *Gospel of Thomas*, 64.

of reconciliation and as its fulfilment. It would seem to share with later practice the notion of a sacred event for which purity was the pre-requisite. However, this is to read the passage within a legal hermeneutic of process, where a consequent has a necessary condition as its cause: if you do not confess, you cannot take part. But the logic of this document is that people do want to take part; so they need to acknowledge their faults to one another, and because they are taking part, they must be prepared to settle disputes with neighbours. It is participation in the meal that is the cause of the confession and reconciliation – when it is seen as 'the pure sacrifice' the prophets desired – rather than its outcome. A community could hardly stay together, eating with one another, if its members did not seek to be reconciled with one another; for without such efforts the community would fall asunder.[63] Lack of reconciliation at the meal was just one more threat to its survival.[64]

The key point to be derived from the *Didache* is that the eucharistic meal – the spiritual universal sacrifice – is the realization of that reconciliation that must characterize the community of disciples when they eat together. They cannot realize who they are at this gathering without active reconciliation with their neighbours. Moreover, this ecclesial *Sitz im Leben* allows us to hear other traditions on reconciliation, such as Mt. 5.23-6, in the context of gathering for community meal. Recently, Robert Daly has written that Christian sacrifice 'is first and foremost, a mutually self-giving event that takes places [sic] between persons'.[65] Viewed in this light the reconciliation that is implicit within early gatherings becomes indistinguishable from the activity of sacrifice.

While it is not difficult to demonstrate intellectually that reconciliation with one another and with God was inherent to the early Christian meals, there is a danger that this is viewed as a matter of theological abstraction: another piece of 'teaching about' their eucharistic activity; but such an approach fails to recognize their practical starting point. It is very difficult to share food with someone with whom one is in dispute or with whom one has 'fallen out'. If one is going to share food, give one's food to another or be in table-contact with someone, then one must as a matter of human relations sort out the problem or else there will be the proverbial 'bust up' that destroys so many family meals and celebrations! If they believed they were called to eat together they had to sort out their differences or division was the result. That this happened is a clear implication of the way Paul wrote to the Corinthians; and it was probably the inability of members to practice actual reconciliation at meals that was one cause of their attenuation in a subsequent time. Faced with conflicts that could not be 'sorted out' or with factions, it was probably the way of least resistance

---

[63]See Milavec 1995 and 2003a.
[64]See Milavec 1994.
[65]Daly 2009, 5.

to isolate the 'eucharistic' dimension from an actual meal and so produce a ritual which avoided the real interpersonal encounters that actual meals involve. Once again, what is sometimes presented by those who see historical outcomes as intentional perfections as the 'emergence' of 'the Eucharist' as an independent reality can also be seen as a failure of communities to accept the call to reconciliation while having the illusion that one could have the 'outcome' – the encounter with the Lord – while ignoring its fundamental relationship to discipleship. A conundrum that could then only be resolved by making full participation in the resulting Eucharist dependent on a judicial process of penance. And in the process, the new ritual was more a reward for the process – for its denial was the sanction in the process – than a celebration of the new life of reconciliation which Jesus preached and enacted when he ate with sinners.

The place of encounter

No aspect of the Eucharist has received so much attention within the various strands of Christian tradition than that of the liturgy being, or resulting in, an encounter with the risen Jesus. Indeed, this 'presence' of Jesus has been seen as a rationale of the sacrament, while the nature of that presence, as instanced in the controversies over the nature of 'the change of the elements', has been a source of dispute and division among Latin Christians like no other. So can we say that the early communities thought of their meals in terms of an encounter with the risen Jesus?

Before we can approach this question we need to recall our own assumptions at the outset. For most western Christians today, if the question of presence appears at all on their religious horizon, then it comes up in an either/or form of 'presence' and 'absence' as complementary terms. This then can be coupled with questions about the nature of the presence: is it 'real' or 'symbolic' again viewed as opposed complementary terms. These theological proclivities then take very concrete shape in the actual cult whether that be the notion of 'receiving the Eucharist' or the notion of 'presence' indicated by a burning 'sanctuary lamp'. And even if we avoid the notions of 'physical presence' found in the retraction demanded of Berengarius of Tours (c. 1010–88)[66] or that of medieval popular piety in the form of 'eucharistic miracles', we need to acknowledge that the notion of 'presence' which dominates much of our sixteenth-century inheritance belongs more to a forensic quest – 'is it/he there?' – than to a theological search for what disciples mean by seeking the presence of the Lord. The inadequacy of those older approaches has even been tacitly recognized in the formal documents of the Roman liturgy when it seeks to locate the

---

[66]*DS*, 690; and see Chadwick 1989.

Christ's presence in a larger context.[67] But that said, centuries of division still obtrude into our thinking.

The fundamental conviction of the early believers is that Jesus is risen and so present among them. Because the Lord is risen, their faith is not in vain (cf. 1 Cor. 15.14) and they can rejoice because the Bridegroom is with them (Mk 2.20). The Christ, risen from the tomb, was with them, and it was this presence that was celebrated and recalled when they gathered – and expressed formally in logia as 'For where two or three are gathered in my name, there am I in the midst of them' (Mt. 18.20). Because their entire kerygma was based in the continuing presence of Jesus – expressed in a wide variety of theologies – the question of (to use a later terminology) 'sacramental encounter' can be reformulated thus: did they see their meal gatherings as celebrations of that presence? This is a far more fruitful approach than that of asking the meaning of particular phrases in the tradition such as 'this is my body'[68] with the assumption that what was intended was reference to some manner of specific ontological presence/absence.

That the gatherings for the meal were special occasions of encounter can be seen in many ways. In the gospels of Matthew, Luke and John the risen Lord appears to his followers on the first day of the week (Mt. 21.1-10; Lk. 24.1-12; Jn 20.1-18) which was the day of their gathering. This is reinforced by other Sunday meetings: in the Upper Room (a tradition found in both Lk. 24.36-49 and Jn 20.19-23), the Emmaus meeting (Lk. 24.13-35) and the meeting with the disciples *and* Thomas a week later (Jn 20.26-9). Those meetings at Emmaus and the Upper Room as recounted by Luke are explicitly meetings involving a meal; and this theme is also found in the breakfast by the Sea of Tiberias in the appendix to Jn (21.1-23) and the meeting on the roadside with James in the *Gospel according to the Hebrews*. In the Emmaus and James meetings we have explicit references to the meals being thought of as paradigm instances of the churches' own eucharistic meals.[69] When they gathered and ate together, the risen One was among them.

Moreover, the fundamental assumption of their action of offering thanks to the Father, in the manner attributed to Jesus, was that this thanks was given in, through and with Christ. It is this assumption that makes the eucharistic activity referred to by Paul and the *Didache* explicable. Meals were the moments of real encounter with one another as followers, as such they constituted them as the community that was the church, and with the risen one in their midst, and recalled in their memories, they praised the

---

[67]*Missale Romanum* 1969, 'General Instruction', n. 7; this document does not acknowledge publicly any failure, weakness nor excess in earlier approaches as it is written within a hermeneutic of that church's own perfection in every historical moment, but the mere fact of adding to that legacy undermines that hermeneutic.
[68]Mk 14.22 (Mt. 26.26; Lk. 22.19).
[69]See Nodet and Taylor 1998, 48–55.

Father. It was because the risen Jesus was their High Priest who was among them that they could stand in the divine presence as a priestly people and offer the new and universal act of praise to God.[70]

Memory, recollection and events

Memory is thought of by us as either a store of information which can be accessed for reuse – in this a text of the Scriptures on a shelf or a 'Hard Drive' are similar – or it is thought of in terms of mental recollection when someone goes over their recollections in a story or a meditation.[71] When memory takes place in an event – as when we celebrate a birthday party – another process, which I think of as 'layering', occurs. Here we recall an event of significance in the past, but create another event of significance in the present: now both are in our memories.[72] And if we seek to recall the original event again in, for example, a year's time: that celebration inevitably recalls the earlier acts of memory. We know how to celebrate a traditional Christmas because we have memories of celebrating Christmas. This is the phenomenon noted by liturgists – it was one of Baumstark's Laws[73] – and by ritual studies' scholars.[74] A memory somehow contains all remembering of the memory, and it is that whole extent that gives value and significance to the each memorial act.

For the Jews of the second temple period, all meals were ritualized as proper by the act of blessing, but meals of the past were also re-remembered as their celebration of identity, and none more so than Passover. So all the meals of the early followers of Jesus came with existing layering and then upon it was added the new significance of Jesus's final Passover in Jerusalem. That meal, his last meal, was already charged with value, and this value could but grow. To remember him at table would be to remember as significant a meal as there could be, such that it became the community's 'stock image' for all their eating and drinking together. Hence that one meal took on a variety of emphases in the early traditions – 'on the night he was betrayed' (1 Cor. 11.23), the Passover with his disciples (Mk 14.14), the earnestly desired Passover (Lk. 22.15-6), the last Passover before his crucifixion (Mt. 26.2), and the meal of meals (Jn 13.1-17.26) – but always with the focus that

---

[70]See the invocation of Mal. 1.11 in the *Didache*, quoted above.

[71]Contrast this view of memory with that put forward in many recent studies of the dynamics of memory, for example, Connerton 1989 or Schwartz 2005.

[72]The work of Czachesz on how memory of the stories of Jesus is linked to the social gatherings of the early communities is especially relevant here. He has argued that 'the eminent place given to meals in the gospels' is a reflection of the influence of their social gatherings and the structures of those gatherings: see Czachesz 2010, 432.

[73]See Baumstark 2011, 178–88.

[74]See J. Z. Smith 2001.

that was *the* meal.[75] Indeed, all the rest of the meal practice became either footnotes to that meal or had to be related to it such as we see in John's location there of mutual footwashing as a key to discipleship in the early traditions. And this layering – which had begun for them long before they heard of Jesus in their celebrations of the Passover in their childhoods – was reinforced with every celebration of the Christian meal and every retelling of the story of its origins. So we have two memorializing processes working in tandem. On the one hand, all the memories of the meals of Jesus collapse into this one, great layered image of the Lord's Supper. On the other, the narratives of the rich meal memories, of events, conflicts and stories of Jesus, and the remembered context of Jesus,[76] which continually opened out the significance of that memorial act of dining together.

So what did this meal celebrate within their memories? Nothing less than the whole of the gospel, and it could model every aspect of discipleship not only for those eating and drinking at the meal, but also for those recounting the gospel, those who were their evangelists, it was the context of their recollecting. So we could ask whether their actual meal was a modelling of the new community, whether it was to exemplify the ethics of discipleship, the ideal forms of their inter-relationships as disciples, and we could find traces of all these themes. Yet recalling such themes as a sequence runs the risk of missing the wood for the trees. The community was never more conscious of itself than at this gathering, and the whole gathering was a celebration of the whole of their identity. The meal was the Christian universe in miniature. Their new world was experienced in the *convivium*, and the totality could be imagined as a feast.[77]

Week by week the meal came and went; it gained specific names to distinguish it from other gatherings and it became a highly layered memory that was keyed to the memory of Jesus such that it celebrated the whole of that memory.[78] In fact, this eating together could be seen – as it was by Pliny the Younger and later by Justin – as what was most characteristic of their activity. And in these meals there was need to bless God not just in any form, or indeed in the form they might have known in other meals, but by using a distinctive form that they believed was in imitation of the way Jesus had blessed. To this we can now turn.

---

[75]This is not the place to enter into the question of those who in addition to the quest for the historical Jesus quest for the historical 'Last Supper' and seek to locate this or that element from the tradition at that precise meal (cf. Meier 1995). Suffice to say that there was a last supper on the night Jesus was arrested, but that The Last Supper, of the tradition's memory, needs to be seen as a theological event which encapsulates Jesus as one who showed them how to be disciples around a table.
[76]What Christians refer to as, using a theological shorthand, 'the Old Testament'.
[77]See Wolter 2009.
[78]On the notion of 'keying' past memories to present realities, see Schwartz 1996, 911: 'Keying is not just analogical thinking but rather it 'transforms memory into a cultural system . . . because it matches publicly accessible (i.e. symbolic) models of the past . . . to the experiences of the present. Keying arranges cultural symbols into a publicly visible discourse that flows through the organisations and institutions of the social world'.

6

Distinctive memories: The acts of blessing and their recollection

'We do not know exactly when the full meals ... were abandoned by Christians (or, in the case of those consisting principally or exclusively of bread, were reduced in quantity to purely symbolic amounts) to produce the kind of eucharistic rite with which later generations were familiar'.[1] This development of a tradition belies the existence of two great ironies that have echoed just beneath the surface of the book thus far. The Eucharist is a most highly valued event in the churches and proclaimed as the great sacrament of unity: it is that which bonds individual disciples into the body of Christ – a Pauline theme – and then bonds the churches to form the *catholic* Church. Yet, the time of the Eucharist on a Sunday morning is the moment when Christians are most divided and ensconced in their divisions,[2] and often most sectarian in their behaviour towards one another.[3] Indeed, many churches use the Eucharist as a litmus test for who among the baptized they are prepared to see as fully members of the *catholica*. The Eucharist, in effect, becomes an instrument of disunity and is used as a hardening

---

[1]Paul Bradshaw and Max Johnston 2012, 25.

[2]See Hunsinger 2008, 21–46; and Lindbeck 1999.

[3]It is easy to imagine sectarianism as just a mild species of religious hatred, but it has a more profound meaning in regard to the actions of Christians. When one deliberately excludes from Christian fellowship another *baptized* person who wishes to enter one's communion, then one is acting in such a way that the church is no longer coterminous with the community of the baptized who are seeking to follow the Way, and this is sectarianism. Carried to its logical conclusion – as often happens – any disagreement on practice or doctrine would be the basis for exclusion from the church and make it a selecting group of the elect. One cannot affirm an acceptance of the Christ's universal call to discipleship with its hand held out to sinners, and affirm a sectarian practice without contradiction. The *catholica* of its nature is the antithesis of a sect.

[4]One sees this most poignantly in the case of inter-church marriages when the laws of one church are used to exclude partners from a full sharing in the family thanksgiving meal of Christians. For a classic exposition of the alternative view, see Ware 1978.

agent for existing divisions.[4] Then, as is the way with groups which define themselves against others, they almost unconsciously are able to find ever new depths in their mutual disagreements thus making common ground, much less common eating, ever more difficult.[5] In parallel with this division in practice, there have been few areas of formal theology where vituperation has more been the order of the day than in discussions of the event once called 'the Agape'. Bitter exposition of others' faults has been seen as a more fruitful way to defend the value of the *Synaxis Christianorum* than any searching for new insights towards complementary approaches and reconciliations.[6]

The other great irony is that Christianity is the religion of Jesus who is 'called "Emmanuel": God is with us' (Mt. 1.23). The basis of Christian faith is that in an historical individual, Jesus of Nazareth, we are shown the way to the Father. Jesus was not a hierophantic entity appearing among us, a position we formally condemn, but one who lived as we live, and who ate and drank at our tables. He was remembered as proclaiming the expansion of the domain of the holy from the temple bounds to the whole of life (cf. Jn 4.21-4), and whose proclamation was understood to extend the land of promise to the very ends of the earth (cf. Lk. 24.47). Even death was brought within the range of God, such that human life can stand anew in the presence of God (Phil. 2.8-9). So Christians confess Jesus to be, in his whole humanity, their great High Priest (cf. Heb. 3.1). Conversely, while claiming, as we should in such an incarnational religion, that the Eucharist is at the centre of Christian life, it is actually marginalized to a ritual periphery. Screened from life – sometimes literally – it is often seen, and portrayed in its manner of celebration, to be the work of a distinct *sacerdotium* acting on behalf of that 'chosen race, [that] royal priesthood, [that] holy nation, God's own people' (1 Pet. 2.9). For many Christians, the only way to approach the Eucharist – either in liturgy or theological description – is by stressing how it differs from the ordinary world of the creation: it is not an ordinary meal, it is not ordinary food, it is not an ordinary meeting, the president is not acting in his human capacity, and the whole event is not in this world but in the temple court of heaven.

---

[5]Johnson 2006 not only gives a more optimistic reading of the situation, but also notes how far is the journey ahead and how in many churches there are those who positively reject an engagement with modern liturgical scholarship with its inevitable ecumenical dimension.

[6]There has been a remarkable coming together among theologians in the past 50 years, but this ecumenism disappears when it comes to practical action where the previous positions are re-asserted in law, albeit in less strident language, without recognition of the reality of the eucharistic activity of other Christians. The 1998 Catholic document, *One Bread One Body* is an example of such a refusal to recognize eucharistic activity outside a boundary defined by a legal notion of 'valid order'; while Ware 1978 is an Orthodox statement of virtually the same position save that it includes Roman Catholics in its exclusion. Both ignore the actual location of the Eucharist in basic Christian activity, preferring instead to see it as some sort of capstone on a systematic theological edifice.

Liturgy is often located against the backdrop of a theological conundrum. What we preach about the incarnation is the very opposite of many of the ways we have modelled the Eucharist in practice where we have presented it with the iconography of a heavenly vision from the apocalyptic tradition.[7] Many Christians are far more comfortable with the notion that one encounters the divine in a hierophantic sacral event barely touching earthly existence than with the notion that we worship the Father in the incarnational setting of a meal of baptized brothers and sisters around a kitchen table. Yet if the assumptions of this liturgical practice that is based on the distinctiveness of our cultic activity were to be expressed in the formal language of Chalcedonian orthodoxy, then the practices would have to be condemned as failing to represent the nature of the Christ-event.

These two great ironies are closely paralleled by two others in the domain of eucharistic practice. The first is that any observation of the actual practice, interest and devotion of Christians points to the Eucharist being a way of remembering Jesus, celebrating him and encountering him. It is *the* sacrament wherein Christians recall and encounter the Christ. It is his supper, his sacrifice, his meal. However, even a cursory glance at the texts we use in the liturgy or at the earliest records we possess which seek to give explanation to the eucharistic activity of Christians[8] shows that its focus lies in the praise of the Father. Jesus blesses the Father, thanks the Father, and his followers believe they are to imitate him. Moreover, we address formal prayers to the Father, through the Christ, and in the Spirit.[9] This gap between most *believers' interest* and the *dynamic of the texts* to which they give authority both intellectually and in the practice of repetition, has been, and remains, a fecund seedbed for all sorts of quarrels among Christians. Because there is this fundamental difference between what the ancient texts state and later basic interests, all sorts of confusions and contradictions appear from time to time as a result of trying to square this circle. Thus one theologian has proposed this useful rule of thumb: 'every dissension concerning the Gospel necessarily expresses itself in dissention over the Lord's Supper'.[10]

The other practical irony is that the Eucharist is built around eating and drinking, uses the human grammar of meals, items of food and expresses itself in language that is well located in the human world. But, once it comes to practical expression, it is not a meal in any real sense compared with the ways we take part in a meal whether that is the simplest shared meal or a special banquet. The Eucharist is not experienced as a meal, while many Christians go out of their way to distance its eating/drinking from 'ordinary

---

[7]Much of the liturgical imagery of the 'Exposition of the Blessed Sacrament' (a practice which exercises a powerful hold on the explication of the Eucharist among Roman Catholics) is derived from the apocalyptic imagery of the adoration of the Lamb in Rev. 21-22; see van der Meer 1978, 237–40.

[8]See McGowan 1999b.

[9]See Chapter 2 above.

[10]Sasse 1959, 3.

food'. There is little chance that anyone unfamiliar with communion wafers would, on tasting one, ever imagine that it was claimed to be bread.[11] While drinking, if it occurs, at a Eucharist would hardly compare as a human encounter with that of a quick cup of coffee with a friend.[12] So there is a constant experiential discord: the Eucharist is to be the earthly banquet of a people that gives a taste of the heavenly banquet of the Kingdom (*pignus futurae gloriae*), but it is experienced all too often as an individual's private spiritual moment, with the token meal barely visible in the background. The clearest demonstration of this is among Roman Catholics where, in recent years a shortage of presbyters has led to the practice of 'Communion Services' using the reserved Sacrament. But few of those 'ordinary' Catholics attending such services have noticed how inadequate they are in terms of Catholic theology; and that this experiential confusion is widespread is verified by the fears Catholic authorities have expressed that such practices are being confused with the Eucharist.[13]

The fundamental problem can be expressed in this way. First, eucharistic activity is supposedly located as close to human experience as shared meals and the common events of a community. It is an incarnational reality. Second, the ritual event of 'the Eucharist' has become a token affair in terms of sharing food and taken on the dominant shape of a series of readings and exhortation combined with prayers and hymns. Third, therefore, its value within the Christian life is now presented conceptually, it functions at the level of concepts, and has to be affirmed conceptually (if at all). Little wonder then, on the one hand, that many Christians just cannot see what all the fuss is about: faith and ethical discipleship in living seem so much more real, while on the other hand, for many Christians the ritual is so distinct from living that every detail has to be seen as pertaining to the divine and the minutiae of the *opus operatum* take on the seriousness of that careful observance of every step that is proper to carrying out a dangerous chemical process, or are seen as fulfilling the demands of God as if those could include a series of ritual requirements. Christians are often presented with a dilemma of extremes: an ethical seriousness that devalues ritual *or* a ritual seriousness that seems too detached from ethical behaviour and which

---

[11]On the origins of these wafers in the West, and then their confirmation as 'the only way' as a result of a quarrel with the east, see Woolley 1913. On how the criticism of the East made the Roman churches unwilling to admit the possibility of being in error, and thus making unleavened bread a litmus test of orthodoxy, see Erickson 1970. Roman Catholic authorities, despite historical studies demonstrating the contrary, still make official claims that this is the 'ancient' Latin church practice, see Canon 926 (*Codex Iuris Canonici* 1983). This failure for the bread to be perceived as real food is tacitly admitted today by the Roman Catholic Church (see Smolarski 2004), while they still want to preserve their traditions of unleavened bread.
[12]Johnson 2006, 5, has a lovely irony on this point: Methodists in their Eucharists use real bread, while Catholics use real wine. The implication is that *all* have a great deal to learn – and to learn from one another.
[13]See O'Loughlin 1998a.

expresses its liturgical concerns in a way that borders on the magical. While both extremes ignore the anthropological fact that, as social creatures, we are both ritual and ethical agents.

The Last Supper

We need to recall these related sets of ironies before we can look at the distinctive features of the community meals of the early Christians. They saw these features as coming from Jesus himself and they saw their own meal practice as in continuity with him. We see an example of this belief of the early communities that there was a specifically 'Jesus manner' of blessing the Father at a meal – and that their own practice continued in that style – in the account of the post-resurrection meal in Emmaus in Lk. 24.30-31.[14] In that story Jesus is presented as taking a loaf, blessing the Father, breaking the loaf and giving it to his table companions – and this was done in so specific a manner that from the manner of his actions they were able to recognize him, and then retell the event as 'how [Jesus] had been made known to them in the breaking of the loaf' (24.35). The common assumption of Luke and his audience is that there was a specific way of offering the table blessing that was linked with Jesus, and they all know this because they imagined themselves carrying on his manner of blessing God at table. Given that early shared assumption, can we establish the form – be that actions or words or both – that those early communities used and which they held to be the continuation of the practice of Jesus?

For most of our history that has not even been a question: the answer lay in the accounts of the Last Supper in Paul and first three Gospels. Here was direct evidence of the continuity of exemplar to all later repetitions; or, in more recent times, here at least was the direct echo of actual liturgy in the early churches. There were, of course, differences in the canonical accounts but these could be reconciled by a comparative method so that, if the task was pursued diligently, one could arrive at so close an approximation of the events and words of that Last Supper as made no difference. However, despite any number of attempts – assuming that the genre of gospels could provide such precise details – the results were usually anything but clear. Moreover, the quest itself assumed that the events of that supper were intended by Jesus to establish a specific ritual very much like that which the researchers knew and cherished. Similarly, this quest was not simply confined to the doctrinal

---

[14]This account falls into the category of 'legend' and the sub-category of 'cult legend' – which implies that it is a theology in the form of a narrative from which the audience are to draw theological conclusions: see Betz 1969, 38 and note how Betz insists on the importance of it being a 'common . . . normal evening meal' (p. 41) if this legend is to perform its task in helping the early communities make sense of the basic understanding of the risen Jesus's presence among them. It is worth recalling that a *Sitz im Leben* must be a common experience of those who recall a story.

appeals to history that began in the aftermath of the Reformation, but it underpinned much of the work of the modern liturgical movement. It has been elegantly summarized by Bradshaw and Johnson:

> The pioneers of modern liturgical scholarship ... generally presumed that Jesus would have left precise instructions to his disciples as to what they were to say and do when they continued the practice established by him at the Last Supper, and so by comparing ancient liturgies with one another it ought to be possible to discover from what was common to them all the core elements that went back to apostolic times. This was never an easy task, because these ancient rites varied so much from one another, and it became increasingly difficult to maintain the thesis as more evidence for early eucharistic practices emerged in the late nineteenth and early twentieth centuries.[15]

Indeed, as the awareness of the complexity of the gospels grew among scholars, and the amount of other new evidence steadily grew, sometimes historians of liturgy simply avoided the issues. On one side they ignored the issues raised by biblical scholars as foreign to their concerns, while, on the other side, they ditched, with as little fuss as possible, any ancient materials that contradicted their views. We see this strategy even in such eminent scholars as Gregory Dix who disposed of the evidence of the *Didache* in a single footnote.[16] Meanwhile, many theologians retained earlier confessional structures for the debates, while up-dating usage of traditional biblical passages.

Is another quest possible?

However, if we avoid seeing 'the Last Supper' as the solitary foundation moment and see it as the dramatic climax in the kerygmatic narratives of the meals of Jesus,[17] then we can see that it is possible to uncover certain features within the memories of the meals of Jesus which were held by his followers as distinctive of his practice. This does not mean that we can isolate a 'core' beneath a plethora of details for such a discovery there would need to be many distinct but comparable strands of evidence (e.g. the Synoptics are variations on a single strand of evidence) and we would need far greater consistency across the evidence than exists (it was this very lack of consistency that wrecked the dreams of biblical scholars to isolate the 'original' Last Supper by comparison of the gospel evidence). Likewise, we

---

[15]Bradshaw and Johnston 2012, 19–20.
[16]Dix 1945, 48, n. 2 (on the background to this dismissal of the single most important piece of 'new' evidence regarding the Eucharist, see O'Loughlin 2013a).
[17]This is the approach taken in the previous chapter.

should note that we cannot identify some ubiquitous structure such as that made famous by Dix.[18] This is because such a structure supposes some kind of absolute and formal institution of a self-contained ritual such as would be the corresponding historical moment to the later doctrinal statement – a particular urgency during the Reformation period[19] – that 'the Eucharist is a sacrament instituted by the Lord'.[20]

However, as we survey the strands of evidence we notice that while there is almost no evidence for any uniformity of practice at the disciples' meals, much less of interpretation of what their eating together meant to them, there are recurrent elements and these can form the basis for a theological vision in the present. These practical commonalities combined with their allegiance to Jesus as the Christ, when thought about against the background of a network of travelling teachers, prophets and evangelists allow us to speak of 'the eucharistic practice of the early church'. There is a danger of falling into the extremes of 'clumping or splitting' in such a search: the 'clumpers' tending to take the various 'bits' of evidence and then present them as the surviving *tesserae* of a mosaic. In turn, there is the risk of treating the reconstructed mosaic as if it were a uniform ideal which was reflected, more or less, in individual cases. The 'splitters', by contrast, imagine that each church went its own way, acted differently and adapted its Jewish inheritance differently. Consequently, any notion of commonality is a later development that, in retrospect, draws lines together, harmonizing understandings into an orthodoxy. Rather than seek a middle way between these extremes, this study will proceed by looking at how we as *homines coenarii* act, and interpret out actions through our memories.[21]

The presupposition of any meal is a shared set of table conventions, manners, be they simple or elaborate. Such manners are usually shared widely across a society: the presupposition of all the books on table manners that have been produced down the centuries of which we might take those in Sir. 31.12-32.13 as a signal example.[22] But table manners, or perhaps we should refer to these as 'the grammar of our food sharing', also vary with every group that regularly eats together. Each group develops its own customs, patterns and idiosyncrasies. The visitor to any family gathering knows this well: the common pattern of eating together is well understood, but there are always details in the family's practice that are different to that of others. Indeed, it is this sort of variation between the manners at one banquet and another that underlies the advice in Sirach. This variation

---

[18]Dix 1945, 48.

[19]See O'Loughlin 2012a.

[20]See the preface to the Decree on the Eucharist of the 13th Session (1551) of the Council of Trent (1551), DS 1635, for the historical claim. The tag '*sacramentum a Christo Domino institutum*' is found in several places (e.g. DS 1773).

[21]See Uro 2011.

[22]For the most adequate translation of this passage, see Skehan and Di Lella 1987, 384–6.

within a common pattern[23] can be seen even more clearly if one is the guest in the refectory in different houses of the same monastic tradition. In such cases there is a highly formalized set of meal customs (one can but recall the table manners described by Philo in *De vita contemplativa*), and while these can be traced back genetically to common mother houses, and each custom is imagined as based in the same tradition, they are different in each house and the variations are even recorded in books of customs. Likewise, just as there were common expectations in the Greco-Roman world about what should happen at a symposium, each group's practice was also distinct. So too each church's meal practice took on particular shapes (perhaps the sharing of the cup took place before the sharing of the loaf, or vice versa) and emphases (in one place it was they imagined themselves as the re-gathered Israel and in another as the one body of the Christ). That there were such variations, particularly between Jewish-Christians and Gentile-Christians, has not been in doubt as we have direct evidence from Paul (Gal. 2.11-4); and that it became an ongoing problem can be seen from Luke's stress of being willing to participate at one another's meals.[24] But we should see variations as being part of the life of each gathering, and the historical quest as taking note of the common strands between them. Always bearing in mind two other caveats: first, that our evidence is fragmentary; and second, that every human event, such as meal, is always greater as an event than can be known in the traces it leaves in material capable of holding a record that can be accessed, intellectually, by anyone else (much less people two millennia later).[25]

The common strands

1 Blessing activity takes place at a meal

The most obvious common strand is that all eucharistic activity takes place during a meal, it belongs to the meal, it is part of the meal. Moreover, it is very hard to find any reference in the literary remains of the early disciples of Jesus where food was involved where there was no act of blessing. Indeed, given the place of blessings of God at meals in Jewish life, to find such a practice among the followers of Jesus would itself be abnormal.[26] Be it a miraculous

---

[23]It is the phenomenon that underlies the sociological process of deciphering meals as begun by Mary Douglas (Douglas 1972).

[24]Acts 10-11.18 (see O'Loughlin 2013c).

[25]It is this awareness of the inadequacy of our sources in providing an account, much less an account adequate to the needs arising from our theological disputes, that separates contemporary theologians from those of even a generation or two ago. The work of Bauer which appeared in 1934 (although it was not until 1971 that it appeared in English) can be seen as marking the boundary between the different sets of expectations.

[26]We have looked at the evidence in the previous two chapters: see Smith 2010 for a summary; and one should always note the pioneering work of Finkelstein 1929.

feeding narrated in the context of a meal, an account of an encounter with the risen Jesus at which there is eating, or the occasional references to meals among the disciples in Acts referred to as 'the breaking of the loaf' (2.42 and 46; 20.7 and 11; and 27.35), the blessing of God at a meal was a basic activity. Paul's experience of the ritual of early communities – which he made his own and then used as a model for instructing the Corinthians – was that being at table (1 Cor. 10.21) the community experienced the *koinonia* that was the decisive experience of Jesus' followers with him. Now at this table, this supper of the Lord (11.20) there was an experience of *koinonia* of women, slaves, Jews, gentiles and the poor.[27]

We can go further and state that the general thrust of all the evidence of gatherings of the followers of Jesus was to come together and eat together. Christianity was a feast,[28] its assemblies were meals, be they simple or lavish. This conclusion is forced on us not only by the direct evidence for such gatherings (such as references by Paul in 1 Corinthians and Romans), but also by the fact that it imagined its encounters with Jesus, both during his lifetime and after the resurrection, in terms of meals.[29] The litmus test of this assertion is not any of the great meals well remembered in the *kerygma* (be that in parable[30] or narration)[31] but the meal whose eucharistic dimension never enters discussions of the Eucharist: Luke's presentation of Paul's meal while adrift in the Adriatic.

Just before daybreak, Paul urged all of them to take some food, saying, 'Today is the fourteenth day that you have been in suspense and remaining without food, having eaten nothing. Therefore I urge you to take some food, for it will help you survive; for none of you will lose a hair from your heads.'

After he had said this, he took bread[32]; and giving thanks to God in the presence of all, he broke it and began to eat. Then all of them were encouraged and took food for themselves. (We were in all two hundred seventy-six persons in the ship.) After they had satisfied their hunger,

---

[27]See Keightley 2005, 144–7.
[28]Cf. Wolter 2009.
[29]Cf. Czachesz 2010.
[30]For example: Lk. 15.11-32 ('The Prodigal Son') which Luke sees as a direct response to the commensality of Jesus ('This man receives sinners and eats with them') in 15.2 and whose conclusion is that those who eat at the feast are now 'found' (15.32) within the Father's kingdom.
[31]For example, Lk. 19.7 (the account of the meeting with Zacchaeus) which is seen to make Jesus defend his commensality against critics (19.9: 'He has gone in to be the guest of a man who is a sinner') and which concludes with a statement that Zacchaeus has been sought out by the Son of Man and is now 'saved' (19.10) within the Father's kingdom.
[32]This phrase, *labón arton*, should be rendered (as the NRSV does on other occasions such as Mk 14.22; Lk. 22.19; and 1 Cor. 11.23) as 'taking a loaf'. See O'Loughlin 2004.

they lightened the ship by throwing the wheat into the sea. (Acts 27.33-8;
NRSV)

This account offers a valuable insight into Luke's understanding of how what
we call 'the Eucharist' was located within Christian life and imagination
in his time. The context is, explicitly, an extreme: the life or death of the
entire ship's company of 276 people, who fear being lost at sea (27.20). Paul
has encouraged them (27.21-6) but is concerned that they have been going
without food (27.21) for a fortnight and is anxious that they eat if they are to
survive. This fasting by the ship's company is unexplained – it may have been
religious in intent[33] – but Paul's advice is severely practical: if they are going
to survive in those conditions (as is promised by the angel: 27.23) then they
must have the strength that comes from nourishment: this is not going to be
a symposium nor a gathering of believers – a fact that Luke emphasizes –
but as close to 'raw' alimentation as we find. Yet even in this case, Luke
is so imbued with Christian meal practice that he has Paul 'eucharistize'
and 'break a loaf' before he can eat.[34] That it is *not simply* a memory of
alimentation, but a recollection transformed through Luke's experience of
Christian commensality is easily seen: bread would not have survived that
length of time they were at sea unless they baked some afresh, but this break
in the 'continuity' of the narrative is indicative to us of how deeply embedded
the blessing of a loaf was within their shared ritual memories. Every act of
eating by a Christian is a eucharistic occasion; and the eating by those with
Paul – it is one of the 'we' passages – was a eucharistic meal after the fashion
of all the other Christian meals.

The cumulative effect of this evidence from the early communities – and
we could cite examples until well into the second century with Justin, Ignatius
or the apocryphal *acta* of the Apostles[35] – is that the older approach of seeing
'the Eucharist' emerge/evolve/develop out of the meal is wholly wide of the
mark. One cannot force the evidence into an evolutionary process which
is imagined by analogy with an original 'emulsion' of oil and water which,
over the course of time, separated into their 'pure' components of oil (the
Eucharist) and water (a community get together with shared food perhaps
labelled 'the agape'). Such notions do not do justice either to the evidence

---

[33]Commentaries usually see it as the result of some sort of sea-sickness or having too many
other cares; but because these problems do not prevent them from eating once Paul has begun
to eat, it is more likely that Luke intends us to understand this as a case of deliberate fasting to
appease the gods.

[34]This verse is generally passed over in commentaries on Acts; while Munck's comment (1979,
251) 'that Paul himself sets a good example by saying grace [before] beginning to eat' seems
to miss the point that this is not ethical example, but the specifically religious act of thanking
God for his goodness.

[35]See the meal events in *Acta Iohannis*, 4–85, 89 and 109–110; or in the *Acta Thomae*, 29,
49–50, 121, 133 or 158: the significance of this material for our understanding of eucharistic
evolution is rarely acknowledged, but see Czachesz 2010, 432.

before us, nor to the early communities' memories of what they saw as the mandating practice of Jesus for their common activity. It has often been noted that because the Eucharist continued to involve token eating/drinking, then it must be the case that eating and drinking were inherently linked to it. However, for those who saw 'the Eucharist' as mixed-in with 'a meal' but substantially distinct, that linkage was problematic because the purpose of the gathering was a spiritual one. Faced with this 'fact', many Reformation churches wondered about all the fuss over bread and wine because the purpose could be just as well fulfilled without them. Similarly, Catholics could so play down the actual eating (Catholics did not drink), while separating the act of 'receiving' from 'attendance', while they could also conclude that a 'spiritual communion' – without any eating – bestowed the same spiritual benefits as an actual 'communion'. So what was the purpose of this token eating and drinking? Either it was simply as an aid to memory of the Last Supper, or as the fulfilment of a sacramental type (the manna was eaten, so the new manna too needed to be eaten to fulfil its 'sign' value), or for catechetical purposes among the simple.

Few, in the period before the rise of modern historical consciousness, ever progressed the argument to see that if eating and drinking remained, problematic as they were, then it must have been the case that it was not the Eucharist that emerged, but the meal that became atrophied and redundant. So unusual did any such thought seem, that as the evidence mounted from the 1880s onwards, many scholars were reduced to postulating that the early disciples had two separate events which were confused in the early 'inchoate' period: a token affair uncannily like what later happened and which belonged explicitly to the 'sacral' domain; and an 'ordinary' meal which promoted collaboration and expressed practical concern for the poor and which could be called 'an agape'.[36] Even fewer realized that while they appealed to the early examples as mandates for later theology and practice, they simultaneously had to dismiss the early practice as chaotic and not having the clarity or coherence they actually sought.[37]

Reflecting on the historical actuality that eucharistic activity is meal based, the task facing Christians today is to see that the incarnational dynamic involved in every meal of Christians has a eucharistic dimension. And coupled with that understanding is the appreciation that any Christian gathering, which claims descent and continuity with the historical Jesus and his companions (the basis of the claim to 'apostolicity'), should take the form of a real meal, at which there is a blessing by the person who is the host

---

[36]See McGowan 1997.

[37]J. H. Newman seems to have been aware of the conundrum in his *Essay on the Development of Christian Doctrine* 1845 but did not press the point (see O'Loughlin 1991 and 1995). The problem becomes explicit in the attempts to remove any eucharistic dimension from the *Didache* (see O'Loughlin 2013a) while continuing to appeal to antiquity as warrant (see O'Loughlin 2012a).

of the meal. This is a challenge of *ressourcement* and renewal greater than anything so far undertaken by most churches.

This may seem extreme to those Christians for whom the Eucharist is a sacral event presided over by a presbyter endowed with the 'power of orders' and whose hands are made holy for this task through an anointing. But the basic ritual forms which underlie this eucharistic understanding and practice are themselves evolutions from what was originally done and from those sources which they see as the primary witnesses to the 'deposit of faith'. Likewise, for those Christians for whom the Eucharist is but an occasional event,[38] and for whom this gathering is mainly a matter of words, this too may seem ludicrous, yet the very texts to which they ascribe authority portray a radically different practice and vision of gathering. If the evidence of the early churches, and their memories of Jesus, have any value for Christians today, then Christians need to see a blessing as a part of every meal, and having a meal together as central to their common worship. In such a situation, not only does the dissonance between the texts cited and their actual practice disappear, but also the claims of Vatican II that the Eucharist is the 'centre' and 'the summit' of Christian life take on a genuine and direct meaning.[39] Meanwhile, it is only from this incarnational starting point of liturgy in the midst of human life that the full implications of those theologians – such as Henri de Lubac (1896–1991) – who have stressed the links between 'Eucharist' and 'Church' (a theme taken up in Vatican II), can be seen to have practical meaning for Christians over and above being beautiful ideas.[40]

2 Blessing is addressed to God as Father

In the case of every meal the community addressed its prayer, or recalled Jesus addressing his prayer, to the Father. The actual words used in this prayer of thanking God varied: in some places it was based on words related to *eucharisteo* and in others on *eulogeo*, and this variation reflects that found in Jewish table prayers some of which used the form *berakah* while others used *hodayah*.[41] That these words, in whatever language, were understood as synonyms within early Christianity, and that there was a variety in early Christian practice based in this linguistic distinction, can be seen from Mark's equal employment of both terms. But this well-known concern over a linguistic detail has often obscured the larger issue: the prayer

---

[38]Perhaps it is occasional because it is only carried out infrequently simply because it is mentioned in the Bible that it should be done; but it may also be occasional because it is linked to church-going at Christmas and Easter, or, possibly, a wedding.

[39]See *Sacrosanctum concilium* 1964, n. 10; and drawn out more in *Eucharisticum mysterium* 1967, I, B.

[40]See McPartlan 1993.

[41]Bradshaw 1981, 11–16; 2002, 43–4; and 2004, 8–9.

is addressed to God for all his goodness of which the food was an instance and an occasion of blessing.

For many Christians this is too obvious to be noted; it is simply clear from the textual evidence as in the case of Luke's presentation of Paul on the ship: he took a loaf and 'he gave thanks to God' (Acts 27.35). However, for many Catholics this has become so obscured through a confusion in Latin phraseology resulting from the use, together, of two verbs (*gratias agere* and *benedicere*) in the liturgical institution narrative that it has created the notion that Jesus gave thanks to the Father and 'blessed' the bread. This confusion has then been followed up in theological writing, in rubrics and in art. Over time it has become a commonplace to imagine that Jesus (and so the liturgical presider) blessed the bread and wine (and by analogy there are many formulae for the 'blessing' of objects – such as salt or water or eggs – in the *Rituale Romanum*), and this, in turn, gave ever greater focus to the actual elements: they were the object of attention and action. Today, a return to the perspective of having the loaf and the cup of wine as God's gifts and, therefore, blessing the Father for this goodness and all his goodness, most especially for the Christ, will require not only changes in liturgical practice, but also a shift from a well-embedded cultural understanding.[42]

From the time of the first attempts to reconstruct the historical 'Last Supper' until very recent times, one central quest was to find the actual words of Jesus (his *ipsissima verba*) not only as part of a general search for the words of Jesus in the gospels, but also because here would be the ideal liturgical text, which might also prove to be the key to resolving disputes about the Eucharist arising from the Reformation.[43] This quest suffered its first major reversal with the discovery of the *Didache*, became even more untenable with increasing awareness of the complexity of the gospels' tradition within an oral culture, and was finally recognized as futile in the face of our steadily growing knowledge of the ancient forms of Eucharistic Prayers. However, despite churches continuing to declare that only specific verbal formulae could have any 'validity' (often equivalent to stating that only those words could effect consecration) or were 'genuine' (often treated as equivalent to the notion of Jesus's *ipsissima verba*), all churches with rigidly fixed verbal formulae have to come to terms with the fact that originally there were no fixed formulae – and so, at the very least, learn to respect one another's differences or even wholly *ex tempore* (*chez* Justin) eucharistic praying.[44] The task of the prayer was clear, to bless/thank the Father, but there were no specified words, much less the use of the words of Jesus as found in the gospels.

---

[42]See O'Loughlin 2013h.

[43]Higgins 1952; Jeremias 1966 are examples of the quest for the 'original words' – and so the original theology; see Wandel 2006, 256–62 on the notion that the origins would reveal the true theology.

[44]Johnson 2006, 20, draws attention to the fact that implications of the 2001 Roman acknowledgement of the authenticity of the *Anaphora of Addai and Mari* [cf. Taft 2003] are 'mind-boggling'.

The evidence can be laid out very simply: first, there is no liturgical formula in the gospels, and the use of an 'institution narrative' (i.e. gospel materials in a euchological setting) is itself a later development. Second, while the *Didache* offers a formula, it is not prescriptive but offering help to those presiding who may not have the skills to compose a euchological prayer *ex tempore*. It is clear that when there is 'a prophet' present – who was probably a disciple who moved from church to church[45] and who should know how to offer such a prayer – he is to be let pray as he wishes (10.7). Moreover, the prayers found in the *Didache* are better seen as an assortment of forms, reflecting varying usages, than any attempt at a specific form.[46] All we can say is that those prayers represent a Christian adaptation of blessings in use in contemporary Judaism.[47] Third, when in the middle of the second century we get a description from Justin of a presider *(proestos)* offering prayers of thanks to the Father of all, the only fixed formula appear to be the community's 'amen' at the prayer's conclusion, and the prayer itself is to be made 'as best he can'.[48] Lastly, given the ambivalence about prayer-formulae which we find in the Synoptic Tradition,[49] it seems that any attempt to have long, formalized prayers would have probably met with opposition.[50] If this scenario is accepted, then attempts to find 'the earliest form of a Eucharistic Prayer' need to be seen as the archaeology of the extant evidence, rather than the process of looking for the origins through sifting the evidence of later developments.[51] This state of affairs should then be seen as setting a full stop over many medieval and modern disputes about what elements are necessary for a Eucharistic Prayer and, because it is a prayer of blessing the Father rather than 'a formula of consecration', who can utter it.

So how did the relatively fixed forms – those prayers we label 'paleoana-phoras' – emerge? The answer probably lies in the phenomenon of custom developing from repetition. As activity became more and more a matter of expected custom, the variety that was initially present did not continue to expand, but rather contracted as individuals drew upon forms of blessing which they had heard and used many times already. In such a manner phrases long familiar in Jewish table prayers came into Christian use; and once they

---

[45]That the prophets were seen as having special skills and moved from place to place forming the network of the *oikoumene*, see Milavec 1994, but note the comments of Draper 1998.

[46]See van de Sandt 2011.

[47]The most convenient collection is by Louis Ligier in Hänggi and Pahl 1998, 5–57; and see Mazza 1995, 12–41.

[48]*Apologia* I, 65, 3.

[49]Mk 12.40 followed by Lk. 20.47 – where the problem is presented as one afflicting 'the scribes', but it may well be that it is a reflection on those community members who were overly prolix in their prayers.

[50]That disciples should pray *ex tempore*, as a response to the gift of the Spirit, is not seen as a basic principle of Christian liturgy in those churches with a tradition of fixed liturgical formulae, but this is an aspect of worship that needs to be recalled to act as a balance to formalization. See Abba 1960, 7–9.

[51]This process is implied in Mazza 1995, 10.

were familiar in Christian use, it was but a small step from them being familiar usage to their being considered 'our' style, and very soon anyone not adopting that style was seen to be breaking with the tradition. Memory tends to repeat patterns and series – what is referred to by psychologists as 'serial recall'[52] – and this means that forms repeat one another until a moment comes when it is a departure from the form that causes alarm.

It may be the case that Christian prayer 'in the Spirit' should reflect the spontaneity of an interaction with the living God that cuts across customs and formulae, but such existential awareness does not take sufficient account of how repetition affects us as ritual animals. It is the propensity of human beings to endow familiar ritual forms with authority, and then to imagine that those authoritative forms take their status from some specific moment of 'institution'[53] – a moment in history, but of such unique quality that it has the ritual status of being '*in illo tempore*'.[54]

3 There is a loaf

While the many searches for 'the original words' (be that those of Jesus or some hypothetical archetypal prayer) have proven fruitless, the same cannot be said for the archaeology of certain actions. While words and interpretations varied in the early communities, actions – which tend to be more stable in imitation – seem to have been far more consistent between groups.[55] All our evidence points to a leader taking a loaf of bread and then breaking it so that portions of it can be taken and eaten by others.[56] While Dix's famous set of four constituents of a Eucharist may have come in for much criticism in recent decades, it is true that he drew attention away from the search for words and concentrated on the 'shape' of the activity. Dix

---

[52]Rubin 1995.

[53]The notion of a moment of institution by Christ lies just beneath many of the disputes at the time of the Reformation – and that desire for a single authorizing moment fitted with their legal approach to Christian origins (just as a charter needed a moment when it came into force, so any action regulated by law, such as the consecration at Mass, needed an authorizing warrant); but just as that approach to history has withered, so too should the theological arguments that were derived from it.

[54]The notion that ritual forms can be traced back to a primal moment *in illo tempore* – a time hovering on the borders of historical time – is taken from Mircea Eliade (see Eliade 1954, 21–6). But we should also recall that the historical elements in religious memory are not just memories of when something happened, but of the particular moment the event of religious significance came 'into being' in our world. This memory is, therefore, more than an historical statement; as Maurice Halbwachs remarked: 'every religious representation is both general and particular, abstract and concrete, logical and historical' (Halbwachs 1992, 174).

[55]This is an approach taken by Nodet and Taylor 1998, 88–125.

[56]The question of when the blessing was said is a distinct issue, and we will come to it later in this chapter.

noticed that this involved taking a loaf (he did not use the word but it is implied in that he asserted that it was subsequently broken), giving thanks to God, breaking it and this being shared (or as he imagined it: 'distributed').[57] While we have many descriptions of Jewish table prayers, including those where the leader of the table offered the blessing for all at the table,[58] this emphasis on the breaking of one loaf into portions for sharing seems to be peculiar to the followers of Jesus. This is one of their distinctive practices – and as such Luke can assume that it would be the 'historical' basis for the moment of recognition in the Emmaus story (24.35).

While we are next tempted to ask whether this breaking of a loaf was intended as a symbolic action or was a distinctive action which was then interpreted symbolically, such an approach is very wide of the mark for several reasons. First, it ignores the fact that any formal action done in public is an act of ritual communication[59]; second, it supposes the Renaissance distinction between action and 'meaning' which underlies much sixteenth-century controversy[60]; and, third, it imagines that humans behave as if they were performing roles in a pre-determined pattern be that a laboratory experiment, following a recipe, acting out stage directions, or following rubrics in a formal liturgy. By contrast, most public actions are understood, repeated without conscious awareness that they involve exact repetition, and understood afresh day after day and week after week. Moreover, in real life there is no way of knowing how many different understandings there were of such actions, except that all believed they were acting together. That said, understandings, and sometimes explanations, become enwrapped into actions by which their distinctiveness is valued, and the part played by the action within the community underlined. So do we glimpse how this action of breaking a common loaf was understood?

For Paul the singularity of the loaf is a realization of the unity of the new people: 'Because there is one loaf, we who are many are one body, for we all partake of the one loaf' (1 Cor. 10.17). The unity of the loaf, a unity which can be shared in through each having a portion of it when it has been broken, is their unity in Christ. Moreover, just as 'the people of Israel' are 'partners in the altar' in Jerusalem through eating what has been sacrificed (1 Cor. 10.18), so their eating of 'the loaf which we break' makes them participants 'in the body of Christ' (1 Cor. 10.16). The body of Christ is the community who have, as individuals, consumed a fraction of the one, common, loaf.[61] And as a table community is a natural unity, so the common loaf shared by those at table is expressive of the basis of that unity: their faith in Jesus.[62]

---

[57]Dix 1945, 48.
[58]Bahr 1970.
[59]See Rothenbuhler 1998.
[60]See J. Z. Smith 1987.
[61]See Hollander 2009.
[62]See Rouwhorst 2006.

In the *Didache* this theme of the loaf representing the singularity that is the community of those on the Way of Life invokes a different range of images, but with the same key element of being a people, in Christ, praising God. Here the unity of the loaf, a unity created out of the many individual grains which are milled and baked to produce it, is seen as parallel to the unity of the community of believers which is formed from scattered individuals (9.4). Because this image starts with what are seen to be really separate, but similar, items – grains of a cereal – and then imagines these being transformed into what is also immediately recognizable as a single reality, a loaf, it is a richer image than that of the body used by Paul. No one sees a member, for instance an arm, actually detached and alone which was still capable of being a part of the whole.[63] The independence of the members of a body is only known notionally in that I can imagine my arm distinct from my leg or from me. But the grains in the *Didache*'s image are really separate at the start of the process by which they are brought to the finality for which they have been sown and reaped. And what those grains become in the human transformation is both radically different from their origins, yet truly a real individual entity: a loaf. While Paul's image is static and based on what the Christ has done, the *Didache*'s image is dynamic and embraces what the Christ is doing in forming and transforming the Holy People who are offering the thanksgiving over the loaf.[64]

This image of many individual seeds and one transformed loaf is then presented in the *Didache* in messianic terms of Israel, which having been scattered over the hills is now being reunited in the work of the Anointed One, and the reunion is seen in the community of the meal.[65] The loaf, of which each has a share, is a symbol not only of unity and the nature of that unity which began in isolated individuality,[66] but is a symbol of the work of the Father's servant, Jesus, who brings the history of Israel to the desired moment of the scattered-being-gathered again. It is the action of this child of the Father that transforms – as the grain was transformed into bread by human processes – these scattered human beings into the People of God. This regrouping by Jesus both fulfils the ancient promise and is the joyful basis for their celebration. The unity of the diners in the *Didache* is the result of the transformative work of the promised Messiah, and this is experienced in the loaf of which each has a portion.[67]

---

[63] I am told that this is now medically possible; suffice to say that imagery as used by Paul to make his point about the nature of the Church assumed a less developed state of medicine.

[64] See van de Sandt 2006 who locates the imagery of being scattered and re-gathered both within its context in Second Temple Judaism, and in particular the writings of Philo, and within early Christian literature such as the Letter to the Hebrews and 1 Peter.

[65] See O'Loughlin 2010, 97–8.

[66] That the churches were willing to dwell on the nature of cereal grain as providing metaphors and images for the impact of the Christ-event is clear from the use of grain-imagery in stories (Mk 2.23), the 'Parable of the Sower' (Mk 4.1-9 and parallels), and another use in Jn 12.24.

[67] On the subsequent uses of this imagery, see O'Loughlin 2003a and 2013.

Reflection that the single loaf related to the single body of believers as the body of Christ – and this time with an emphasis on that body of believers being the truly human, incarnate, Jesus – can again be found in Ignatius' letters in the middle of the second century. His imagery is based on both 1 Corinthians and the tradition of the *Didache* in that for him the loaf stands for the church, and as it is one, so must each church be a single unified harmony. As Klawiter has summed it up:

> Ignatius identifies himself with the bread, a symbol for the unity of the members of the church with the flesh of Jesus Christ who offered himself as a sacrifice of agape.[68]

So in this oft-quoted line from Ignatius, 'breaking one loaf as the medicine of immortality' we have a statement that in being part of the real body of the Christ, the church, they are joined to his immortal humanity; and they can see this in the single loaf of their community meals.[69] Moreover, Ignatius is not alone among second-century writers in seeing the loaf in this, already traditional, way as a symbol of their incorporation into the Christ because the same imagery can subsequently be found in Irenaeus of Lyons.[70]

There is also one other possible indication of the symbolic value attached to the loaf in the earliest churches: Judas is identified as the reprobate traitor in that not only is he at table (Lk. 22.21) but he 'is dipping [a piece of] bread into the dish with me' (Mk 14.20). Just as the symbolism of the kiss is inverted in the Synoptic Tradition to draw out the perversity of Judas,[71] so having a piece of bread from the same dish emphasizes his treachery. If so, it obliquely shows the value attached to partaking of a single loaf as a symbol of the community's communion with one another and with the risen Jesus. Having Judas have a portion would then highlight in ritual communication that he was with Jesus within the group, bounded by the common table, and yet *then* betrayed Jesus and the rest of that community.

---

[68]Klawiter 2007, 136. This article overturns a long standing tradition of modern scholarship which has read Ignatius's eucharistic notions in terms of a sacramental 'realism' – that is, it is the actual elements that are the body and blood of Christ – and has shown that both loaf and cup are symbols of the community, which is the real flesh and blood of Jesus Christ. Klawiter's argument would have been even clearer if he realized that using 'bread' in this context is a hangover from the medieval theological paradigm (see O'Loughlin 2004) and although he used loaf on occasions (e.g. on p. 136 he notes 'flour . . . is baked into one loaf') he should have done so consistently. His overall argument is now even more telling than when he published it in 2007 as then he had to develop his reading of Ignatius on the assumption that he wrote early in the second century, whereas now we can locate him much later (see Barnes 2008) and so far closer in time to Irenaeus whose work Klawiter used as corroboration for his reading of Ignatius. Indeed, we can see Ignatius' letters as a mid-point between the *Didache* and Irenaeus.

[69]Ignatius, *To the Ephesians* 20, 1–2; and see Klawiter 2007, 142–4.

[70]*Adversus haereses*, 3, 17, 2; the text is cited in Klawiter 2007, 137.

[71]Mk 14.44; Mt. 26.48; Lk. 22.47-8.

Looking at the various hints – and they are little more than that – about how they interpreted the breaking of the loaf should not obscure the basic action of sharing a single food item, and its human significance to us as *homines coenarii*. Every human act of sharing the food establishes a bond between those who share it. Whether it is the close informality of 'let's share it' of two spoons and a single pudding, thirsty men sharing a water canteen, the implication of welcome when food is shared in a desert camp, or the celebratory cake that is part of many special occasions: this deliberate act serves to express common humanity, the fact of community, and a degree of intimacy.[72]

All interpretations, from the few-sentences-length interpretations of Paul and the *Didache* to the most complex of eucharistic theologies, are, in the last analysis, appendages to this basic human experience. And to the extent that any 'explanation' (and every explanation is less than the reality which is its focus) of the Eucharist is not founded in this basic understanding, which implies a Christian community actually thanking the Father while actually sharing a loaf; that explanation is simply an accretion to a corpus of ideas. While such a presentation of belief may or may not appeal to certain Christians, it will risk distracting them from the basic Christian symbol in which Jesus' followers understood themselves as continuing with his practice when 'they devoted themselves to the apostles' teaching and fellowship, to the breaking of the loaf and the prayers' (Acts 2.42).

At first sight this appreciation of the place of the loaf in Christian eucharistic activity does not pose any serious challenge to contemporary practice or teaching within the churches. After all the eastern Churches present a large real loaf of bread for their celebrations (although whether or not they have any sense of sharing a portion of a single loaf when they receive communion is another matter).[73] Meanwhile in the west, with the exception of some worries about the practice of fraction in some German-speaking Protestant Churches in the aftermath of the Reformation,[74] it has been part of the western rites throughout their history (albeit vestigially, and with almost no appreciation of its significance through the use of individual pre-cut round wafers).[75] Moreover, there is an awareness among liturgists of its historical importance since the work of Duchesne (1889),[76] Wilpert

---

[72]See Vera 2004, 36–7, on how this human hospitality with food can be the basis of a eucharistic understanding.

[73]A common practice is for each person to bring their own little loaf (*prosphora*), or buy it at the church door, which is sent to the altar with a list of people to be prayed for. The priest cuts a tiny piece out of the little loaf and it is dropped into the cup on their behalf. The *prosphora* is then sent back out to the person who brought it.

[74]See Nischan 1984.

[75]See Craig 2011.

[76]See Duchesne 1923, 218–22 – this study, originally published in French in 1889, was the first modern study to draw attention to the fraction as a significant moment in earlier forms of the liturgy.

(1895)[77] and Dix (1945),[78] while the 1969 *Missale Romanum* makes allowance in its rubrics for a fraction that is more than simply the president breaking his own wafer in two before consuming both portions himself.[79] Moreover, there have been parallel developments introducing a real fraction in the renewed rites of other Churches.[80]

Today, many churches are happy to invoke the imagery of the fraction in discussion, song and art, but then avoid the practice. The problems, it seems, relate to 'pastoral practicalities'. For instance, it would be difficult to obtain a suitable large loaf to have sufficient portions for modern-sized gatherings; or perhaps it would take too long and bore the gathering; there is still the western familiarity with using unleavened wafers[81] – hence change would disturb people; and, though less often voiced, there is the long-standing concern in some traditions about 'crumbs'. Such dismissals of liturgical problems as matters of 'practical logistics' must be viewed with caution. These practical matters are theologically significant precisely because the Eucharist is a practice: being eucharistic is an activity. Indeed, over the centuries, some of the greatest theological confusions have begun life in seemingly innocuous changes in practice: concern over the cost of providing fresh, white loaves in the early medieval period – which led to the use of unleavened bread and eventually contributed to a schism with the east[82] – being a case in point. Because the Eucharist is an activity and meals are part of human life – and are then rationalized and explained in relation to actions – dismissing the practicalities is theologically and pastorally irresponsible.

But a renewed focus on sharing a portion of a single loaf also poses strictly theological challenges to several churches. The long-standing focus in many churches is not on the portion-of-a-whole shared, but on the reality of the commodity received. 'What it is' is what makes it valuable and sacred, and what makes the Eucharist a religious event of the highest order. For anyone thinking within this framework of quiddity, if what one has *is* the body of the Lord, then whether it comes as a fraction of a loaf or as a pre-cut unleavened wafer is irrelevant, if not positively a distraction with

---

[77]See Wilpert 1895.

[78]Dix considered 'breaking' one part of the invariable four-fold 'shape'; and his work was influential on the Roman Catholic liturgists who produced the rubrics of the 1969 missal. In the very first formal lecture on liturgy I ever attended in September 1977 which was given by Dr J. H. Murphy c.m. (the last of the eminent rubricians of the former rite), he introduced the key elements of the Eucharist in terms of the four-fold shape of taking, thanking, breaking and eating directly from the work of Dix.

[79]Rubric 131 of that missal reads: *Quod etiam pluries repeti potest* [of the *Agnus Dei* chant], *si fractio panis protrahitur*. Clearly, the reformers foresaw the possibility of a 'protracted fraction' but, however, saw such an event as exceptional and clearly of limited importance. See Smolarski 2004 for developments since 1969.

[80]See valuable summary by Bradshaw, Giles and Kershaw in Bradshaw 2001, 129–30.

[81]On the rather sordid origins of this usage which coincide to a large extent with the disappearance of a real fraction, see Woolley 1913.

[82]See Erickson 1970.

material details. At best, any such concern could only relate to the level of catechesis and communication, while what is at issue is the ontological status of the object which appears to the eyes as a product of baking flour and water. Moreover, any refocusing on the form of what is broken, shared and eaten would severely challenge the whole interest in the change in substances that has been at the heart of so much Christian controversy, as well as the cult of the reserved sacrament that has played such a part in the spirituality of western Christians (either as an activity engaged in or one positively rejected) since the twelfth century. While such an approach ignores the reality of liturgy as a matter of signs, to its adherents such issues are of little account.

For anyone who thinks of the Eucharist in Aristotelian-style categories, taking proper account of the basic activity of breaking a loaf is likely to pose what are, probably, insuperable obstacles. The question of what it is, because it related to the category of 'substance' will always have such priority in thought that any issue about the differences between 'a loaf' and 'bread-stuff' will seem but a debate on peripheral 'niceties' – the shape, form, size, colour, texture and overall appearance are 'accidents' secondary to 'substance'. But while these categories might have been excellent tools of scientific analysis in the pre-modern age, they were *never* the categories with which human beings assessed their own food, described their banquets either real or imaginary, nor were they ever used to express the depths of our humanity nor our relationships with one another. A warm, freshly baked loaf is a treat to all the senses; while a cup of wine 'foaming' (Ps. 75.8) and 'spiced' (Song 8.2) speaks of our hopes and joys: it is at this human level where food is much more than the quiddities of alimentary substances that we encounter each other, the liturgy, and the divine.

Likewise, for many focused on a traditional notion of 'presence' any issue about breaking a loaf is secondary because activity is always secondary to something that is: *agere sequitur esse*. Hence, it is the static that has priority, because activity is merely a function of 'being'. However, one cannot appreciate the basic eucharistic activity of the early communities, and its symbolic worldview based in its belief in following Jesus while imagining the Eucharist in Aristotelian terms using a hermeneutic designed to assist in formal intellectual analysis (analogous to what we would term 'science') of collections of material objects. The contemporary Christian quest must be, in the first place, for an appreciation of the common activity that gave unifying shape to those communities' desire to thank God for all that has made them 'God's people'. Then, having looked at origins, the quest must seek out the elements from that inheritance that still speak within our cultures that can form the basis of our activity of thanking God. And it is the argument of this study that, given that sharing food was at the basis of that early activity and it is still inscribed on our humanity today, it can provide a genuine incarnational location for eucharistic activity.

However, accepting the centrality of the breaking of a loaf, as distinct from focusing on the issue of *what* is eaten will, for many, prove difficult for other reasons. First, we are creatures who like to possess what is valuable, we like what we can hold, and we like to collect and to possess. Indeed, our fascination with 'having' is one of those weaknesses for which we need to seek God's help within our lives. Here the notion 'it is Jesus' we 'have' in the Eucharist can all too easily transform a eucharistic theology into a kind of religious consumerism.[83] We have only to look at how Isidore of Seville presented the Eucharist in terms of the most sacred of possessions and the greatest of relics to see that it is an attractive notion; albeit one which is fundamentally at odds with all that the Eucharist is supposed to be. Somehow 'receiving Jesus' appears, ironically, a better and more earthy reason for all the ritual rigmarole – and the bother of 'going to church' – than sharing a loaf as an expression of our unity as the Spirit-filled new People called into being by the incarnate Anointed One. Second, while shifts in any long held liturgical position encounter cultural resistance due to the habitual quality of the activity, the rituals surrounding the notion of 'sacred presence' are so linked to heightened emotions – and their ritual shape the very opposite of any notion of a broken shared loaf – that they create a barrier to taking seriously any of the evidence from early Christian experience. The 'culture wars' that have developed in Catholicism in recent years about alternative rituals or styles of celebration hide a deeper division than these are presenting problems. The fault lines may relate to fundamental eucharistic paradigms and different understanding of human religious activity.[84] One paradigm is essentially an individualistic relationship with God/Jesus, and the other a view of faith as a community and ecclesial affair. While the current Catholic 'culture wars' are the most public, the same tensions are present, with slightly different presenting symptoms, in most western churches – and come to the surface when they seek to renew their eucharistic rituals.

4 There is a cup

While the common memory of the origin of the Eucharist in the 'Last Supper' is that Jesus took 'bread and wine' (a remembering that emphasizes the distinct materials), by contrast *all* our texts notice that he took 'a cup'.[85]

---

[83]It could be argued that the practical difficulties that were solved by unleavened wafers – ease of storage, shelf-life, and speed of preparation and distribution – is the earliest known example of the logistics that underlie 'fast-food' chains.

[84]Is the Eucharist about sharing and eating portions of a single loaf over which a thanksgiving has been offered to the Father or about the transformation of bread into 'the presence of Jesus' who is, through this physical object, 'present' to those at the celebration? While this question is rarely posed directly in Catholic circles, it is the unacknowledged problem underlying the divergent practices of groups since the 1960s.

[85]1 Cor. 10.16 and 21; 11.25, 26, 27 and 28; Mk 14.23; Mt. 26.27; Lk. 22.17 and 20; and *Didache*, 9.2.

That this cup contained wine is then inferred from a subsequent statement found in the Synoptic Tradition: 'Truly I tell you, I will never again drink of the fruit of the vine until that day when I drink it new in the kingdom of God.'[86] But is the early usage of 'a cup' (and, therefore, on *how* that drinking took place) when contrasted with the later emphasis on what is in the cup (hence, on *what* was actually consumed) of any real significance? After all, logically it should be wine that parallels bread, or plate with cup, so is seeing a specific reason for 'a cup' anything more than an academic curiosity?

That this is important can be seen in a variety of ways. The most obvious evidence that 'a cup' was significant in the churches' memory was that having taken the cup Jesus gave it to those at table so that they each drank 'from it'. It was not that they all drank wine – or any other liquid – which they could do from their individual cups,[87] nor that they all had a drink of the same wine in that it came from one source or flagon,[88] but that they passed a cup from one to another and *each drank from that same cup*. When we recognize this we see at once that 'the cup' was of, at least, equal significance to them with what it contained. The focus of early memory was on the *how* of their drinking, not upon *what* they drank.

First and foremost, we need to recognize just how unusual was this action of sharing a drinking vessel. There was no equivalent to it in any known Jewish practice such as Shabbat or Pesach meals, there is no mention of anything like it in any other Jewish sect such as the Essenes or the Therapeutae/Therapeutrides, nor are there any literary references to such a practice either in Jewish documents that are certainly earlier than Jesus (be they canonical or not), roughly contemporary with him (e.g. in Philo or Josephus), nor those which are of uncertain date but ancient (e.g., the Mishnah). Making the sharing of a cup part of one's table manners is confined exclusively to the followers of Jesus. Moreover, that those disciples considered it to be a deliberate and significant ritual is seen by the fact that they located it, and remembered it, explicitly in relation to Jesus' own action and wishes.[89] Here we have a practice unique to the churches. Indeed, it is so

---

[86]Mk 14.25; Mt. 26.29; and Lk. 22.18.

[87]This is the normal meaning we take when we share a moment of common drinking. If I say 'we had coffee together after the meeting', the implication is that each had her/his own cup of coffee but we had these in company with one another. Likewise, if I said about a friend 'we went for a pint together', I do not mean we had one pint between us, much less that we drank from the same glass, but that we each had our own pint in our own glasses. The intimacy of friendship implied in 'going for a pint' together does not extend to sharing cups.

[88]This is the understanding implied when a flagon is placed on the table for the Eucharistic Prayer and 'blessed' (understood as blessing a creature)/'consecrated' so that a variety of cups can be filled from it. This practice considers the flagon as a container for a sufficient quantity of a ritual material by parallel with a ciborium – a vessel distinct from a paten – which can contain hundreds of wafers. See O'Loughlin 2008.

[89]This is already in evidence in Paul when he wrote to the Corinthians assuming there is a single cup (10.16) and that they all drink 'the cup of the Lord' (11.27); and that this is a practice 'received from the Lord' (11.23).

distinctive that its features of being 'disruptive of expectations' with 'multiple attestation' (Paul, the Synoptics, the *Didache* – and, as we shall see, possible John) that we can view the action as one that goes back to Jesus himself.[90]

Because most contemporary Christians have seen participants in a Eucharist share the cup there is a danger that the human implications of this action are opaque to us, while its Christian implications become invisible. While drinking is, quite naturally, a part of the meal rituals of all cultures (we need hydration more urgently than alimentation), the notion of *regularly* passing a cup from mouth to mouth is, to my knowledge, not otherwise attested. There are many instances of shared drink – the same liquid (a group each drinking a particular substance) or the same body of liquid (the liquid drunk coming from a single bowl or a single source) – but not of sharing the same cup. There are, of course, some exceptions such as the sharing of a special victory cup and 'loving cups' but these are both rare and unusual – and it is this very rarity that gives the action of sharing its special significance on those occasions. While we humans love to share meals, we also have a deep aversion to sharing our drinking vessels. Only in an emergency – for instance sharing a canteen of water – or in moments of exceptional informality – two friends with but a single bottle of beer and no drinking vessel – will we drink from a container in sequence. Even then, we might wipe the lip of the container before drinking after someone else. Certainly, we would not in 'normal' circumstances, that is, when there is an ordinary meal at a table,[91] presume to have shared drinking vessels – although we happily share jugs, bottles or decanters from which those vessels will be filled. It seems to be hard-wired into *Homo coenarius* that she has her own cup at table. This anthropological insight allows us to see that, first, the widespread adoption of this action of sharing a cup cannot be dismissed as some minor practical detail: something so unusual was a very deliberate choice. Secondly, it allows us to appreciate why, in virtually every Christian tradition, there has been an unspoken aversion to its full implementation. This has resulted in a plethora of strategies (sometimes bolstered by theologians in 'justifying the status quo' mode) to avoid having to drink from a cup that someone else had drunk from or of allowing someone else to drink from one's 'own' cup.

That it was the action of sharing one cup that was at the heart of this ritual action rather than drinking from a common volume of wine is also seen indirectly in evidence from the second century, and slightly later, when the uniformity of practice between the churches was steadily becoming more important. One of the practices that came under increasing criticism

---

[90]J. P. Meier set out a list of criteria for determining which 'sayings of Jesus' in literary artefacts are likely to be based in actual statements by Jesus (Meier 1994, 237–43) but these criteria can equally be used in the case of an action which is as distinctive as this one and so is analogous to an utterance. See Meier 1995, 349–50; Meier, in that article, is exceptional among exegetes working on the Last Supper narratives in noting the significance that the disciples are portrayed drinking from the cup of Jesus rather than their individual cups.

[91]Even an 'ordinary meal' assumes some level of planning and provision.

was that of sharing a cup of *water* at the Eucharist.[92] This practice was both widespread and deep rooted; and it cannot be dismissed as some sort a later-developing deviation. We have noted in an earlier chapter how water was central to the solemn banquets of the Therapeutae/Therapeutrides and how Philo presented them as rejecting wine as a loss of self-control while being too evocative of the pagan *symposia*.[93] It may be that this practice was adopted by some of the churches who likewise wished to distinguish their sober common meals from boisterous drinking of other voluntary societies.[94] It may be that the use of water was an act of asceticism, brought into the churches by those who had been disciples of John the Baptist who was noted as 'not drinking' [wine] (Mt. 11.18). Similarly, avoiding wine may have been a form of waiting for the eschaton: a reflection in the community of the waiting implied in Mk 14.25 and parallels.[95] Or avoiding wine may have been an aspect of the interest in fasting and the renunciation of food that was continued unchanged among those familiar with it in Judaism, as we see in the fasting practices of the *Didache*, and which soon would become a standard part of Christian practice.[96] My own suspicion for the widespread use of water in eucharistic activity is that because they knew it was the sharing of the cup that was the issue, and we know that Christianity spread at every level of society (and wine was not nearly as common among the poor as we often imagine) and there were disputes over the interaction of rich and poor, water avoided the practical problems of cost – the meal was not provided by a benefactor – and divisions between rich and poor, and between those who were happy to drink wine and those who suspected the practice.[97] Water, then as now, was neutral. Using water did not limit the ability of a group of disciples to act eucharistically at every shared meal, while it also prevented factions at this key moment in the meal.[98] Moreover, when later bishops wrote about the practice, it is interesting that they did not deny the reality of those Eucharists, but rather stressed the better practice of

---

[92]The evidence is set out in McGowan 1999a; and note how the argument has been taken forward in Daly-Denton 2007.

[93]See Chapter 3 above.

[94]See Ascough 1997 and 2008 for the comparisons; while the fears of drunkenness in Jude 12 are a symptom of this desire for distance between the behaviour at the Christian meal and common behaviour.

[95]Such a waiting is hinted at in the Eucharist in the *Gospel to the Hebrews* where James will not eat until the Lord returns, and part of the *kerygma* of this passage is that he can because the Lord *has* returned: he *is* risen and with his disciples. Cf. O'Loughlin 2009b.

[96]See O'Loughlin 2003.

[97]Analogously today, many western churches use grape juice, wholly unfermented, or 'must' (the first fermentation giving an alcohol content less than beer) rather than wine. See the ironic comment of Maxwell Johnson 2006, 5 cited at n. 11, above.

[98]Robert Jewett has suggested that the Christian meal became the very characteristic of the early communities, and as such even the poorest urban groups could have, through discipleship, access to meal-community – in such situations the use of water in the common cup made that commensality feasible as a frequent and regular occurrence. See Jewett 1994.

using wine. The implication of the argument of these episcopal correctives is that they recognized that what was fundamental was the sharing of a cup. It was the common cup that mattered.

When we take these pointers to the significance of the common cup, we can see that the paralleling, mentioned above, of 'bread' with 'wine' is faulty in that that parallel is based on materials. An accurate paralleling should be in terms of their formal use within a meal. One 'loaf of bread' (which can be shared by breaking) is paralleled by 'one cup' (which can be shared by being passed from one to another). Paul's use of 'eat of the loaf and drink of the cup' (1 Cor. 11.28) is, therefore, a precise statement of the central ritual actions.

Are there any traces of how this most unusual gesture was understood? Clearly, by parallel with the sharing of portions of the loaf, a key element in the significance of the shared cup may have been the gathering's unity with one another and with the risen Lord. If sharing a loaf indicated the intimacy of the table, and the unity of those around it, then the level of intimacy of passing a cup around the table is even greater. However, hints linking the cup to the unity of the community are not found in our earliest sources. In the *Didache* where the unity of the community and the work of Jesus in gathering it, is presented by analogy with grains and the forming of a loaf, we do not find any parallel notion such as that of the individual grapes being combined to form wine – a parallel which would emphasize the content of the cup rather than the sharing of the cup. Likewise, Paul points out that 'since there is one loaf, we who are many are one body, because we all partake of the one loaf' (1 Cor. 10.17), but there is no parallel statement about sharing the cup. For Paul the choice facing those who share the cup is between 'the cup of the Lord and the cup of demons. You cannot partake of the table of the Lord and the table of demons' (10.21). This choice between the Christ and the demons was a choice that faced all Gentile disciples: were they willing to turn from the idols that were part of the social and domestic fabric of Greco-Roman urban life? If one wanted to express the new discipleship then one not only turned from that which had been offered to idols, but one partook of the common cup of the disciples of the Christ. Drinking from the common cup was a 'boundary ritual' that expressed commitment to discipleship, and as such was a serious matter: they had to be willing to answer for their decision to drink from that common cup (11.27-8). Because it is the action of declaring both commitment to discipleship and rejection of idols, it is a participation in the life-blood of the Christ (10.16) and makes them part of the new covenant which was sealed in Christ's blood (11.25).[99] For Paul discipleship is about being part of the new covenant and sharing in the new life offered by the Christ; and taking the common cup – not a gesture that one would do lightly in any case – was accepting that discipleship and taking

---

[99] See Meier 1995, 349–50 who develops this understanding of sharing the cup from Paul to the Synoptics. See also Theiss 1994.

that life-blood of the Christ into one's own body.[100] We are accustomed to think of the act of baptism as *the* boundary ritual of the new community, but for Paul at the time he first wrote to the Corinthians, the sharing of the cup was also a demarcation ritual – and because it was repeated weekly it was the ongoing declaration of willingness to continue along the Way. That such a paralleling of drinking from the cup with baptism was present in Paul's mind when he wrote about that church's meals is confirmed by his remark about the Spirit being present in that church: 'for by one Spirit we were all baptized into one body – Jews or Greeks, slaves or free – and all were made to drink of one Spirit' (12.13). Just as the Spirit united them in baptism, so the Spirit was now what they drank in common. In short, if they wanted to be part of the new people, then they drank from the common cup accepting the consequences. They were becoming blood brothers and sisters in the new covenant.[101]

The *Didache* has no similar claim for 'the cup' being an act of commitment to discipleship, but it does dovetail with Paul's statements. It is the assumption of the *Didache* that those who are eating at the meal have already made a choice between the 'Way of Life' and the 'Way of Death'; it is explicit that only those who are baptized are to eat and drink (9.5). Willingness to eat from the loaf and drink the one cup are marks of continuing commitment; and, moreover, it places those eating in a holy situation that is their equivalent presenting a sacrifice in the temple in Jerusalem.[102]

This relationship between baptism and drinking from the common cup as boundaries may seem strange to us who put these 'sacraments' into different theological compartments: one is about joining and is a once-off event, while the other is about continuing and is repeated over a lifetime. However, such a neat system of 'outcomes' does not fit with how ritual establishes and maintains identity. One-off events need to be constantly recalled, while that which is an ongoing concern needs to be seen to have a moment of establishment. They were living as disciples, and day-by-day facing its challenges, so they declared themselves day-by-day while looking back to the moment when discipleship was established. The two rituals, baptism and drinking from the eucharistic cup need to be seen as complementary within living a life of commitment, rather than as distinct from one another with different functions in a theological system.

When we look at the Synoptic Tradition, we see that this notion that the one cup of the Lord is be taken as willingness to accept what discipleship involves is reinforced, while being given a narrative expression, within a paradigm encounter of would-be disciples with Jesus. The scene appears in

---

[100]For this aspect of commensality as part of Paul's gospel, see Jewett 1994.

[101]Megivern 1962, 55 uses this image of 'blood brothers' in the covenant as part of the significance of drinking the cup.

[102]See van de Sandt 2002 on the presence of a second temple understanding of purity/holiness in the communities using the *Didache*.

Mk 10.35-40 where James and John, the sons of Zebedee, ask if they can sit beside Jesus in glory. This prompts a challenge that links drinking from the same cup as the Lord with baptism: 'Are you able to drink the cup that I drink, or be baptized with the baptism that I am baptized with?' (10.38). And when they reply that they are able, they are told that 'The cup that I drink you will drink; and with the baptism with which I am baptized, you will be baptized' but that still will not guarantee them their desired places. To accept fully what it is to be a disciple is both to share in the baptism of Jesus and to drink the same cup as him. In Mt. 20.20-23 the story reappears but now the question is asked by their mother and the reference to baptism has disappeared, but the message is just as stark: to be a disciple means drinking from the same cup that Jesus drinks – and this invites from the audience a ritual conversion: if you drink the ritual cup, then you consciously declare your readiness to accept the cost of discipleship.[103]

This theme linking the cup with discipleship is further developed in that Jesus's own discipleship to the Father is presented as his willingness to drink the cup that the Father offers him. In both the Synoptics and John the suffering that the Father's Anointed must undergo is presented in terms of his 'cup' and Jesus' willingness to drink it. In Mk 14.36, followed closely by Mt. 26.39 and Lk. 22.42, this is presented as part of his prayer in the garden: 'Abba, Father, for you all things are possible; remove this cup from me; yet, not what I want, but what you want'. And thus with obedience he accepts where his discipleship has led. In Jn 18.11 Jesus is presented as doing the Father's will without hesitation or any sign of human fear, but again he is drinking 'the cup' that the Father has given him. This identification of the acceptance of martyrdom, as the acceptance of the 'drinking from the cup' continued to develop in the second century and is a distinct theme in the letters of Ignatius, when the imagery comes full-circle and taking the cup of martyrdom is understood in terms of taking the cup at the meal of the church.[104]

Drinking from the one cup is a declaration within the community of acceptance of a common destiny as a community, and its common destiny with the Christ; as such it formed a very real, and possibly physically dangerous, boundary for the people of the New Covenant. It was also an act that was intended to shatter other boundaries such as those of race, social status and factions within the churches, and implied a willingness for a new fictive community and a new intimacy in Jesus. As such, it is the presumed social backdrop for the logion on being friends in Jn 15.13-5: friends with one another and with the Lord.

The meal envisaged in Sir. 31-32 as a Jewish symposium may give us the general shape of the churches' eucharistic meals, but the sharing of the loaf,

---

[103]This notion of a ritual conversion between the cup of the meal and the cup of martyrdom comes out in a developed form in Ignatius' letters, see Lawlor 1991, 286–7.

[104]See Klawiter 2007, 157–9; and Lawlor 1991.

and especially the sharing of a single cup, be it of wine or water, made this event stand out as forming a table community with a very distinctive view of their common destiny and what might lie in store for them as the consequence of having embarked on The Way. This understanding of the cup, when located within the overall setting of the meal in the presence of the risen Jesus, can then form the basis for its being seen as an anticipation of the Kingdom (Mk 14.25)[105] and the banquet of the Kingdom (Mt. 8.11-2).[106]

Does this call to drink from the one cup pose a challenge to contemporary Christian practice and theology? It could be argued that sharing the cup is common in many communities: it is virtually universal in Anglican celebrations of the Eucharist, and in other Protestant churches it is carried out in some way or another. Even the Catholic Church, despite a residual fear that it might be seen as having been mistaken in its condemnation of the Utraquists in the early fifteenth century,[107] has since 1969 made limited provision for 'communion under both kinds' (although in reality, apart from some parts of the Anglophone world, the cup is never touched by the laity).[108] Meanwhile the Orthodox churches claim that they have always done this and they, unlike the west, have no history of any controversy over this. However, in reality while they receive liquid from the common cup, usually by way of a spoon, they do not actually drink from the cup. Most Protestant churches equally claim to have no problems here – and this is true in that all can receive some common liquid – but in fact, the situation is far less clear: individual thimble-sized glasses are as destructive of Jesus' bold symbolism as pre-cut Catholic wafers, while both transmit signals far different from the early interpretations of this distinctive action, and communicate a message that appeals greatly to an individualistic consumerist culture.

In almost every community, drinking from a common cup is a source of stress and contention in some way or other: and possibly that is the true value of this symbol in that it demands that each ask whether they can accept the implications of discipleship. Meanwhile, these stresses are rationalized through a mix of practicality, hygiene and theology. While in one tradition this will be expressed in terms of the fear of 'a spillage of the precious blood' through someone mishandling the cup, in another the unease will be presented as concern over hygiene or fear over the spread of a flu

---

[105]See Meier 1994, 302–9.

[106]See Meier 1994, 309–17.

[107]This is the term applied to those who in the late fourteenth and early fifteenth century, often linked to the name of Jan Huss, demanded the restoration of the cup to the whole assembly. The name of the movement, Utraquism (sometimes 'Subutraquism') comes from the Latin liturgical term 'sub utraque species' ('under both species'), that is, communion should be received under both the appearances of bread and wine. The Catholic Church's response can be found in Session 13 of the Council of Constance (*DS* 1198–1200); cf. de Vooght 1960. The need to be seen to be upholding this decree still exercises a major influence on official Catholic practice as expressed in law.

[108]See Huels 1986, 37–53; and Roppelt 2005.

virus, while somewhere else it will be the length of time and awkwardness involved, or the problem of alcoholic wine . . . and the list of problems – all with some factual basis – grows longer and longer. People do not like the idea of such sharing a cup, and then find serious reasons which justify this aversion. Likewise, faced with need, in order to fulfil the Lord's command, to share the cup's contents in some way (already a shift in attention from the action to the material), they develop subterfuges to avoid my lips having to touch a vessel after your lips have touched it. So we find the use of a spoon among the Orthodox; the use of straws (*fistulae*) or dipping ('intinction') in other churches; the use of trays of individual thimble-sized glasses; and, of course, the most extreme, but most common, deviation: confining the cup to the president or clergy. Sharing a cup is a counter-instinctive gesture, so we naturally avoid it. But in the manner in which they do this, they miss both the central imagery of the action (a spoon or a straw or a dipped wafer stress a common material rather than a common commitment; while individual glasses fail to recognize the body of Christ in the community), and the 'shock' that is at the gesture's core: will you share a cup and a common destiny in discipleship that might demand 'obedience unto death'? (Phil. 2.8). Paul's final word on the meal is worth recalling: 'Examine yourselves, and only then eat of the loaf and drink of the cup' (1 Cor. 11.28).

The sharing of the common cup as a central moment in any Eucharist should not be seen as merely the fulfilment of a biblical/dominical command (Mt. 26.27) or an item of traditional ritual. Rather it needs to be recognized as a constituent moment in Christian identity. It needs to be seen on a par with baptism, a uniquely christ-ian moment, that marks the gracious transformation of disciples into friends. Moreover, the actuality of sharing the cup must be seen as a direct linking with the actions and proclamation of Jesus rather than in terms of some vague 'fuller sign value'[109]: the Lord instituted a radical sign of discipleship *and* he drank the cup, and so, in the midst of convivial rejoicing, we have the challenge that we too must drink from the cup and accept the radical call of discipleship.

The widespread abandonment of a common cup is also a warning for those involved in inter-church dialogue and for theologians as a group within churches. Most ecumenical debates get bogged down in details of eucharistic practice and often take on an ontological dimension such that there is question as to whether the other group are actually celebrating a Eucharist at all? The implicit assumptions are, first, that there is a fixed list of criteria, *a Christo instituto*, and if anyone fails one criterion, then their acts of thankfulness are but simulacra of reality, and, secondly, that the judge's own practice is in no way wanting in its continuity with 'the moment of institution'/'apostolic times'.[110] In the face of these assumptions, we should

---

[109]See Megivern 1962, 56.
[110]I place these in inverted commas as these are theological ideal states rather than temporal points in actual human history.

recall these two historical facts. First, it was the cup, not its contents, that was significant in the period referred to as 'apostolic times'. Moreover, there was a variety of practice on issues that would today be highly divisive: they lived with the variety of water, wine, mixes of both, and perhaps other liquids.[111] Second, given that the witness of the 'apostolic' period is unanimous on the importance of common drinking from a cup, as difficult then as later, perhaps churches today should be careful about their claims to constancy and continuity of practice. Every church must start and painfully reflect how it can communicate with others in the Eucharist in the future, each acknowledging that all have failed in one way or another in the past.

Likewise, theologians need to take warning about how one can create a very satisfactory theology, after the event, to justify a development in practice that was itself a serious deviation from the earliest tradition. When the cup – or perhaps more precisely the contents of the cup – had disappeared from the laity in the west to the extent that *only* the president could drink it, theologians on the whole did not question this, but proceeded to explain it through 'the doctrine of concomitance' whose only basis in the tradition was the bad practice it sought to defend.[112] Moreover, those who did challenge this, such as Jan Huss (c. 1372–1415) and the sixteenth-century Reformers, were rejected as heretics. While the call for 'the restoration of the cup' was often ridiculed as a case of biblical literalism, such that if '*bibite*' (Mt. 26.27) were to be interpreted physically, so too should Mt. 19.24 on camels getting through the eye of a needle. Catholic theologians, in particular, have little to be proud of in the millennium-long custom of actively defending a practice that was, and remains, a perversion of the tradition.

Before leaving the common cup, one other matter which was of major concern in the earlier quests for the structure of the Last Supper needs to be mentioned: the matter of the order of the loaf and the cup. The traditional liturgical order, once an institution narrative became part of the Eucharistic Prayer, is clear: Jesus took a loaf and 'after the meal' he took a cup. The early descriptions, however, are less consistent. Paul mentions the cup before the loaf on one occasion (1 Cor. 10.16) and then places the loaf before the cup on another (1 Cor. 11.23, 25 and 27). Because he is writing a single letter to one church, this difference cannot be explained by development of practice or by reference to different settings. The *Didache* (9.2-3) assumed that the cup is first and then the loaf. While Mk (14.22-3) assumes that it is loaf before cup; and in this is followed by Mt. (26.26). However, Luke, also

---

[111]There have been many debates about whether cups of milk, milk and honey, and references to fish (or fish-dip: *opsarion* in Jn 6.9 and 11, or 21.9-13), should be seen as eucharistic or not (McGowan 1999a, 127–40 is an example of such discussions), or about water in the cup in Johannine circles (see Daly-Denton 2007), but all such references should be re-examined in the light of the fundamental theological assumption that the whole of the Christian life should be an eucharistic action towards the Father whose creative love is 'made delectable' in food (see Wirzba 2013).

[112]See Megivern 1963.

following Mark, has, first, a cup (22.17) – the cup that is assumed to be filled with the fruit of the vine (22.18) and so this is the cup that parallels that in Mark and Matthew – then the loaf (22.19) and then another cup (22.20).[113] While it would make a fascinating study to trace these variations, how they combined to form the liturgical text, and how later theologians sought to harmonize Luke's text with a single historical story,[114] this would be out of place here. The evidence points to a variety of practices regarding the order in the meal practices of the churches, and, in all likelihood, in the manner of presiding by different people in those gatherings. Such variation in meal patterns is no more than can be found in any two households with regard to their table customs. Equally, if we acknowledge that there were varieties of formulae in blessing God – and that uniformity was a later development – it would be hard to imagine that in this matter there was already an invariable and fixed pattern. This variety, and the realization that uniformity was a later phenomenon,[115] should serve as a warning to all those who would declare a eucharistic celebration 'invalid' because it failed to meet a checklist of uniform ritual details within a lawyer's view of liturgy.[116]

5 Giving and sharing of food

Most Christian consideration of 'the meal aspect' of the early Christian gatherings has focused on food as commodities: did they use bread, was

---

[113]This text of Luke (which is that found in Byzantine texts, the Latin texts and modern editions) is sometimes called 'the longer text' because several shorter forms exist which only mention a cup once. These shortened forms are best explained as later adaptations of Luke in order to accommodate his gospel text to the other Synoptics and to the liturgical tradition. For a comparison of the various forms of the text of Luke, see Metzger 1975, 173–7, or Omanson 2006, 147–9.

[114]Until recently some Catholic editions with notes (e.g. the *Jerusalem Bible* 1966; the *New Jerusalem Bible* 1985 or the Colunga and Turrado edition of the Sixto-Clementine Vulgate 1946) attempted to harmonize the text by placing a heading 'The Institution of the Eucharist' after Lk. 22.18 and so removing the first cup from the debate and maintaining the canonical order of loaf before cup. However, this common 'solution' failed to note that it is the *first* cup in Luke which is the cup in Mark and Matthew. If one approaches this as an historical riddle (an *antikeimenon* in strict sense) – that is, contradictory evidence stemming from one moment in space/time – then one must face the fact that is cannot be resolved.

[115]That was already recognized by Anton Baumstark in 1923 when he famously wrote: *Einheitlichkeit ist nicht der Ausgangspunkt, sondern das Ziel der liturgischen Entwicklung* (uniformity is not the starting point, but the result of liturgical development). See Baumstark 2011, 89–97, and see R. F. Taft's comments on this on p. xv of the forward to that edition of Baumstark.

[116]There was an encouraging sign of the abandonment of this approach in the 2001 recognition by Rome of the 'Prayer of Addai and Mari' as a real Eucharistic Prayer, albeit with some obfuscation that it contained 'an implicit' use of the words of Jesus (see Taft 2003); however, the continuing arguments over 'gluten' in the flour used for wafers and over translating Latin suggests that this legalist view of theology, and history, is far from dead.

it unleavened, did they use wine, was it mixed with water, were other foods eaten, and, if so, how were these distinguished from the 'eucharistic' foods. However, from the few hints we have about their gatherings what is significant *with reference to foods* is that there is an absence of any attention to the nature of the food and drink *per se*, and a very noticeable emphasis on how it was used. The concern is that the food be shared and on the manner of the sharing: that there are not divisions based on status and quality of food, and that they 'wait on one another' (1 Cor. 11.33).[117]

Just as we have seen that there was more interest in the forms 'loaf' and 'cup' rather than the materials eaten or drunk, so there was more concern over the behaviour, the 'manners', of the meal than over its food content.[118] Likewise, while most social meals reflected the stratified nature of Greco-Roman urban culture, there was a Christian emphasis on their meal behaviour reflecting their vision of society where all were brothers and sisters. In such a society competition for the best seats was clearly out of place, as we see in the Letter of James.[119] This concern with behaviour that modelled their vision of themselves as the new People of God and as disciples committed to an ethical way can still be seen in the mid-second century in some of the comments of Ignatius of Antioch on what a properly harmonious Eucharist should be like and how they should share food.[120]

Knowing that community-focused behaviour was a concern among those early Christians who commented on their meals allows us to note other early references to sharing food as being, in all probability, pointers to their correct meal practice as much as more general 'ethical instructions'.[121] References in the gospels to sharing with the hungry (e.g. Mt. 25.27), to not taking the higher place (Lk. 14.10) or to avoiding making social or ethnic distinctions at meals (e.g. Lk. 5.30), and the list could be extended, take on a distinct immediacy when heard as pointers to actual community meal behaviour. The meal, in the view of these teachers, was to reflect the communities' ethos, recall the table practice they remembered as that of the Christ, and also model their vision of the God's love as a feast and of the eschaton as a banquet.[122]

In recent years there has been a steady growth in theological interest in the interplay between a Christian ethic that strives for justice in the face of poverty and a view of the Eucharist that sees such concerns as intrinsic to an adequate eucharistic theology.[123] And consequently, there has been a

---

[117]See Hollander 2009.

[118]This can be seen in the many studies of Paul's concerns over divisions in the Corinthians' gatherings, see Theissen 1982, 147–63.

[119]Smit 2011.

[120]See Klawiter 2007, 152.

[121]That this was so can be seen in the fact that Luke used meal behaviour to model the nature of interaction between Jewish and gentile Christians: see O'Loughlin 2013c.

[122]See Wolter 2009.

[123]For example: Sagovsky 2009; or Méndes Montoya 2009.

new emphasis on the significance of sharing food with the poor which is exemplified in the sharing presumed in the Eucharist.[124] While there has been a wider concern, indeed unease, that the way we celebrate – complex rituals, expensive vestments, elaborate paraphernalia – might actually model power relations within the group contrary to the Gospel or suggest a comfortable self-satisfaction. There is an awareness that massive displays of pomp by a group of clerical leaders does not accord well with the liturgical memory of Jn 13.1-10[125]; or that aesthetically elegant liturgies might not accord with prophetical memories such as Isa. 58.7 or Mic. 6.6-8. These fears are usually expressed in terms of reflection and communication: the Eucharist should *reflect* our ethical concerns and it must *signal* that care of the needy and hungry is a more fundamental part of the liturgy of the Church. However, this anxiety that the Eucharist recall such concerns is itself a result of the separation of the eucharistic activity from the real coming together of a community to share food. Not only must the Eucharist reflect and communicate the ethical demands of discipleship, but also it must be a paradigm event of such actual community, actual sharing, with each participant acting as the servant of others.

This has both direct and corollary implications for contemporary practice. It implies that when we read the concerns of Paul, James and Ignatius on the sharing at the eucharistic meals we are listening to the voices that eventually went unheeded in the way practice developed. This implies that if Christians look to the past for understanding of what they are about, that those calls to act ethically when eating together, at which they offer thanks, are still relevant even if they have been long ignored. They have not been superseded because what eventually became standard Christian practice is derived from the very customs – prevalent in the larger society – that those early teachers were seeking to condemn. Moreover, there is a corollary for liturgical style. There has been a long-standing tendency in the 'high' liturgical churches for ritual to take an 'other-worldly' aspect, stressing in ritual communication its distance from the everyday: one need only look at the ritual style of Pope Benedict XVI (2005–13) or the 2011 Roman Catholic translation of the *Missale Romanum* into English to see examples of this phenomenon.[126] But such ritual distance from the domain of the everyday, and thus the sphere of the ethical, is not merely a failure of 'joined-up thinking', but runs counter to this basic insight into eucharistic origins: they were not called together just to eat and drink, they were called together for a feast where all were to share the food and drink available. The Eucharist must exhibit this fundamental ethic of the New People.

---

[124]See Méndes Montoya 2013.

[125]See O'Loughlin 2014a.

[126]See O'Loughlin 2013e. That this was a deliberate policy to distance liturgical activity from everyday practice can be seen from reading the Vatican's 2001 document *Liturgiam authenticam* (see Jeffery 2005, 88–120).

6 There is *anamnesis* of Jesus

When in the mid-second century Justin describes the eucharistic meal, he stresses the place of 'the recollections (*apomnemoneumata*) of the apostles' at the gathering: a reference that is usually seen in terms of it being one of the earliest indications of a 'liturgy of the word'. However, when we put together all the disparate fragments of information – be it the travelling prophets who offer the thanksgiving in the *Didache*, the meal memories in the gospels and Acts, or the evidence that performances of the good news took place at a *symposium*[127] – it becomes clear that recalling Jesus' life and death, his words and deeds, was a central part of the churches' meals. Moreover, we know from 1 Corinthians that the meal gathering was viewed, explicitly, as being in the tradition of Jesus (11.23), that they believed that when they spoke of him he was present (*Didache*, 4.1) and that when they gathered in his name he was among them (Mt. 18.20), and that their eucharistic activity took place through him (*Didache*, 9.2 and 4). As such, he was not only with them as risen Lord,[128] but was with them so that they could see themselves as 'his body' who were 'in him'.

Arguably, this notion of Jesus' 'presence' is the great continuity with modern practice, but a moment's thought shows that while some churches emphasize a 'realism' of presence often identifying such presence with the food objects; others almost ignore presence except in so far as there is a presence in biblical reading or that which might be generated psychologically by historical remembrance. Both of these positions fail to express the community's reality of being as a community 'in Christ'; while generating an alternative vision of being 'the community in Christ' and finding a means to express this, which is true both to our historical origins and our cultural values, is the core challenge of all renewal in our practice of the Eucharist.

Going through these common strands of evidence, searching out the general thrust of the witness of the early churches for us today, will seem to many to be a case of building much on little. Hence, it is worthwhile to bear this comment by a Mennonite theologian in mind:

> In the New Testament, we have only hints of how the Lord's Supper was practiced. After spending years pursuing a pristine theology and practice of communion, I have concluded that this sparse record is a blessing, lest we imitate the form rather than the spirit of the event.[129]

---

[127]See Chapter 4 above.
[128]See O'Loughlin 2009b.
[129]Rempel 2001, 5.

What then of the Last Supper?

If the 'Last Supper' accounts in the Synoptic Gospels (and its earlier mention by Paul) are not snippets from the liturgical practice of early churches,[130] then what role did that memory play in the understanding of the Eucharist by those early churches? The answer lies in the nature of the stories which constitute our identity, and in noting the dissimilarity between that early remembering and its later recollection.

The evangelists brought their stories of Jesus to focus and conclusion in the last days in Jerusalem. In their common narrative arc, all the stories led to these final hours and the mystery of his Passover. Mark's narrative has been described as a 'passion narrative with a prologue'; but it is worth recalling that in John's narrative 155 of the 878 verses in his gospel (18 per cent) are located at just one meal on the evening before Jesus suffered – and bear in mind that John alone has a 3-year ministry for Jesus, and, moreover, he did not include a story of eucharistic origins at the final meal. By locating a narrative of the origins of the Eucharist on that evening, the early preachers – and it is a tradition older than Mark (we hear Paul referring to it) – were underlining the importance of the communities' continuing practice. Here the repeatable and recurring sign that was at the heart of the communal activity was given a narrative location in the greatest of their great historic moments. The Last Supper narratives are explanation and location, not paradigms for imitation.

Likewise, it worth noting the different sequence between the memory exhibited in Mk 14.22-5 (and also the other Synoptics) and that which, under the liturgy's influence, has dominated later remembering. In Mark, Jesus is remembered as taking a loaf, blessing God, breaking it into pieces, giving it to the disciples, and then, presumably while they were eating it, saying: 'Take; this is my body'. In the liturgy the actions of the president are those of taking the loaf, referring to the act of blessing the Father, then saying 'the dominical words', and then, subsequently, the loaf is broken, distributed and eaten. So in Mark, the narrative is about an action of Jesus – the action with the loaf – which is subsequently given an interpretation: 'this is my body'. While in the liturgy, that statement of interpretation moved to the centre of the action, and so became the dominical formula that declares what the eating *will* involve (and for many Christians, it came to be seen as 'effecting' the Eucharist). By inserting a gospel-derived narrative into the existing liturgical structure of a Eucharistic Prayer a new sequence of actions was created. Now the words of Jesus came *after* taking a loaf *but before* its fraction and distribution; while his action of blessing the Father slipped further from view. The very nature of the sequence of this new liturgical narrative caused those dominical words to alter in our perception from being *midrash* and reflection to cause, and the 'formula of consecration' came into being.

---

[130]See Ligier 1973 and McGowan 1999b.

The same transformation in memory, and later theology, occurred with the cup. In Mark, Jesus took a cup, gave thanks, gave it to the disciples 'and they all drank of it'; and then comes the statement: 'This is my blood of the covenant which is poured out for many'. While in the liturgy we have the recollection that Jesus took a cup, a reference to his action of giving thanks, then the statement – focused on the object in the president's hands – that they should take it and drink from it (with the implication that the words precede the act of drinking and that it is a command to be carried out after Jesus has finished speaking and given them the cup) for 'this' – what the president holds before them – 'is the cup of my blood', and then later this cup is offered to those present and they drink from it. The shift in sequence, due to dropping a harmonized gospel account into the existing liturgy both transformed the words to the disciples into an act of consecration, however understood, and focused on what was in the cup that they were being instructed to drink.

These shifts can be seen schematically thus:

Gospel Narratives (Mark's gospel is used as the representative text)	**Liturgical Narratives** (the Roman Canon is used as the representative text)
1. While eating	
	1. The community is fasting
2. Jesus took a loaf	2. President takes a loaf.
3. Jesus blessed the Father	
	3. A reference is made to Jesus' act of blessing
4. Jesus broke the loaf	
	4. Reference to Jesus's breaking
5. Jesus gave it to them	
	5. Reference to Jesus giving it to the disciples
6. Jesus spoke: 'Take, this is my body'	6. Jesus spoke: 'Take this all of you . . .'
7. Jesus took a cup	7. President takes the cup
8. Jesus gave thanks to the Father	
	8. A reference is made to Jesus' act of thanking
9. Jesus gave the cup to them	
	9. Reference to Jesus giving the cup

10. They all drank the cup	
11. Jesus spoke: 'This is my blood of the covenant . . .'	10. Jesus spoke: 'Take this all of you and drink from it . . .'
	11. The loaf is broken
	12. The loaf is eaten
	13. The cup is drunk

Moreover, the dynamic of this liturgical narrative became an ever more powerful lens towards viewing the Eucharistic Prayer as little more than a context for the consecratory formulae due to other developments in the liturgy. Once the actuality of the loaf was replaced by wafers, eating of the loaf became ever more rare allowing 'Mass' and 'Communion' to be seen as distinct events, while the disappearance of the cup except for the president, and the recitation of the Eucharistic Prayer in silence removed any sense of it being a recollection of an ecclesial dialogue. Even today, so embedded is this liturgical sequence within Christian memory – and the disputes about its meaning – that few even notice the gospels' sequence is not identical, nor attend to the way the liturgical location and sequence skews understanding towards viewing the purpose of the Eucharistic Prayer towards 'consecration of the bread and the wine'.[131]

One other difference between the gospels' narration of the Last Supper and that of the anamnesis of the liturgy should be noticed. For the liturgy, the president's prayer – and most especially the *verba Christi* – constitute not only the high point of prayer, but indeed the moment of greatest sacrality.[132] Yet we are not told what words Jesus was remembered as using in his actual prayer: we are merely told that he blessed/thanked. This omission points to the evangelists' focus of attention, which was not upon Jesus' prayer, which they probably assumed to have been like one of the Jewish table prayers with which they and most of their audiences were familiar, but on the interpretation their audiences might bring to their own eucharistic actions.

When we keep these points in mind, we see that the question is not 'what did Jesus do at the last supper' but what view of discipleship did the evangelists wish to convey to an assembly about the significance of the meal their audiences were sharing as they listened to their accounts? That this should be the focus of the question may not be immediately obvious, so some preliminary comments are needed.

---

[131]The depth of this understanding can be seen in the number of Catholic and Anglican churches which still today, nearly half a century after their liturgy's reform, at the consecration there is still a ringing of bells. That ringing is a noisy reminder of an older theology.
[132]See Jungmann 1955, 2, 205.

First, there has been an important debate among New Testament scholars as to the historicity of the Last Supper, and, in particular, the extent to which it can be seen in terms of a Passover meal in the Second Temple period.[133] And, assuming that, if it can be seen as the original Eucharist.[134] But this interest in the events of that single night, however important in terms of the search for the historical Jesus or our reconstruction of his times, is distinct from the role of that meal in the understanding of the early Christians of their regular meals.

Second, while the Last Supper was remembered as the great historic moment of formal inauguration of their repeated eucharistic practice, that a moment is seen as 'the founding moment' does not imply that every successive moment is seen as a repetition of that moment. This can be seen in some very simple ways: by the time of Paul the regular, probably weekly, meal was being seen as having its foundation moment in an annual Passover meal. This apparent disjunction, which would cause such worry to many of the sixteenth-century reformers, is a reminder that community practices and customs have their own dynamic of continuity quite distinct from any formal and spoken rationale given to account for them. Here the regular weekly meal of the disciples – probably the continuity of the Shabbat meals Jesus ate with them – remained a regular weekly occurrence even when they had begun using the final Passover meal as its great foundation moment in memory. Similarly, the practice of the earliest communities was to bless the Father over a loaf of bread (*artos*) which would have been leavened – and it is this practice that forms the basis of Paul's simile in 1 Cor. 5.6-8 and his imagery of the loaf in 1 Cor. 10.17; and this would remain the unbroken usage of the churches until the tenth century in the west.[135] However, the Passover used *matzah/azymes*, yet the memory of the Last Supper as the inauguration moment did not lead to any desire for a 're-presentation' of it.[136] Likewise, while the actions and instructions of Jesus stand out as a dramatic climax in Mark, and are further elaborated in Matthew and Luke, they did not figure in early Eucharistic Prayers which we possess or can reconstruct.[137]

Third, while later Christians would conflate *great historical signs* (which are of their nature once-off, unrepeatable events) with *remembered signs* (of their nature repeatable and indeed regular), there is little evidence of this happening in the early period.[138] The great historical signs are moments remembered such as the annunciation, the birth, the baptism, the Sermon on the Mount, the Last Supper, the death and, above all, the resurrection. The repeatable signs were the proclamation of the gospel – a day to day

---

[133]See Marcus 2013.
[134]See Meier 1995.
[135]See Woolley 1913.
[136]That linkage only occurred as a *post eventum* justification after unleavened bread had been adopted in the West for practical reasons: see Woolley 1913.
[137]See Ligier 1973.
[138]See Kreider 2001.

reality, the call to follow the Way of Life, the baptism of new members of the covenant community, the need to pray, fast and give alms, and the need to gather on a weekly basis to bless the Father in Christ while sharing in the loaf of Christian identity and drinking from the cup of discipleship. The great signs are recalled as the sources of identity; the remembered signs are regularly celebrated as part of the life of the community asserting and reasserting that identity.

Only when repeated, remembered signs are viewed in a *one-to-one relationship* with the great historic signs, in some manner of cause to effect, does one need to understand the great sign in order to understand the remembered sign. Then, once that linkage has occurred, there is a consequent need for a sacramental metaphysics to explain the causation. That can be a scholastic causal explanation that takes virtually no account of human ritual, or a more liturgically sensitive form such as that developed by Odo Casel (1886–1948) in his theology of 'mystical causality',[139] but the need for such explanation is itself a product of a particular way of seeing remembered signs. If, by contrast, one sees the two kinds of sign in parallel – with the latter borrowing anyhow from the former for yet another 'explanation' – one can understand the flexibility with which the repeatable sign of the regular meal could look at any and all meals/feedings in their memory – from the manna to the Passover and from the feeding of the multitudes in the desert to the meals with tax-collectors and sinners – as sources for their own appreciation of what they were doing in small crowded rooms week after week.[140] Moreover, this way of viewing the two kinds of signs is in harmony with the way we view all the signs around us in our lives: a married couple can look back to the wedding day, and value special relics of it such as a photo album, but equally they must exchange signs continually which express their ongoing identity as partners. A once-off event can change our lives, but the living of life is ongoing and not merely a sequel to a once-off event. When we bury a loved one we are struck by the finality of the event of death altering ontologically our relationship with the deceased, but the richness of memory is more than a recollection of the fact that that person is dead. Great historic signs and ongoing signs interweave in our consciousness, but, unless we are cursed in the manner of Dickens' Miss Haversham, we mostly manage to keep them distinct.

Moreover, we know that a confusion/conflation of these two kinds of signs had not yet taken place in the first century. If they had, then given the fact that John's gospel has no institution story, we should then assume that he has no theology of the Eucharist – yet we know that not to be the case.[141] We see this even more clearly in that, again within a Johannine perspective, the

---

[139]Casel 1999; see Jungmann 1955 who seeks to combine the traditional scholastic metaphysics with one derived from Casel using Karl Rahner's early theology as the link.
[140]See Horrell 2004.
[141]See Macgregor 1963 for a classic statement of the theme; and see Kobel 2011 for a more recent statement in terms of what we now know of meal practice in the early communities.

regular meal that looks back to *that* meal finds in the footwashing its pattern for communal behaviour and an ethic for the new covenant community of mutual service: they were to '*agapate* one another' (Jn 13.34) at their Agape. Again we have the interplay between a great historic sign – that event when Jesus washed their feet on that night – and a regular remembered sign – their ongoing practice of washing one another's feet at their gatherings.[142] And that was just one of many ways of viewing the significance of the meal in terms of the presence of the risen Christ in the community.

A key connecting theme, apart from providing an inauguration moment from which regular practice was recalled as flowing, in all the institution accounts is that this is the event of the new covenant:

> In the same way he took the cup also, after supper, saying, 'This cup is the new covenant in my blood. Do this, as often as you drink it, in remembrance of me' (1Cor. 11.25);

> He said to them, 'This is my blood of the covenant, which is poured out for many' (Mk 14.24);

> . . . for this is my blood of the covenant, which is poured out for many for the forgiveness of sins (Mt. 26.28); and

> And he did the same with the cup after supper, saying, 'This cup that is poured out for you is the new covenant in my blood'. (Lk. 22.20)

The death of Jesus, the Passover at which he was the paschal victim (1 Cor. 5.7), had established a new covenant between the people, not just his disciples, and the Father. The participants in the meal of the baptized formed the new covenant community; and that community as a people of the covenant, only existed because Jesus had sealed this new covenant in blood as covenants between the people and God needed to be sealed (Heb. 9.15-22).[143] So recalling back to Jesus' Passover Supper was a re-statement of their own covenant identity as the new People of God and sharing in the discipleship that is implied in drinking from the cup was the assertion of their acceptance

---

[142]See O'Loughlin 2013f.

[143]This is but an emblematic reference to Hebrews – the theme of covenant and the blood of the covenant run right through the letter. This use of Hebrews as a guide to how the supper was remembered might seem problematic, but it should be borne in mind that the covenant–blood link is there prior to Paul, and if Hebrews reflects a situation prior to 70 CE (see Witherington 1991, 151), then Paul, Mark and Hebrews are independent witnesses of a common tradition – I am not suggesting any direct contact between them – and such a liturgical/ritual context, such as the common meal, for that memory fits well with exegesis of those passages in Hebrews and the significance its attached to 'blood' (see Dunnill 1992, 115–49 (on a liturgical reading of covenant renewal) and 231–4 (on the symbolism of blood)). See also Hahn 2004 on the confusion of *diathéké* as *testamentum* rather than *covenant*. This confusion has obscured the eucharistic dimension; and this is confirmed, from a different perspective, by Cahill 2002.

of that covenant status, and their participation in that covenant. They were taking the cup and the cup was Jesus' covenant blood.

Traditionally, concerned with the ontological status of the elements in relation to the presence of the Christ we have read these texts as 'this *is* my blood' and then read the rest of the phrase adjectivally: 'the blood of the new and everlasting covenant'.[144] However, given the cultural assumption that a covenant is sealed with blood – the classic memory of Moses in Exod. 24.3-8 as recalled, for instance, in Zech. 9.11, we should read those words as 'this is my blood-of-the-covenant which is poured out for . . . the forgiveness of sins' (Mk 14.24). Put another way, what Moses did with the blood of bulls and goats (see Heb. 10.4), Jesus was recalled as doing with his own blood on Golgotha (see Heb. 13.12). Then this covenant was remembered in the cup shared at the meal. That this way of reading the text is the most ancient one (i.e. 'this is my blood-of-the-covenant' rather than 'this is my-blood, [the blood] of the covenant') can easily be seen: no Jewish group, attempting to keep the laws of *kosher* as we know the early Jewish followers did attempt to do, could ever have contemplated drinking any cup that claimed, even symbolically, to be a cup of blood.[145] Such shocking language – so easily confused with a later 'sacramental realism' – would only become possible in a later Greco-Roman milieu, such as we find in John's gospel and even later in Ignatius, where it would be used to underline the real humanity of Jesus.[146]

Sharing that cup could be viewed, recalled, proclaimed as re-affirming one belonging to the covenant people, just as it affirmed willingness to undertake the way of discipleship. These are two intersecting understandings about being the people with the new Moses. As Moses proposed to the people the ways of life and death (Deut. 30.15)[147] and sealed the covenant between the people and God, so drinking from the cup declared one's covenant choice of discipleship. And, as the covenant established a two-way relationship, so this act of recollection – drinking from the cup – was future oriented: a renewal of the group's affirmation and commitment to that covenant.

The memory of the Last Supper was a frame within which the audiences were to imagine their own suppers as focused on the covenant that now exists between 'the people' (*laos*) and the Father, and recalls Jesus as the new Moses who established this covenant: in the language of Hebrews, the new High Priest who is the 'mediator of a better covenant' (8.6) and they have gathered at a new Mount Zion, a heavenly Jerusalem, an angelic feast, 'and to the sprinkled blood that speaks a better word than the blood of Abel'

---

[144]What I have cited at this point is a standard liturgical text, but it should be remembered that this text is confused by conflation – as such the later liturgical text, which dominates *our* memories, obscured what early Christians would have heard.

[145]See Cahill 2002.

[146]See Kobel 2011, 251–70; and Klawiter 2007.

[147]See O'Loughlin 2010, 29–38 on the paralleling of the Christian covenant with 'the summary' of the covenant in Deut. 30.

(12.22-4). In a later language, Jesus, and his meal, is the sacrament between the community and the Father. However, in so far as Jesus, the Christ, became the focus of Christian attention – the shift from 'the good news proclaimed by Jesus' to 'proclaiming that Jesus is the good news' – this focus of the meal would also shift. From being the meal where, with Jesus, the Father is blessed and the covenant reaffirmed, the focus moved to being the meal where Jesus is encountered, and his action as High Priest recalled, celebrated and re-enacted. And it is this christocentric view of the Eucharist that would dominate in the later tradition.

However, for those early communities, the loaf, and more especially the cup, as covenant recollections were symbols of their whole reality: this is what their story telling told them.[148] This memory was not only interpreted through the supper, but the supper gave it constant presence in their consciousness. Their story of Jesus' final supper – itself independent of our textual witnesses – could tell them that the loaf and cup of their regular ritual were symbols of the whole Paschal Mystery. They had embraced that mystery, that covenant, by drinking from the cup,[149] this was a serious business (see 1 Cor. 11.27-9), and it was a pledge of what they must face as brethren of one who was crucified (see Mk 10.39). The Last Supper was an important site of memory for the early communities, but those recollections were primarily *midrash*, incidentally history, while in no way being ritually paradigmatic.

Sed contra . . .

At this point, many who have grown up with the understanding that the Eucharist is a 'real, if unbloody, sacrifice' and that Jesus is 'really present', will explode with rage and declaim that their celebrations are not mere memories, memorials or symbols.[150] While the reasons why someone might take such a position are manifold, its weakness can be pin-pointed exactly. Remembering, when done communally as a church, is done in the presence of the Risen One; and because it is in the presence of the Risen One, it is no mere mental act, but an act of attention by disciples to the divine. Remembering in

---

[148]On the practicalities of what this would have been like in a darkly lit room full of people eating and talking, see Dewey 2004.

[149]See Hahn 2004, 429.

[150]It is not the intention of this book to present a theology of eucharistic presence (see, e.g., Schillebeeckx 1968 which focuses on the topic), but it should be noted that the notion of presence has shifted quite remarkably in the period since Vatican II (see Kilmartin 1998, 300–39; and the very fine overview by Witczak 1998); however, this more nuanced view of 'presence' is still rare in Catholic preaching, and indeed, as Witczak, 698, observes: 'theological literature . . . is still driven by the Tridentine emphasis on transubstantiation and real presence and ends up dealing with ontological issues surrounding presence'.

the presence of God constitutes an encounter with God.[151] Likewise, symbols are those realities by which we humans live, move and love:

> [anyone downplaying the significance of symbol] should also avoid poetry, concerts and the theatre, language, loving another person, and most . . . attempts at communicating with one's kind. Symbol is reality at its most intense degree of being expressed. One resorts to symbol when reality swamps all other forms of discourse. This happens regularly when one approaches God with others. . . . One learns to live with symbol and metaphor or gives up the ability to speak or to worship communally.[152]

Other contemporary Christians will argue that giving such power to anything done in the community, particularly with 'ritual overtones', is liable to confuse the unique atonement of Jesus with an earthly activity. The Catholic extremism of 'real presence' finds a counterpart in the extremism of Balthasar Hubmaier (c. 1480–1528) who insisted that if the risen Jesus was in heaven then he could not possibly be in the community's supper.[153] As such, the Lord's Supper is really little more than a three-dimensional mnemonic exercise, whose only rationale within a literate community is that it carries out an 'ordinance' in Lk. 22.19. Such a cosmos assumes as complex an ontology as that underlying a notion like 'transubstantiation': the Divine is imagined to act in a manner that is conformed to a radically secularized creation where human consciousness of empirical reality marks the boundaries of the real. Indeed, so limited is its view of what constitutes a real historical action to that which we encounter within the physical world of interacting materials, that this cosmology silently invokes such a barrier between matter and spirit that it is difficult to see how it could possibly accommodate the incarnation. Likewise, Kavanagh's warning, aimed initially at Catholics who downplay symbol, applies: anyone who imagines that Jesus is really absent from the community supper cannot really ever have a celebratory meal with loved ones, while considering it anything more than an occasion of material nourishment of one's physical body.

From servants to friends

Rather than try to draw a set of conclusions to this chapter which might give the impression that there was some dominant theological vision

---

[151]As expressed in lapidary form in the *Didache*: My child, remember always, day and night, the one who speaks to you the discourse of God, and honour that person as you would the Lord: for wherever the things of the Lord are spoken about, there the Lord is present (4.1).
[152]Kavanagh 1982, 103.
[153]See Finger 2001, 30; on this reductionist cosmology – which impacted on their symbology – of such theologians, see Smith 1987, 96–103.

within early Christian meal practice, I want to leave the last word to John the evangelist, and yet one other insight into their commensality. In the Johannine recollection of the final supper,[154] a central moment is when the group of disciples are told that Jesus will no longer call them 'servants' (*doulai*) but rather 'friends' (*philoi*) because he has made known to them everything he has learnt from the Father (Jn 15.15). This text usually escapes attention in discussions of the Eucharist, even in studies devoted to this theme in John,[155] and it is only recently, and peripherally, that it has had any influence on liturgy.[156] However, its narrative location in the middle of a discourse that is to be imagined as taking place at table surely provides a *prima facie* case for interpreting it within the meal *Sitz im Leben* of those who first heard it.

I believe that John wished the story to be read at two levels. The first level is that those at table (and it is already clear from the footwashing in Jn 13 that those at the narrative table represent all Christians at their tables) should hear it in terms of their own behaviour at the Christian meal. They have been masters and servants together, one knowing and ordering, the other not knowing and subservient, but now they must view themselves as friends around the table. Friendship, as all knew in the Greco-Roman world, is a reality between social equals. This is the Lord's Supper in which they are taking part, and in him the former distinctions of status are abolished (at least temporarily) and they must behave as friends should towards one another. Such a community/liturgical reading could be seen as the Johannine equivalent to Paul's concerns over inequalities at the table and to the similar concerns in the Letter of James. Moreover, this equality as friends in Christ, equal members of The Way, would show them to be responsive to Wisdom[157] and directly parallels the equality that Philo imagines for the meals of Therapeutae/Therapeutrides.[158] The status of the group, in Christ, as

---

[154]On the structure of this meal in Jn, see Witherington 2007, 63–85.

[155]Kobel 2011, the most extensive recent treatment of the eucharistic activity in John, has an index item to the verse (p. 351), but this is a misprint for 13.15 – and so this verse is left out of account; this is in keeping with virtually all commentaries.

[156]In the 1975 Catholic additional 'Eucharistic Prayers for Masses with Children I' there is this phrase: 'he broke the bread, gave it to his friends, and said' (and there are parallel phrases in Prayers II and III); while in the 'Eucharistic Prayers for Reconciliation I' there is this phrase: 'Again he gave you thanks, handed the cup to his friends, and said'. These phrases have, however, provoked negative reactions from some quarters on the basis that 'people are disciples of Christ, but friends with other humans' – one hopes such critics have not recognized the Johannine origin of the words.

[157]Brown 1966, 682 notes that Wis 7.27 imagines wisdom passing into holy souls makes them the *philoi* of God.

[158]*De vita contemplativa*, 70–1 where Philo states that 'in the sacred symposium there is no slave' but all are free people; this is a theme in the work in that in n. 17 he points out that all in the community are equal; in n. 19, that they are not like slaves (*douloi*), that their banquets are not like pagan meals with slaves (n. 50), and that their places at table are ordered by age, not status (nn. 30 and 67).

friends is a practical challenge to their own vision of themselves at table and dovetails with the command to love one another by washing one another's feet – where each is to act as a slave to each. That call for behaviour as friends at the table was a real challenge to their ritual practice, one whose importance would become more significant in the face of social pressures to avoid any real meal sharing among Christians, and one that John knew was difficult as we see from his portrayal of Peter in 13.6-9. This willingness to act as friends is a key challenge for discipleship in John, and one which remains valid today.

The Johannine story is also narrated in such a way that its author intended it to be read in another context or level.[159] That is that friendship with God is a characteristic of the covenant: the Lord spoke to Moses on Sinai as a man to his *philos* (Exod. 33.11).[160] In recollecting the Last Supper as a source for their understanding of their own community meals, their sharing in the cup of the covenant can be imagined as moving from the domain of being a servile people to being those who are the intimates of the Father, and who through Jesus' high priestly ministry (Jn 17), are his friends. The community meal is the intersection between people and intersection between the People and the Father. Therefore, they can bless him, in words that were, in all likelihood, known to John:

> We give you thanks, holy Father, for your holy name which you have made to dwell in our hearts, and for the knowledge and faith and immortality which you have made known to us.

> Through Jesus, your servant, to you be glory forever.[161]

---

[159]That it is located between the footwashing (Jn 13) and the High Priestly Prayer (Jn 17) – and can be read in terms of both these themes in the Final Discourse – demonstrates that John was deploying these memories at two level.

[160]See Brown 1966, 683.

[161]*Didache*, 10.2; Brown 1966, 746 notes the links between the high priestly prayer in Jn 17 and *Didache*, 10.2. This connection is of significance in that both texts invoke the image of Jesus as 'the Vine'; see Schwiebert 2008, 137–45.

7

The common meal and
the common good

From the standpoint of the theologian, the history of the Eucharist – as memory, practice, reflection and teaching, with each generation overlaying, altering, rejecting and adding to what it received – has to be seen as a series of displacements. I imagine these displacements under four broad and interconnected headings, all of which took place relatively early in Christian history but in no specific sequence: we cannot chart the developments in detail but merely note that a displacement has occurred at a later point when definite evidence of the alteration in practice has occurred. However, with the changes in practice a new situation was brought about in the churches such that as they recalled their origins in the action of reading their sacred texts, they validated and revalidated their existing practice while rendering discontinuities all but invisible. In this situation the dissonance caused by particular memories was either marginalized (for example, the appearance of unleavened bread in the early medieval west or the fifteenth-century call for the use of the cup) or treated as a problem confined to some specific item of interpretation (e.g. the long-running disputes over the nature of the change of the elements or what constituted an adequate expression of 'presence'). The force of inherited practice, for better and for worse, invariably set the parameters of understanding.

Displacements

'A ritual is "falsified" to the extent to which it cannot serve as a paradigm for significant action outside the ritual itself and is validated to the extent to which it does function in this way'.[1]

---

[1]Theodore Jennings 1982, 119–20.

The first, and perhaps the most far-reaching displacement, is that by which the ritual event of the Eucharist became separate from a real meal among a gathering of disciples. In becoming a ritual which was reduced to, and so focused upon, the recognizably 'religious' elements of the symposium – the formal remembering that today would be called the Liturgy of the Word and then the explicit action of blessing the Father so as to share a loaf and cup: the overall significance of the action was lost to view. What led to this displacement? We simply do not know but probably the mixing of ethnic groups, social and economic levels, and genders all made a purely token meal – if it was even perceived as a meal rather than as individuals each receiving a marvellous edible object – a far less daunting prospect for all concerned.

The original whole, the meal, was more than its parts, and, once sundered, what were thought of as 'parts' no longer made obvious sense to those who took part in the activity. In the new token meal situation, where the significance of the event had to be found in words or in purposes apart from a community eating together, the 'theology' of the Eucharist, unfettered from the original situation, could develop in any number of ways – and did so – and it was but a matter of time before a desire for consistency within doctrine was confronted with either destructive contradictions or ever more elaborate harmonizations. Moreover, the further matter of eating and drinking became but a minor part of a larger ritual, the ability of communities to appreciate the fundamental thrust of their inherited symbols was diminished – and into this gap in understanding came successions of new meanings.

The second displacement is the shift in the theological and ritual focus of participants in the Eucharist. From being the action of praising and thanking the Father for all his wonderful goodness, the *magnalia Dei*, it became the event at which the Christ became present in a special way in the Church. There he could be encountered anew, beseeched and adored. While in the doctrinal background the Eucharist was the sacrifice to the Father – and so the Father was its focus – this aspect was a concern of a theological elite: it played little role in the beliefs of ordinary members of the Church nor in preaching. And when it was invoked it became so entwined with the issue of that sacrifice being the death of Jesus on the cross that it became *de facto* another aspect of the presence of Jesus: was this a new offering on the cross, the one offering on the cross remembered, or the one offering on the cross made present? Whether or not this second displacement was a result of the first is impossible to answer (we simply did not have enough surviving evidence from second and third centuries) but it is clear that by the fourth century both displacements had taken place and cohered well with one another. Once it was clear that the people gathered so that they could encounter Jesus among them, any number of other changes flowed as simple consequences: most obviously that the *anamnesis* aspect of the Eucharist became one of historical re-enactment in time; the *eucharistic* prayer –

already long severed from being a table blessing – became a *consecrating* prayer; while in the realm of theology the nature of Christ's presence and the relationship of the Eucharist to the cross and his sacrifice to the Father – itself an issue not free of confusion – could all come to the fore as matters of dispute. Likewise, once the Eucharist was identified as Christ's action, then in western theology where issues of the relation of 'grace' and 'work' regularly generated new controversies, the issue of presence, sacrifice and the involvement of the people was another fertile seedbed of confusion and controversy.

It is the problems arising from this second displacement that have attracted most attention from individual theologians and from ecumenical endeavours over the past century. But the displacement that generated these controversies is so embedded in marrow – the history, practice, law, identity – of the disputing churches that many are still willing to completely ignore it. It is true that most engage in academic discussion and may face up to the problem when it appears on their peripheral vision as has happened in the recognition by the Roman Catholic Church of the liturgy of Addai and Mari in 2001, but on the whole confronting this displacement seems just too difficult for many. One merely has to observe a celebration of the Eucharist in an average Catholic Church where the president may announce that he is using a particular 'Eucharistic Prayer' but will in fact perform a consecratory prayer – and so long as this occurs there will inevitably be controversy over presence, modes of presence, and a string of complex questions over the relationship of 'sacrifice' and 'Eucharist'.

The third displacement concerns the agent of the eucharistic action. Given its origins in table prayers of a gathering, and the focus of Jesus' actions in sharing a loaf and a cup, it should be obvious that this is a collective activity, a matter of the Church, an involvement of the Holy People. However, it soon became primarily the business of a specialist group acting not simply as leaders of a church but in virtue of special powers as a service to the church, and then, indeed, performing a sacerdotal action – *in persona Christi* – on behalf of the church. From being the action of the community it became the action of those with the 'power of order' for the group, to such an extent that their presence was accidental to action. Again, the process and sequence of steps by which this transformation took place are largely hidden from view, but it is clear that from the time – the beginning of the fourth century at the latest – that Christian ministers considered themselves as a distinct group, the clergy, within the Church, and as an *ordo* within society, the role of presidency of the Eucharist became a matter of special concern to them – indeed it became the very basis of their identity, their sacred power, and their unique defining characteristic. In becoming a matter for the clergy, and an expression of power within the society of the Church, the Eucharist could not but be altered in the perception of Christians: it became the supreme expression of sacred government, hierarchy. Moreover, as a function of power – one has but to recall that the highest sanction in western canon law is referred to as 'excommunication' – the Eucharist became part of the mystique of power on the one hand, and an instrument by which power could be exercised on the other. Now any dispute over authority within Christendom could not but involve the Eucharist in some way or other, and when the Church's sacred leaders – sacred in the final analysis in virtue of their power to consecrate at the Eucharist – acted as if the Church was a toll house, then the Eucharist became the toll gate. It is not surprising that every movement of opposition to clerical power had the effect of making the Eucharist, which was so much their private concern and interest as can be seen in the practice of private Masses, ever more peripheral to Christian life. It was 'their [clerical] thing': they did it for the merely baptized, and it was attended by others 'under pain of sin'. In such a view, it would indeed have been surprising if the Eucharist were not marginalized, and indeed sidelined as an aspect of a more general anti-clericalism. While when the Eucharist did figure closer to the centre of Christian life it took the form of devotions to the reserved sacrament which was seen as something that the clergy renewed rather than controlled.

One other aspect of this displacement from being the action of the community to being the action of the priest – now more accurately designated a *sacerdos* rather than a *presbyter* – is that it ritually separated the Eucharist from other prayer. In the case of the community leader offering table prayers at the Christian meal, that eucharistic praying was the summit of all the prayers and praises that the community offered whether individually or in groups, privately or publicly. Whether it was the prayer to the Father that was a cornerstone of discipleship, the Lord's Prayer, or its most elaborated form, the Liturgy of the Hours, or the simple act of thanks before every meal or the elaborate thanksgiving of a public *Te Deum*, all these were somehow distinct from the Eucharist rather than being seen as being part of the whole People's song of thanksgiving to the Creator and the Father of Jesus the Anointed. If the Eucharist is to be 'the centre and summit of the Christian life', then it has to be in continuity with the simplest prayer of 'thank God', and each Christian's prayer. The displacement such that the Eucharist was a function of Holy Orders, put all other thanksgiving into a secondary category while destroying the essential unity of Christian prayer. Other consequences flowed from that such as that Order was seen to be the key to some of the basic aspects of the Church's life rather than baptism; and the availability of the Eucharist followed from the availability of the ordained, which in turn rested on how the origins of ministry were imagined – another area where confusion abounds. For instance, the ongoing disputes about who can be ordained, in effect who can be a cleric, exist within the paradigm built upon this displacement. A far better approach would be to look to the nature of Christian thanksgiving, how this is expressed in the *ekklésia*, and then how this takes its more Christ-ian form in blessing the Father, Jesus-fashion, in the midst of the community's banquet which celebrates their memory, identity and hope. A theologian recently remarked after a lecture on the question of women's ordination that 'if you can't ordain them, you shouldn't baptize them'; but perhaps we could express it even more accurately: 'if you do not offer thanks at the breakfast table, you should not seek to offer thanks at the community's table' or, yet again, 'if you can offer thanks to the Father for his goodness in providing a bowl of cereal, then you can offer thanks in the midst of the community before sharing the loaf and cup'.[2] It is, after all, Jesus' call and then baptism that makes us, in the words of a second-century writer: 'a chosen race, a royal priesthood, a holy nation, God's own people, that you may declare the wonderful deeds of him who called you out of darkness into his marvellous light' (1 Pet. 2.9).[3]

The fourth displacement does not have a distinct historical origin but is such a significant theological consequence of the other displacements that it needs to be noted as a distinct problem. At the core of Christian faith is the conviction that 'the Word was made flesh and lived among us' (Jn 1.14). The distinction of sacred/profane becomes outdated: every aspect of human life can be a locus of encounter with God, and the human person becomes the temple of God's Spirit. It is in this 'temple' of our redeemed humanity that we stand in the Father's presence and offer praise. Put another way, we can assert that the whole universe is thereby made sacred; and consequent on this is that Christian worship is not a temple-based activity: 'the hour is coming when you will worship the Father neither on this mountain nor in Jerusalem. . . . God is spirit, and those who worship him must worship in spirit and truth' (Jn 4.21-4). The room and the table around which his disciples ate their eucharistic meal was as holy as the temple in Jerusalem, there they gathered in his presence, and the Holy One was praised in midst of life and creation. Where, for instance, is the purity and holiness of the Jerusalem temple to be found for the communities using the *Didache*? Wherever a group of disciples eat together and bless the Father 'through Jesus Christ forever'.[4] The coming of 'the holy vine of David' had transformed every table potentially into being a place of the divine presence. However, this vision that every table is potentially the holy table because of the mystery of the incarnation was displaced by the 'mysteriousness' of the Eucharist as a sacral event understood by analogy with pagan cults – the table retained its shape but took on the functions of an altar – and the cult of the Old Covenant whereby the place of gathering took on the theology of the temple. Indeed, so 'holy' did the event become that it had to be cut off as far as possible from the locus of the incarnation: where we live within the creation. The language we

---

[2] See O'Loughlin 2013i where this is examined in more detail.

[3] On should not ignore the fact that there is an incipient clericalism in this early second-century document; see Elliot 1970.

[4] It has often being noted how purity was an issue for this community (van de Sandt 2002), but while such purity was not restricted to the temple (see Poirier 2003), that their eating was conceived in terms of the temple is clear from Did 14.2-3 (see van de Sandt 2011).

use to describe the eucharistic liturgy – it takes place in a 'sanctuary', the whole event is a 'most holy mystery', a desire for a hieratic language that seeks to refer to a cup as a 'chalice' – and ritual codes employed within its liturgy – a special area marked off from the profane and perhaps shielded from their eyes, special vesture and any number of arcane details – set the celebration outside the world of everyday life into which the Christ had entered. The Eucharist became the domain of the specially consecrated person – inheriting the identities of the *cohen* as well as the *pontifex* – who performed it on behalf of 'the rest' behind the veil whether that was made of wood or words. That our memory also included that the temple's veil had been ripped 'from top to bottom' (Mk 15.38 and parallels) by the priestly work of the Christ slipped from our liturgical consciousness. It has often been remarked that it was too much to ask people – with their desire for the numinous *ganz andere* – to accept a radically incarnational liturgy; but that merely restates the situation and cannot be offered as a theological justification.

We may have roundly condemned docetism, thinking of it as an ancient and obscure heresy now long in the past, but for most churches the eucharistic liturgy is functionally docetic. The worship of the Father does not take place from the midst of our world, from the midst of our human existence, but arises from a sacral event that is marked off in every way from life, from anything that could be seen as impure: it is something that is 'attended' and has sacral value as a ritual commodity rather than from it being the action expressing our fundamental relationship as a baptized People with God. Once this displacement had occurred a chasm was set up between our ritual activity of the Eucharist and the ethical demands of discipleship. But because it was also part of our memory that participation in the Eucharist was intertwined with fulfilling the Way of Life, this could only be viewed by way of a distinct moral demand that participation in the Eucharist demanded freedom from sin. Eventually, when seen in terms of 'worthiness', the Eucharist came to be seen as a 'reward' for avoiding sin, and became further distanced as that which demanded a 'purity' that was seen not to belong to 'ordinary living'. Yet the chasm still remained: if one were to ask how is the feast of the Eucharist related to the fact that there might be famine in another community, most Christians would not see any inherent link in terms of their behaviour as the People of God, but might propose that at the Eucharist the famine might be recalled, in prayer and homily, while they might be encouraged to contribute to famine relief while the 'grace' of the Eucharist might move people's hearts to help. But the notion that sharing one's food with the hungry, while acknowledging God as the source of all sustenance, would not spring to mind. Ritual belongs within the *fanum*, while ethical action outside in the *profanum* – with a code of morality throwing across a kind of makeshift bridge. Yet all truly meaningful ritual must not only model our vision of our collective place within a created cosmos, but also 'serve as a paradigm for significant action outside the ritual itself'.[5] And perhaps here we have one of the keys as to why the Eucharist, despite all the emphasis it has received in the tradition, can be seen of marginal value in the actual lives of so many Christians.

Confronting the past in the future

However, faced with these displacements, we need to be aware that the Church is not only always forgetting (largely an unwitting process) but always remembering afresh (an activity which is engaged upon with earnestness). Moreover, one of the great strengths of modern Christianity is the level of skill and the clarity of insight which it can bring to the study of its past and its activity of recollection and self-examination: we can see the past more clearly than most of the generations before us; and we can establish a vantage point on the processes that have brought us to the present which allows understanding of the tradition and our present that is unmatched in Christian history. This does not mean that we can simply reconstruct the past or create afresh as if we did not have the baggage of centuries pushing us forward. The shallow impression of the very limited reforms of the liturgical movement of the twentieth century upon actual practice after more than half a century should remind us how inherently conservative is human ritual activity. But perhaps recollection can serve us in other ways. I believe that careful historical recollection serves the community of faith in three overlapping ways.

First, remembering allows us to see new dimensions in what is happening around us in the world. We are always in danger of producing a theology of the Eucharist that is simply an exalting exposition of our particular liturgical experience; but recalling displacements can make us look at what is happening in areas that are, apparently far removed from the liturgy. One of the most intriguing developments in the humanities in the latter half of the twentieth century was the discovery of the human significance of food and eating. It has manifested itself in the study of the history of food, the rituals of our eating and, more recently, the developments of theologies of food. But new interest in food is not confined to the humanities: development studies, dieticians and even security experts looking at 'food security' now put food and eating at the core of human existence in a way that would not have occurred just decades ago. Food has always been 'big business', but we approach our central ritual with a conscious appreciation of eating and drinking unparalleled in history. A few decades ago it was common to find books on the theology of the Eucharist where, unless one knew otherwise, a reader might not realize that it was an

---

[5]See Jennings 1982, 120; and note that there is some empirical evidence that there is a relationship between ethical behaviour and the content and style of Christian worship: see Brown 2013.

action involving eating and drinking – and alas I have read several such books written in the last couple of years; but anyone who approaches the Lord's Supper today without that consciousness of food, meals, and their place in communities is already looking at the activity of Eucharist in an impoverished way.

This new consciousness of food and its sharing is not merely an academic affair or a matter for those who work in the background of supplying society with its needs, it can be found all around us. In the face of globalized 'fast food', we have the 'slow food' movement; the awareness of how our food habits affect the environment; and the concern for the carbon footprint of our eating habits with 'food-miles'. While we may have lost the sense of seasonality, which was such an important underpinning to the ritual and liturgical year, we have lots of other indications that the links between food and religion are growing stronger. In those churches where a harvest thanksgiving is part of the liturgical year, this is increasingly seen to relate to both the Eucharist and the engagement of the assembly with poverty and with the environment. In other churches – where in the past the Eucharist was not a significant element in communal activities – it is being rediscovered as a 'feast' of the community formed by their shared memory of Jesus. In such a situation, to use the expression of one contemporary theologian: the Eucharist is 'the real meal deal',[6] while another has expressed the contemporary view of Christian origins as 'in the beginning was the meal'.[7] And, at the conclusion of one book on the Eucharist, one cannot but envy the title, *Making a meal of it*, as a recent biblical exegete seeks to link biblical investigation and liturgical practice in a way that would have been unthinkable a generation ago.[8] Such events, small in themselves, are beacons of hope not only for a renewed theology of the Eucharist, but also for a location of the Eucharist outside of the inherited animosities that were consequent of the displacements, major and minor, that have scarred our memories of the Love Feast.

Then there are those developments, minor in themselves, which seek to re-locate Eucharistic activity in the community and outside of 'the sanctuary'. Many churches have begun to experiment with small-group settings for the Eucharist, celebrations in domestic settings, and even such simple things as 'tea and biscuits' after the service all serve to remind the Church that the Eucharist exists in the community of faith as part of the life of discipleship. Even in the Roman Catholic Church, whose liturgical evolution is doubly hampered by its restriction of eucharistic presidency to a professional clergy of male celibates which means that there are fewer celebrations for larger numbers and by a formal clampdown on liturgical experimentation since

[6]Snyder 2001.
[7]Taussig 2009.
[8]Witherington 2007.

1980,[9] there is a growing realization that the liturgy must ground itself in the reality of discipleship or be untrue to its own nature.[10] While as church after church adopts renewed liturgical forms, there is a conscious creativity in the celebration of the Eucharist that is without parallel in Christian history.[11] And all this takes place at a time when cultural factors are making worship a more complex form of social interaction.[12] And, one must not forget the rediscovery of the value and importance (and effectiveness) of eating together as a church that is now a firm part of so many endeavours to evangelize in a post-modern environment – efforts that deserve to be studied as instances of an 'anonymous Eucharist'.

An appreciation of the complex depth of Christian involvement in the Eucharist, which is in stark contrast with the older model of unfailing organic continuity from the moment of the Last Supper,[13] allows us to appreciate what may be of value in these contemporary movements, evaluate their internal dynamics and locate them within a larger picture of many forms that discipleship can take.

Second, remembering reveals links between various parts of both the theological and ecclesial enterprise. It is all too easy for a study of the Eucharist to forget that this activity is part of the larger pattern of the lives of the followers of Jesus. There has been a deep-seated tendency to think of the Eucharist as an object, an 'it', to be analysed (not helped by the focus on 'presence') rather than a form of Christian behaviour and engagement with the world which must take that world fully into account. Equally, we must constantly recall that the Eucharist is primarily an action (*ergon*) rather than a 'thought' or a 'discourse' (*logos*).[14] It is an experience we share and which we react to, for good or ill, as an experience.[15]

Bearing this in mind, how should we approach our ancient sources? What, for example, is the first lesson on the Eucharist we should take from the *Didache*? That eucharistic activity is one more element in the life of a community seeking to follow the Way of Life. As such, a theology of the Eucharist that does not engage with the Christian vision of who the actors are is somehow lacking. The activity must draw on our knowledge of ourselves and project for us an image of how we want to be in the world. For example, given that the Eucharist is a matter of eating and

---

[9]It was on 17 April 1980 that the Vatican issued the instruction *Inaestimabile domum* which effectively presented the form of liturgy as a *datum* to be implemented as uniformly as possible, rather than as a work in progress which was implied in the Second Vatican Council. See Marini 2007.

[10]See, for example, Guzie 1974.

[11]See, for example, the possibilities explored in Giles 2004 which is linked explicitly to the Church of England's *Common Worship*; but there are similar books, although few are as well researched as Giles's work, in every tradition.

[12]See Spinks 2010.

[13]For the classic statement of continuity, see Dix 1945, 744.

[14]See Dooley 2004, 10.

[15]See O'Loughlin 2010a.

drinking together, that eating and drinking must be a model of ecological responsibility. Given that it is a community feast, this must be a challenge to confront both consumerist individualism and the plight of communities in poverty. This larger vision which is to be modelled in our community ritual is not merely a 'moral response' but a direct aspect of the way we remember, ritualize our world and envisage ourselves as a church. Remembering reveals to us that these links have often become tenuous and we have even adopted the very values within the liturgy that are in conflict not only with the vision of the New Creation inaugurated in the Paschal Mystery, but also with some of the fundamental concepts of the eucharistic liturgy itself. When these conflicts are discovered from within the history of the Eucharist, as distinct from being based on an abstract analysis of values, we see how misunderstandings of discipleship can insinuate themselves, often silently, over time and become all but invisible. Historical remembering is, within the body of a church, often akin in purpose to pathology within the human body: knowing the depths of a disease is being a step closer to renewed health.

Moreover, simply recalling that '[t]he first urban Christians established themselves within private, domestic space, wherein the necessary ritual, which was based around a meal, conveniently took place'[16] can have the effect of setting contemporary debates in context. It is a feature of regular human activity, and in particular ritual activity which is seen to link us to a past *in illo tempore*, that we consider our present as a mirror of an ideal, and then expend ever greater energy on ever more abstruse details. Yet all historical moments are but attempts to praise the Father as his People in union with Jesus. It is that *telos*, rather than continuities with past practice, that is the criterion of what we do in liturgy. It is a paradox of human understanding that the more we critically engage with our history – in this case the history of our eucharistic practice, the more we are freed from being entwined in the legacies of the past and the more clearly we can see what we should be aiming for in the future.

Third, remembering reminds us of the relativity of our present within the sweep of Christian history which should inspire a humility in both individuals and churches when we make claims in the name of 'revelation', 'the *depositum fidei*', 'the teaching of the scriptures', 'what the Bible says' or 'the sacred tradition of the church'. The paradox of the Eucharist being the expression of unity in Christ and yet that which divides Christians more than almost any other matter of practice shimmers beneath much of what is written and said about it. Indeed, while there are public gestures (although even these are less common than some decades ago)[17] towards ecumenical understanding, they usually remain firmly within the safe confines of the

---

[16]Billings 2011, 567.
[17]See Johnson 2006; and Wainwright 2007.

academy. And consequently, most teaching on the Eucharist for future ministers is still very firmly fixed within the theological style that Hunsinger has aptly termed 'enclave theology'.[18] Yet a study of the displacements, major and minor, that have occurred over the centuries should demonstrate to us that our enclaves do not have the structural integrity that we blandly claim for them from a mix of pride in our identity and nagging memories of past dissentions. One is tempted to adapt Paul: '. . . all have sinned and fall short of the glory of God' (Rom. 3.23). Put another way, every church, and every group within churches, might reflect on the proverbial wisdom that 'people in glass houses should not throw stones!'

But historical theology does offer something more positive besides: the possibility that we can learn from one another, from our strengths and failings, as we move forward in discipleship. This insight has become widely popular in recent years under the title of 'receptive ecumenism' but it is worth quoting the earliest expressions of the insight which views ecumenical progress in terms of conversion:

> The road to unity is not the return of one church to another, or the exodus of one church to join another, but a common crossroads, the conversion of all churches to Christ and thus to one another. Unity is not the subjection of one church to another, but the mutual regeneration and mutual acceptance of community through mutual giving and receiving.[19]

We all need to learn from one another and from a study of the processes that have brought us to where we are today with its strengths and distortions, areas of impasse and areas of opportunity.

This book has deliberately crossed academic boundaries and has not feared treading on several toes; and many will dismiss it as either proposing an impossible ideal or of failing to value jewels in the *thesaurus ecclesiae*. I shall be happy with the result of my labour if you, gentle reader, when you next sit down to eat a snack or have a cup of coffee with a friend (and this will happen, with virtual certainty, within hours), are struck by the human significance of what you are doing, how this activity is so closely entwined in our *anamnesis* of the activities of Jesus, and that for that food, drink and company one should be thankful.

---

[18]Hunsinger 2008, 1–18.
[19]Küng 1967, 293 – I note that Hunsinger 2008, 21 has also been struck by this statement of Küng, and sees in the approach that Küng outlines there the only real way that union in Christ can ever become more than a matter of academic agreement.

BIBLIOGRAPHY

Ancient and medieval texts and authors[1]

Texts

The Didache (M. W. Holmes (ed.), *The Apostolic Fathers: Greek Texts and English Translations*, Grand Rapids, MI, 1992, pp. 251–69).

The Gospel of Thomas (A. Guillaumont, H.-C. Puech, G. Quispel, W. Till and Y. 'Abd al Masih, *The Gospel According to Thomas: Coptic Text Established and Translated*, Leiden, 1959).

Authors

Columbanus, *Regula Coenobialis* (G. S. M. Walker (ed.), *Sancti Columbani Opera*, Dublin, 1957, pp. 142–69).

Gregory of Nyssa, *Catechetical Oration* (J. H. Srawley (ed.), Cambridge, 1903).

Ignatius of Antioch, *To the Ephesians* (M. W. Holmes (ed.), *The Apostolic Fathers: Greek Texts and English Translations*, Grand Rapids, MI, 1992, pp. 136–51).

Josephus, *The Antiquities of the Jews* (H. St. J. Thackeray (ed.), distributed over several volumes of the LCL).

—*Jewish War* (H. St. J. Thackeray (ed.), distributed over several volumes of the LCL).

Justin Martyr, *First Apology* (M. Marcovich (ed.), PTS 38 (1997)).

Minucius Felix, *Octavius* (B. Kytzler (ed.), Leipzig, 1982).

Philo, *De vita contemplativa* (F. H. Colson (ed.), LCL 363, pp. 112–69).

—*Quod omnis probus liber sit* (F. H. Colson (ed.), LCL 363, pp. 10–101).

Thomas Aquinas, *Summa theologiae* (the bilingual edn produced under the general editorship of Thomas Gilby, London, 1963–80, has been used).

—*Officium de festo Corporis Christi ad mandatum Urbani papae IV (Opuscula theologica*, Rome, 1954, 2, pp. 275–81).

Vincent of Lérins, *Commonitorium* (R. Demeulenaere (ed.), CCSL 64 (1985), pp. 145–95).

---

[1] Unless otherwise noted, all translations are my own.

Ecclesiastical documents

Liturgical texts

Church of England, *Book of Common Prayer* (London, 1966).
—*Common Worship* (London, 2006).
Church of Ireland, *Book of Common Prayer (2004)* (Dublin, 2004).
Roman Catholic Church, *Rituale Romanum* (1614) (Rome, 1952).
—*Missale Romanum* (1969) (Rome, 1969).

Ecclesiastical texts

Bishops' Conferences of England and Wales, Scotland, and Ireland, *One Bread One Body*, London, 1998.
Codex Iuris Canonici [1983], The Vatican, 1983, cited by canon number.
Francis, *Evangelii gaudium*, The Vatican, 2013.
Sacred Congregation for the Sacraments and Divine Worship, *Inaestimabile donum*, The Vatican, 1980.
Trent, texts cited from, and referenced to, *DS*.
Vatican II, texts cited according to A. Flannery (ed.), *Vatican Council II: The Conciliar and Post Conciliar Documents* (Wilmington, DE, 1975).
World Council of Churches, *Baptism, Eucharist and Ministry* (Geneva, 1982).

Modern authors

Abba, R., *Principles of Christian Worship* (Oxford, 1960).
Adams, R., *The College Graces of Oxford and Cambridge* (Oxford, 1992).
Angenendt, A., '*Missa specialis*: Zugleich ein Beitrag zur Entstehung der Privatmessen', *FS* 17 (1983), pp. 153–221.
Angenendt, A. and Schnitker, T. A., 'Die Privatmesse', *LJ* 33 (1983), pp. 76–89.
Ascough, R. S., 'Translocal Relationships Among Voluntary Associations and Early Christianity', *JECS* 5 (1997), pp. 223–41.
—'Forms of Commensality in Greco-Roman Associations', *CW* 102 (2008), pp. 33–45.
Audet, J. P., 'Literary Forms and Contents of a Normal *Eucharistia* in the First Century', in K. Aland, F. L. Cross, Jean Daniélou, Harald Riesenfeld and W. C. Van Unnik (eds.), *SE* (1; Berlin, 1959), pp. 643–62.
—*Structures of Christian Priesthood* (London, 1967).
Bahr, G. J., 'The Seder of Passover and the Eucharistic Words', *NT* 12 (1970), pp. 181–202.
Ball, J., 'Traduttore-traditore? The new translation and mission', *PR* 9, 1 (2013), pp. 55–60.
Barnes, T. D., 'The Date of Ignatius', *ET* 120 (2008), pp. 119–30.
Bauckham, R. (ed.), *The Gospels for all Christians: Rethinking the Gospel Audience* (Edinburgh, 1998).

Bauer, W., *Orthodoxy and Heresy in Earliest Christianity* (Philadelphia, PA, 1971) [ET by R. A. Craft and G. Krodel of *Rechtgläubigkeit und Ketzerei in ältesten Christentum*, Tübingen, 1934].

Baumstark, A., *Comparative Liturgy* (London, 1958) [ET by F. L. Cross of the rev. edn by B. Botte of *Liturgie Comparée*, Chevetogne, 1953].

—*On the Historical Development of the Liturgy* (Collegeville, MN, 2011) [ET by F. West of *Vom geschichtlichen Werden der Liturgie*, Freiburg, 1923].

Berger, T., *Gender Differences and the Making of Liturgical History: Lifting a Veil on Liturgy's Past* (Farnham, 2011).

Betz, H. D., 'The Origin and Nature of Christian Faith According to the Emmaus Legend (Luke 24:13-32)', *Interpretation* 23 (1969), pp. 32–46.

Bhattacharji, S., Williams, R. and Mattos, D. (eds), *Prayer and Thought in Monastic Tradition: Essays in Honour of Benedicta Ward S.L.G.* (London, 2014).

Billings, B. S., 'From House Church to Tenement Church: Domestic Space and the Development of Early Urban Christianity The Example of Ephesus', *JTS* ns 62 (2011), pp. 541–69.

Blackburn, B. and Holford-Strevens, L., *The Oxford Companion to the Year: An Exploration of Calendar Customs and Time-reckoning* (Oxford, 1999).

Boers, A. P., 'In search of something more: A sacramental approach to life and worship', *VJCT* 2, 1 (2001), pp. 42–58.

Bokser, B. M., '*Ma'al* and Blessings over Food: Rabbinic Transformation of Cultic Terminology and Alternative Modes of Piety', *JBL* 100 (1981), pp. 557–74.

—'Unleavened Bread and Passover, Feasts of', in D. N. Freedman (ed.), *The Anchor Bible Dictionary* (6; New York, NY, 1992), pp. 755–65.

Boland, V. and McCarthy, T. (eds), *The Word is Flesh and Blood: The Eucharist and Sacred Scripture – Festschrift for Prof. Wilfrid Harrington* (Dublin, 2012).

Bourdieu, P., *The Logic of Practice* (Cambridge, 1990).

Box, G. H., 'The Jewish Antecedents of the Eucharist', *JTS* 3 (1902), pp. 357–69.

Bradshaw, P., *Daily Prayer in the Early Church* (London, 1981).

—(ed.), *A Companion to Common Worship* (London, 2001).

—*The Search for the Origins of Christian Worship: Sources and Methods for the Study of Early Liturgy* (London, 2002).

—*Eucharistic Origins* (London, 2004).

Bradshaw, P., Giles, G. and Kershaw, S., 'Holy Communion', in Bradshaw (ed.), *A Companion to Common Worship* (London, 2001), pp. 98–147.

Bradshaw, P. and Johnson, M. E., *The Origins of Feasts, Fasts and Seasons in Early Christianity* (London, 2011).

Brent, A., 'The Enigma of Ignatius of Antioch', *JEH* 57 (2006), pp. 429–56.

Brilioth, Y., *Eucharistic Faith and Practice: Evangelical and Catholic* (trans. A. G. Hebert; London, 1930).

Brown, C. G., *The Death of Christian Britain: Understanding Secularisation 1800–2000* (London, 2nd edn, 2009).

Brown, J. E., 'Living the Faith? A Study of Possible Relationships between Ethical Behaviour and the Content and Style of Christian Worship', *Anaphora* 7, 2 (2013), pp. 67–88.

Brown, R. E., *The Gospel According to John XIII-XXI* (New York, NY, 1966).

Brown, S. J., Knight, F. and Morgan-Guy, J. (eds.), *Religion, Identity and Conflict in Britain: From the Restoration to the Twentieth Century. Essays in Honour of Keith Robbins* (Farnham, 2013).

Burkhart, J. E., 'Reshaping Table Blessings: "Blessing . . . and thanksgiving . . . to our God" (Rev. 7:12)', *Interpretation* 48 (1994), pp. 50–60.

Cahill, M., 'Drinking Blood at a Kosher Eucharist? The Sound of Scholarly Silence', *BTB* 32 (2002), 168–81.

Casel, O., *The Mystery of Christian Worship* (New York, NY, 1999) [rept of 1962 translation of *Das Christliche Kultmysterium*, Regensburg, 1932].

Chadwick, H., 'Ego Berengarius', *JTS* ns 40 (1989), pp. 414–45.

Charlesworth, J. H. (ed.), *The Messiah: Developments in Earliest Judaism and Christianity* (Minneapolis, MN, 1992).

Charsley, S., 'The Wedding Cake: History and Meanings', *Folklore* 99 (1988), pp. 232–41.

Collins, J. J. and Harlow, D. C. (eds.), *The Eerdmans Dictionary of Early Judaism* (Grand Rapids, MI, 2010).

Colunga, A. and Turrado, L. (eds.), *Biblia Sacra iuxta Vulgatam Clementinam* (Madrid, 5th edn, [1977] 1946).

Connerton, P., *How Societies Remember* (Cambridge, 1989).

Cook, W. R., 'The Eucharist in Hussite Theology', *AR* 66 (1975), pp. 23–35.

Craig, B., *Fractio Panis: A History of the Breaking of Bread in the Roman Rite* (Rome, 2011).

Crossan, J. D., *The Historical Jesus: The Life of a Mediterranean Jewish Peasant* (Edinburgh, 1991).

Czachesz, I., 'The transmission of early Christian thought: Towards a cognitive psychological model', *SR* 36 (2007), pp. 65–83.

—'Rewriting and Textual Fluidity in Antiquity: Exploring the Socio-Cultural and Psychological Context of Earliest Christian Literacy', in Dijkstra, J. H. F., Kroesen, J. E. A. and Kuiper, Y. B. (eds.), *Myths, Martyrs, and Modernity* (Leiden, 2010), pp. 425–41.

Daly, R. J., *Sacrifice Unveiled: The True Meaning of Christian Sacrifice* (London, 2009).

Daly-Denton, M., 'Water in the Eucharistic Cup: A Feature of the Eucharist in Johannine Trajectories through Early Christianity', *ITQ* 72 (2007), pp. 356–70.

—'Looking Beyond the Upper Room: Eucharistic Origins in Contemporary Research', *Search* 31 (2008), pp. 3–15.

Davies, S., 'The Christology and Protology of the *Gospel of Thomas*', *JBL* 111 (1992), pp. 663–82.

Davies, S. L., 'John the Baptist and Essene Kashruth', *NTS* 29 (1983), pp. 569–71.

D'Avila-Latourrette, V.-A., *Table Blessings: Mealtime Prayers throughout the Year* (Notre Dame, IN, 1994).

Day, J. and Gordon-Taylor, B. (eds.), *The Study of Liturgy and Worship: An Alcuin Guide* (London, 2013).

De Lugo, J., *Disputationes scholasticae et morales* (Paris, 1869).

Denzinger, H. and Bannwart, C. (eds.), *Enchiridion symbolorum, definitionum, et declarationum de rebus fidei et morum* (Freiburg im Breisgau, 4th edn by J.-B. Umberg, 1922).

Denzinger, H. and Schönmetzer, A. (eds.), *Enchiridion symbolorum, definitionum, et declarationum de rebus fidei et morum* (Freiburg im Breisgau, 36 emended edn, 1976).

Dewey, J., 'The Survival of Mark's Gospel: A Good Story?', *JBL* 123 (2004), pp. 495–507.

Dever, W. G., 'Temples: Syria-Palestine', in D. N. Freedman (ed.), *The Anchor Bible Dictionary* (6; New York, NY, 1992), pp. 376–80.

De Vogüé, A., 'Eucharist and Monastic Life', *Worship* 59 (1985), pp. 498–510.

de Vooght, P., *L'hérésie de Jean Huss* (Leuven, 1960).

Diamond, J., *The World until Yesterday* (London, 2012).

Dijkstra, J. H. F., Kroesen, J. E. A. and Kuiper, Y. B. (eds.), *Myths, Martyrs, and Modernity* (Leiden, 2010).

Dix, G., *The Shape of the Liturgy* (London, 1945).

Dooley, C., 'To be what we celebrate: Engaging the Practice of Liturgical Catechesis', *NTR* 17, 4 (2004), pp. 9–17.

Dougherty, J., *From Altar-Throne to Table: The Campaign for Frequent Holy Communion in the Catholic Church* (Lanham, MD, 2010).

Douglas, M., *Purity and Danger: An Analysis of Concepts of Pollution and Taboo* (London, 1966).

—'Deciphering a Meal', *Daedalus* 101 (1972), pp. 61–81.

Draper, J. A., 'Weber, Theissen, and "Wandering Charismatics" in the *Didache*', *JECS* 6 (1998), pp. 541–76.

—'The Holy Vine of David Made Known to the Gentiles through God's Servant Jesus: "Christian Judaism" in the *Didache*', in M. Jackson-McCabe (ed.), *Jewish Christianity Reconsidered: Rethinking Ancient Groups and Texts* (Minneapolis, MN, 2007), pp. 257–83.

Duchesne, L., *Christian Worship: Its Origin and Evolution* (London, 1923) [ET by M. L. McClure of the fourth French edn].

Dunnill, J., *Covenant and sacrifice in the Letter to the Hebrews* (Cambridge, 1992).

Egan, H. D., 'Introduction' to K. Rahner, *I Remember* (London, 1985) [ET of *Erinnerungen im Gespräch mit Meinold Krauss* (Freiburg im Breisgau, 1984)].

Eliade, M., *The Myth of the Eternal Return: Cosmos and History* (London, 1954).

Elliott, D., *Fallen Bodies: Pollution, Sexuality, and Demonology in the Middle Ages* (Philadelphia, PA, 1999).

Elliot, J. H., 'Ministry and Church Order in the NT: A Traditio-Historical Analysis (1 Pet 5:1-5 and parallels', *CBQ* 32 (1970), pp. 367–91.

Eltester, W. and Kettler, F. H. (eds.), *Apophoreta: Festschrift für Ernst Haenchen* (Berlin, 1964).

Engberg-Pedersen, T., 'Philo's *De Vita Contemplativa* as a Philosopher's Dream', *JSJ* 30 (1999), pp. 40–64.

Erickson, J. H., 'Leavened and Unleavened: Some Theological Implications of the Schism of 1054', *SVTQ* 14 (1970), pp. 155–76.

Farber, S. M. and Wilson, N. L. (eds.), *Food and Civilization* (Springfield, IL, 1966).

Finger, T., 'Eucharistic Theology: Some untapped resources', *VJCT* 2, 1 (2001), pp. 28–41.

Finkelstein, L., 'The Birkat Ha-mazon', *JQR* ns 19 (1929), pp. 211–62.

Fontaine, J., Gillet, R. and Pellistrandi, S. (eds.), *Grégoire le Grand* (Paris, 1986).

Freedman, D. N. (ed.), *The Anchor Bible Dictionary* (New York, NY, 1992).

Freestone, W. H., *The Sacrament Reserved* (London, 1917).

Galor, K., Humbert, J.-B. and Zangenberg, J. (eds.), *Qumran. The Site of the Dead See Scrolls: Archaeological Interpretations and Debates* (Leiden, 2006).

Gamber, K., 'Anklänge an das Eucharistiegebet bei Paulus und das jüdische Kiddusch', *OS* 9 (1960), pp. 254–64.

Gihr, N., *The Holy Sacrifice of the Mass: Dogmatically, Liturgically and Ascetically Explained* (St Louis, MO, 1942) [this was the 15th English edn since 1902; it was a translation of a German text which appeared in 1877].

Giles, R., *Creating Uncommon Worship: Transforming the Liturgy of the Eucharist* (Norwich, 2004).

Goering, J., 'The Invention of Transubstantiation', *Traditio* 46 (1991), pp. 147–70.

Goulder, M. D., *Luke: A New Paradigm* (Sheffield, 1989).

Grignon, C., 'Commensality and Social Morphology: An Essay in Typology', in P. Scholliers (ed.), *Food, Drink and Identity: Cooking, Eating and Drinking in Europe Since the Middle Ages* (Oxford, 2001), pp. 23–33.

Guzie, T., *Jesus and the Eucharist* (New York, NY, 1974).

Hahn, S. W., 'A Broken Covenant and the Curse of Death: A Study of Hebrews 9:15-22', *CBQ* 66 (2004), pp. 416–36.

Halbwachs, M., *On Collective Memory: Edited, Translated and with an Introduction by Lewis A. Coser* (Chicago, IL, 1992).

Hänggi, A. and Pahl, I., *Prex Eucharistica: Textus e Variis Liturgiis Antiquioribus Selecti* (Fribourg (Switzerland), 1998) [third edn by A. Gerhards and H. Brakmann; the first edn appeared in 1968].

Häussling, A., *Mönchskonvent und Eucharistiefeier: Eine Studie über die Messe in der abendländischen Klosterliturgie des frühen Mittelalters und zur Geschichte des Messäufigkeit* (Münster-Westfalen, 1973).

Healey, J. P., 'Fertility Cults', in D. N. Freedman (ed.), *The Anchor Bible Dictionary* (2; New York, NY, 1992), pp. 791–3.

Hempel, C., 'Who is making dinner at Qumran?', *JTS* ns 63 (2012), pp. 49–65.

Higgins, A. B. J., *The Lord's Supper in the New Testament* (London, 1952).

Hollander, H. W., 'The Idea of Fellowship in 1 Corinthians 10.14-22', *NTS* 55 (2009), pp. 456–70.

Holmen, T. and Porter, S. (eds.), *Handbook for the Study of the Historical Jesus* (Leiden, 2010).

Homan, M. M., 'Beer and its Drinkers: An Ancient Near Easter Love Story', *NEA* 67 (2004), pp. 84–95.

Horrell, D. G., 'Domestic Space and Christian Meetings at Corinth: Imagining New Contexts and the Buildings East of the Theatre', *NTS* 50 (2004), pp. 349–69.

Hort, F. J. A. and Murray, J. O. F., 'Eucharistia – Eucharistein', *JTS* 3 (1902), pp. 594–8.

Huels, J. M., *One Table, Many Laws: Essays on Catholic Eucharistic Practice* (Collegeville, MN, 1986).

Hunsinger, G., *The Eucharist and Ecumenism: Let us Keep the Feast* (Cambridge, 2008).

Jackson-McCabe, M. (ed.), *Jewish Christianity Reconsidered: Rethinking Ancient Groups and Texts* (Minneapolis, MN, 2007).

—'What's in a Name? The problem of "Jewish Christianity"', in M. Jackson-McCabe (ed.), *Jewish Christianity Reconsidered: Rethinking Ancient Groups and Texts* (Minneapolis, MN, 2007), pp. 7–38.

Jeffery, P., *Translating Tradition: A Chant Historian Reads Liturgiam Authenticam* (Collegeville, MN, 2005).

Jennings, T. W., 'On Ritual Knowledge', *JR* 62 (1982), pp. 111–27.

Jeremias, J., *Jesus' Promise to the Nations* (London, 1958) [ET by S. H. Hooke of *Jesu Verheissung für die Völker*, Stuttgart, 1956].

—*The Eucharistic Words of Jesus* (London, 1966) [ET by N. Perrin of the 3rd edn of *Die Abendmahlsworte Jesu*, Göttingen, 1964].

Jervis, L. A. and Richardson, P., *Gospel in Paul: Studies on Corinthians, Galatians and Romans for Richard N. Longenecker* (Sheffield, 1994).

Jewett, R., *Dating Paul's Life* (London, 1979).

—'Gospel and Commensality: Social and Theological Implications of Galatians 2.14', in L. A. Jervis and P. Richardson (eds.), *Gospel in Paul: Studies on Corinthians, Galatians and Romans for Richard N. Longenecker* (Sheffield, 1994), pp. 240–52.

—*Romans: A Commentary* (Minneapolis, MN, 2007).

Johnson, M. E., 'Liturgy and Ecumenism: Gifts, Challenges, and Hopes for a Renewed Vision', *Worship* 80 (2006), pp. 2–29.

Johnston, W. R. (ed.), *The Encyclopedia of Monasticism* (Chicago and London, 2000).

Jones, M., *Feast: Why Humans Share Food* (Oxford, 2007).

Jungmann, J. A., *The Mass of the Roman Rite: Its Origins and Development (Missarum Sollemnia)* (New York, NY, 1955) [2 volumes ET by F. A. Brunnner of *Missarum Sollemnia: Eine genetische Erklärung der römischen Messe*, Freiburg, 1948 – the ET is cited in this study, but at every point it has been compared with the 5th revised German edn of 1962].

—*Christian Prayer through the Centuries* (London, 2007) [rept of 1978 ET by J. Coyne of *Christliches Beten*, Munich, 1969].

Kavanagh, A., *Elements of Rite: A Handbook of Liturgical Style* (New York, NY, 1982).

Keegan, J., *The Face of Battle: A Study of Agincourt, Waterloo, and the Somme* (London, 1976).

Keightley, G. M., 'Christian Collective Memory and Paul's Knowledge of Jesus', in A. Kirk and T. Thatcher (eds.), *Memory, Tradition, and Text: Uses of the Past in Early Christianity* (Atlanta, GA, 2005), pp. 129–50.

Kilmartin, E. J., 'Sacrificium Laudis: Content and Function of Early Eucharistic Prayers', *TS* 35 (1974), pp. 268–87.

—*The Eucharist in the West: History and Theology* (Collegeville, MN, 1998).

Kirk, A., 'Memory Theory and Jesus Research', in T. Holmen and S. Porter (eds.), *Handbook for the Study of the Historical Jesus* (1; Leiden, 2010), pp. 809–42.

Kirk, A. and Thatcher, T. (eds.), *Memory, Tradition, and Text: Uses of the Past in Early Christianity* (Atlanta, GA, 2005).

Kitzinger, E., 'The Cult of Images in the Age before Iconoclasm', *DOP* 8 (1954), pp. 83–150.

Klawiter, F. C., 'The Eucharist and Sacramental Realism in the Thought of St Ignatius of Antioch', *SL* 37 (2007), pp. 129–63.

Klein, G., 'Die Gebete in der Didache', *ZNW* 9 (1908), pp. 132–46.

Knight, F., *The Nineteenth-century Church and English Society* (Cambridge, 1995).

Kobel, E., *Dining with John: Communal Meals and Identity Formation in the Fourth Gospel and its Historical and Cultural Context* (Leiden, 2011).

Koester, H., *From Jesus to the Gospels: Interpreting the New Testament in its Context* (Minneapolis, MN, 2007).

Kreider, E., 'Communion as storytime', *VJCT* 2, 1 (2001), pp. 16–27.

Kuijt, I. and Finlayson, B., 'Evidence for food storage and predomestication granaries 11,000 years ago in the Jordan Valley', *PNAS* 106 (2009), pp. 10966–70.

Küng, H., *The Church* (London, 1967).

—*My Struggle for Freedom: Memoirs* (Grand Rapids, MI, 2002).

Ladner, G. B., *The Idea of Reform: Its Impact on Christian Thought and Action in the Age of the Fathers* (Cambridge, MA, 1959).

Laeuchli, S., *Power and Sexuality: The Emergence of Canon Law at the Synod of Elvira* (Philadelphia, 1972).

Lathrop, G. W., 'Justin, Eucharist and "Sacrifice": A Case of Metaphor', *Worship* 64 (1990), pp. 30–48.

—'The Lima Liturgy and Beyond', *ER* 48 (1996), pp. 62–8.

LaVerdiere, E., *The Eucharist in the New Testament and the Early Church* (Collegeville, MN, 1996).

Lawlor, J. E., 'Eucharist and Martyrdom in the Letters of Ignatius of Antioch', *ATR* 73 (1991), pp. 280–96.

Ligier, L., 'The Origins of the Eucharistic Prayer', *SL* 9 (1973), pp. 161–85.

Lindbeck, G., 'The Eucharist Tastes Bitter in the Divided Church', *Spectrum* 19, 1 (1999), pp. 1 and 4–5.

Livingstone, E. A. (ed.), *Studia Biblica 1978* (Sheffield, 1980).

Lohse, E., *Colossians and Philemon* (Philadelphia, PA, 1971) [ET by W. R. Poehlmann and R. J. Harris of *Die Briefe an die Kolosser und an Philemon*, Göttingen, 1968].

Lull, D. J. (ed.), *Society of Biblical Literature: 1989 Seminar Papers* (Atlanta, GA, 1989).

Lysaght, P., '"Is There Anyone There To Serve My Mass?": The Legend of "The Dead Priest's Mass" in Ireland', *ASYF* 47 (1991), pp. 193–207.

Macgregor, G. H. C., '*The Eucharist in the Fourth Gospel*', *NTS* 9 (1963), pp. 111–19.

MacNeill, M., *The Festival of Lughnasa* (Dublin, 1962).

Macy, G., *The Theologies of the Eucharist in the Early Scholastic Period* (Oxford, 1984).

—'Of Mice and Manna: *Quid summit mus?* As a Pastoral Question', *RTAM* 59 (1992), pp. 157–66.

—'The Dogma of Transubstantiation in the Middle Ages', *JEH* 45 (1994), pp. 11–41.

Marcus, J., 'Passover and Last Supper Revisited', *NTS* 59 (2013), pp. 303–24.

Marini, P., *A Challenging Reform: Realizing the Vision of the Liturgical Renewal* (Collegeville, MN, 2007).

Markus, R. A., 'How on Earth Could Places Become Holy? Origins of the Christian Idea of Holy Places', *JECS* 2 (1994), pp. 257–71.

Marshall, M., '"Blessed is anyone who will eat bread in the Kingdom of God." A brief study of Luke 14.15 in its context', in C. Tuckett (ed.), *Feasts and Festivals* (Leuven, 2009), pp. 97–106.

Mazza, E., *The Origins of the Eucharistic Prayer* (Collegeville, MN, 1995).

McAdoo, H. R., *The Eucharistic Theology of Jeremy Taylor Today* (Norwich, 1988).

McGowan, A. B., 'Naming the feast: The *agape* and the diversity of early Christian meals', *SP* 30 (1997), pp. 314–18.

—*Ascetic Eucharists: Food and Drink in Early Christian Ritual Meals* (Oxford, 1999a).

—'"Is there a Liturgical Text in this Gospel?": The Institution Narratives and their Early Interpretative Communities', *JBL* 118 (1999b), pp. 73–87.

McGrail, P., *First Communion: Ritual, Church and Popular Religious Identity* (Aldershot, 2007).

McGuinness, M. M., 'Is it Wrong to Chew the Host: Changing Catholic Etiquette and the Eucharist, 1920–1970', *ACS* 11 (1999), pp. 29–48.

McPartlan, P., *The Eucharist Makes the Church: Henri de Lubac and John Zizioulas in Dialogue* (Edinburgh, 1993).

Meeks, W. A., *The First Urban Christians: The Social World of the Apostle Paul* (New Haven, CT, [2nd edn; 1st edn, 1983] 2003).

Meens, R., 'Ritual Purity and the Influence of Gregory the Great in the Early Middle Ages', in R. N. Swanson (ed.), *Unity and Diversity in the Church* (Oxford, 1996), pp. 31–43.

Megivern, J. J., 'Communion under Both Species', *Worship* 57 (1962), pp. 50–8.

—*Concomitance and Communion: A Study in Eucharistic Doctrine and Practice* (Fribourg, 1963).

Meier, J. P., *A Marginal Jew – Rethinking the Historical Jesus: Mentor, Message, and Miracles* (New York, NY, 1994).

—'The Eucharist at the Last Supper: did it happen?', *TD* 42 (1995), pp. 335–51.

Méndes Montoya, A. F., *Theology of Food: Eating and the Eucharist* (Oxford, 2009).

—'Eating and the Eucharist: A Transformation of Desire', *BT* (Summer issue 2013), pp. 8–10.

Metzger, B. M., *A Textual Commentary on the Greek New Testament* (London, corrected edn, 1975).

Meyers, C., 'Having Their Space and Eating there Too: Bread Production and Female Power in Ancient Israelite Households', *NJJWS* 5 (2002), pp. 14–44.

Middleton, R. D., 'The Eucharistic Prayers of the Didache', *JTS* 36 (1935), pp. 259–67.

Milavec, A., 'Distinguishing True from False Prophets: the Protective Wisdom of the Didache', *JECS* 2 (1994), pp. 117–36.

—'The Social Setting of "Turning the Other Cheek" and "Loving One's Enemies" in the Light of the *Didache*', *BTB* 25 (1995), pp. 131–43.

—*The Didache: Faith, Hope, and Life of the Earliest Christian Communities, 50-70 C. E.* (Mahwah, NJ, 2003).

—'The Purifying Confession of Failings Required by the *Didache's* Eucharistic Sacrifice', *BTB* 33 (2003a), pp. 64–76.

—'How acts of discovery transform our tacid knowing powers in both scientific and religious inquiry', *Zygon* 41 (2006), pp. 465–86.

Mitchell, N., *Cult and Controversy: The Worship of the Eucharist Outside Mass* (Collegeville, MN, 1982).

Moonan, L., *Divine Power: The Medieval Power Distinction up to its Adoption by Albert, Bonaventure, and Aquinas* (Oxford, 1994).

Munck, J., *The Acts of the Apostles* (New York, NY, 1979).

Murphy-O'Connor, J., 'Eucharist and Community in First Corinthians' [part 1], *Worship* 50 (1976), pp. 370–85.

—'Eucharist and Community in First Corinthians' [part 2], *Worship* 51 (1977), pp. 56–69.

—*Paul: A Critical Life* (Oxford, 1996).

Newman, J. H., *An Essay on the Development of Christian Doctrine* (London, 1845) [and many later eds].

Niederwimmer, K., *The Didache: A Commentary* (Minneapolis, MN, 1998) [ET by L. M. Maloney of *Die Didache*, Göttingen, 2nd edn, 1993].

Nischan, B., 'The "Fractio Panis:" A Reformed Communion Practice in Late Reformation Germany', *CH* 53 (1984), pp. 17–29.

Nodet, É. and Taylor, J., *The Origins of Christianity: An Exploration* (Collegeville, MN, 1998).

Oliver, S., Kilby, K. and O'Loughlin, T. (eds.), *Faithful Reading: New Essays in Theology and Philosophy in Honour of Fergus Kerr OP* (London, 2012).

O'Loughlin, T., 'Newman, Vincent of Lérins and Development', *ITQ* 58 (1991), pp. 147–66.

—'Newman on Doing Theology', *NB* 76 (1995), pp. 92–8.

—'*Res, tempus, locus, persona*: Adomnán's Exegetical Method', *IR* 48 (1997), pp. 95–111.

—'Eucharist or Communion Service?', *TW* 38 (1998a), pp. 365–74.

—'Medieval church history: Beyond apologetics, after development: the awkward memories', *TW* 38 (1998b), pp. 65–76.

—'Maps and Acts: a problem in cartography and exegesis', *PIBA* 21 (1998c), pp. 33–61.

—*Teachers and Code-Breakers: The Latin Genesis Tradition, 430–800* (Turnhout, 1999).

—'Fasting: Western Christian', in W. R. Johnston (ed.), *The Encyclopedia of Monasticism* (Chicago and London, 2000), pp. 470–2.

—'The *Didache* as a Source for Picturing the Earliest Christian Communities: The Case of the Practice of Fasting', in K. O'Mahony (ed.), *Christian Origins: Worship, Belief and Society* (Sheffield, 2003), pp. 83–112.

—'The Praxis and Explanations of Eucharistic Fraction in the Ninth Century: the Insular Evidence', *AL* 45 (2003a), pp. 1–20.

—'Translating *Panis* in a Eucharistic Context: A Problem of Language and Theology', *Worship* 78 (2004), pp. 226–35.

—'The liturgical vessels of the Latin eucharistic liturgy: a case of an embedded theology', *Worship* 82 (2008), pp. 482–504.

—'Liturgical Evolution and the Fallacy of the Continuing Consequence', *Worship* 83 (2009), pp. 312–23.

—'Treating the "Private Mass" as Normal: Some Unnoticed Evidence from Adomnán's *De locis sanctis*', *AL* 51 (2009a), pp. 334–44.

—'Another post-resurrection meal, and its implications for the early understanding of the Eucharist', in Z. Rodgers, M. Daly-Denton and A. Fitzpatrick-McKinley (eds.), *A Wandering Galilean: Essays in Honour of Seán Freyne* (Leiden, 2009b), pp. 485–503.

—*The Didache: A Window on the Earliest Christians* (London, 2010).

—'Eucharistic Celebrations: the Chasm between Idea and Reality', *NB* 91 (2010a), pp. 423–38.

—'Harmonizing the Truth: Eusebius and the Problem of the Four Gospels', *Traditio* 65 (2010b), pp. 1–29.

—'The Missionary Strategy of the *Didache*', *Transformation* 28 (2011), pp. 77–92.

—'Divisions in Christianity: The Contribution of "Appeals to Antiquity"', in S. Oliver (ed.), *Faithful Reading: New Essays in Theology and Philosophy in Honour of Fergus Kerr OP* (London, 2012a), pp. 221–41.

—'The Prayers of the Liturgy', in V. Boland and T. McCarthy (eds.), *The Word is Flesh and Blood: The Eucharist and Sacred Scripture – Festschrift for Prof. Wilfrid Harrington* (Dublin, 2012b), pp. 113–22.

—*Making the Most of the Lectionary: A User's Guide* (London, 2012c).

—*Gildas and the Scriptures: Observing the World through a Biblical Lens* (Brepols, 2012d).

—'At the Lord's Table', *M&L* 38, 3 (2012e), pp. 10–13.

—'We are one loaf – a way of understanding the Eucharist', *TF* 64 (2013), pp. 412–15.

—'Reactions to the *Didache* in Early Twentieth-century Britain: A Dispute over the Relationship of History and Doctrine?', in S. J. Brown, F. Knight and J. Morgan-Guy (eds.), *Religion, Identity and Conflict in Britain: From the Restoration to the Twentieth Century. Essays in Honour of Keith Robbins* (Farnham, 2013a), pp. 177–94.

—'The Eucharist and the Meals of Jesus', *JMJ* 67, 1 (2013b), pp. 3–11.

—'The ecumenical meal of mission: a re-reading of Acts 10-11:18', *JMJ* 67 (2013c), pp. 118–27.

—'Is every translation a vernacular translation?', *NB* 94 (2013d), pp. 508–17.

—'A liturgy of the Word and the words of the liturgy', *PR* 9, 2 (2013e), pp. 52–6.

—'The Washing of Feet: the Interplay of Praxis and Theology', *Anaphora* 7, 1 (2013f), pp. 37–46.

—'The Eucharistic Table', *D&L* 63, 6 (2013g), pp. 46–53.

—'Blessing and breaking: a dissonance of action and interpretation in the Roman Eucharistic Prayers', *Anaphora* 7, 2 (2013h), pp. 53–66.

—'Ministries', in J. Day and B. Gordon-Taylor (eds.), *The Study of Liturgy and Worship: An Alcuin Guide* (London, 2013i), pp. 82–90.

—'Bede's view of the place of the Eucharist in Anglo-Saxon life: the evidence of the *Historia ecclesiastica gentis Anglorum*', in S. Bhattacharji, R. Williams, and D. Mattos (eds.), *Prayer and Thought in Monastic Tradition: Essays in Honour of Benedicta Ward S.L.G* (London, 2014), pp. 45–58.

—'From as Damp Floor to a New Vision of Church: Footwashing as a challenge to Liturgy and Discipleship', *Worship* 88 (2014a), pp. 137–50.

—'The cup of discipleship', *PR* 10, 1 (2014b), pp. 38–42.

O'Mahony, K. (ed.), *Christian Origins: Worship, Belief and Society* (Sheffield, 2003).

Omanson, R. L. *A Textual Guide to the Greek New Testament* (Stuttgart, 2006).

Otto, R., *The Idea of the Holy* (Oxford, 1950) [ET: J. W. Harvey (2e) of *Das Heilige*, Marburg, 1917].

Pearson, B. A. (ed.), *The Future of Early Christianity: Essays in Honor of Helmut Koester* (Minneapolis, MN, 1991).

Pfann, S., 'A Table Prepared in the Wilderness: Pantries and Tables, Pure Food and Sacred Space at Qumran', in K. Galor, J.-B. Humbert and J. Zangenberg (eds.), *Qumran. The Site of the Dead See Scrolls: Archaeological Interpretations and Debates* (Leiden, 2006), pp. 159–78.

Pocknee, C. E., *The Christian Altar: In History and Today* (London, 1963).

Poirier, J. C., 'Purity beyond the Temple in the Second Temple era', *JBL* 1222 (2003), pp. 247–65.

Polanyi, M., *Personal Knowledge: Towards a Post-Critical Philosophy* (London, 1958).

—*The Tacit Dimension* (Garden City, NY, 1966).

Poorthuis, M. and Schwartz, J., *A Holy People: Jewish and Christian Perspectives on Religious Communal Identity* (Leiden, 2006).

Powdermaker, H., 'Feasts in New Ireland; the Social Function of Eating', *AA* 34 (1932), pp. 236–47.

Priest, J., 'A Note on the Messianic Banquet', in J. H. Charlesworth (ed.), *The Messiah: Developments in Earliest Judaism and Christianity* (Minneapolis, MN, 1992), pp. 222–38.

Pusey, E. B., *The Doctrine of the Real Presence as Contained in the Fathers* (Oxford, 1855).

Rahner, K. and Häussling, A., *The Celebration of the Eucharist* (New York, NY, 1968).

Rausch, T. P., 'Is the Private Mass Traditional?', *Worship* 64 (1990), pp. 227–42.

Rempel, D. D., 'The Lord's Supper in Mennonite Tradition', *VJCT* 2, 1 (2001), pp. 4–15.

Robertson, J. F., 'Temples: Mesopotamia', in D. N. Freedman (ed.), *The Anchor Bible Dictionary* (6; New York, NY, 1992), pp. 372–6.

Robinson, J. M., 'Die Hodayot-Formel in Gebet und Hymnus des Früchristentums', in W. Eltester, et al. (eds.), *Apophoreta: Festschrift für Ernst Haenchen* (Berlin, 1964), pp. 194–235.

—'The Q Trajectory: Between John and Matthew via Jesus', in B. A. Pearson (ed.), *The Future of Early Christianity: Essays in Honor of Helmut Koester* (Minneapolis, MN, 1991), pp. 173–94.

Rodgers, Z., Daly-Denton, M., and Fitzpatrick-McKinley, A. (eds.), *A Wandering Galilean: Essays in Honour of Seán Freyne* (Leiden, 2009).

Roppelt, R., 'A Fuller Light: Communion Under Both Kinds', *Worship* 79 (2005), pp. 2–20.

Rothenbuhler, E. W., *Ritual Communication: From Everyday Conversation to Mediated Ceremony* (Thousand Oaks, CA, 1998).

Rouwhorst, G., 'Table Community in Early Christianity', in M. Poorthuis and J. Schwartz (eds.), *A Holy People: Jewish and Christian Perspectives on Religious Communal Identity* (Leiden, 2006), pp. 69–84.

Rubin, D. C., *Memory in Oral Traditions: The Cognitive Psychology of Epic, Ballads, and Counting-Out Rhymes* (Oxford, 1995).

Sagovsky, N., 'The Eucharist and the Practice of Justice', *SCE* 15 (2002), pp. 75–96.

Sasse, H., *This is My Body* (Minneapolis, MN, 1959).

Schaberg, J., Bach, A. and Fuchs, E. (eds.), *On the Cutting Edge: The Study of Women in Biblical Worlds: Essays in Honor of Elizabeth Schüssler Fiorenza* (New York, NY, 2004).

Schiffman, L. H., 'Communal Meals at Qumran', *RQ* 10 (1979), pp. 45–65.

Schillebeeckx, E., *Christ the Sacrament of the Encounter with God* (London, 1963) [ET of *Christus, Sacrament van de Godsontmoeting*, Bilthoven, 1960].

—*The Eucharist* (London, 1968) [ET of *Christus Tegenwoordigheid in de Eucharistie*, Bildhoven 1967].

Schwartz, B., 'The Social Context of Commemoration. A Study in Collective Memory', *SF* 61 (1982), pp. 374–402.

—'Memory as a Cultural System: Abraham Lincoln in World War II', *ASR* 61 (1996), pp. 908–27.

—'Christian Origins: Historical Truth and Social Memory', in A. Kirk and T. Thatcher (eds.), *Memory, Tradition, and Text: Uses of the Past in Early Christianity* (Atlanta, GA, 2005), pp. 43–56.

Schwiebert, J., *Knowledge and the Coming Kinngdom: The Didache's Meal Ritual and its Place in Early Christianity* (London, 2008).

Sered, S. S., *Priestess, Mother, Sacred Sister: Religions Dominated by Women* (Oxford, 1994).

Scholliers, P. (ed.), *Food, Drink and Identity: Cooking, Eating and Drinking in Europe since the Middle Ages* (Oxford, 2001).

Skehan, P. K. and Di Lella, A. A., *The Wisdom of Ben Sira* (New York, 1987).

Smit, P.-B., 'A Symposiastic Background to James?', *NTS* 58 (2011), pp. 105–22.

Smith, D. E., 'Table Fellowship as a Literary Motif in the Gospel of Luke', *JBL* 106 (1987), pp. 613–16.

—'The Historical Jesus at Table', in D. J. Lull (ed.), *Society of Biblical Literature: 1989 Seminar Papers* (Atlanta, GA, 1989), pp. 466–86.

—'The Messianic Banquet Reconsidered', in B. A. Pearson (ed.), *The Future of Early Christianity: Essays in Honor of Helmut Koester* (Minneapolis, MN, 1991), pp. 64–73.

—'Messianic Banquet', in D. N. Freedman (ed.), *The Anchor Bible Dictionary* (4; New York, NY, 1992), pp. 788–91.

—*From Symposium to Eucharist: The Banquet in the Early Christian World* (Minneapolis, MN, 2003).

—'Meals', in J. J. Collins and D. C. Harlow (eds.), *The Eerdmans Dictionary of Early Judaism* (Grand Rapids, MI, 2010), pp. 924–6.

Smith, D. E. and Taussig, H., *Many Tables: The Eucharist in the New Testament and Liturgy Today* (London, 1990).

Smith, J. Z., *To Take Place: Towards Theory in Ritual* (Chicago, 1987).

—'A Twice-Told Tale: The History of the History of Religion's History', *Numen* 48 (2001), pp. 134–46.

Smolarski, D. C., 'Catechesis Through Liturgy Using the Principles of the 2002 GIRM', *NTR* 17, 4 (2004), pp. 18–29.

Snyder, E., 'Pass-over, morsel, or the real meal deal: Seeking a place at the table for the church's children', *VJCT* 2, 1 (2001), pp. 73–83.

Spinks, B., *The Worship Mall: Contemporary Responses to Contemporary Culture* (London, 2010).

Steiner, S. C., 'The great feast', *VJCT* 2, 1 (2001), pp. 68–72.

Stevenson, K., *Eucharist and Offering* (New York, NY, 1986).

Stewart-Sykes, A., 'The Birkath Ha-mazon and the Body of the Lord: A Case-study of *Didache* 9-10', *QL* 85 (2004), pp. 197–205.

Swanson, R. N. (ed.), *Unity and Diversity in the Church* (Oxford, 1996).

Taft, R., 'What does Liturgy do? Towards a Soteriology of Liturgical Celebration: Some Theses', in Vogel, D. W. (ed.), *Primary Sources of Liturgical Theology: A Reader* (Collegeville, MN, 2000), pp. 139–50 [originally published in *Worship* 66 (1992), pp. 194–211].

—'Mass Without the Consecration? The Historic Agreement on the Eucharist between the Catholic Church and the Assyrian Church of the East Promulgated 26 October 2001', *Worship* 77 (2003), pp. 482–509.

Talley, T. J., 'From Berakah to Eucharistia: A Reopening Question', *Worship* 50 (1976a), pp. 115–37.

—'The Eucharistic Prayer of the Ancient Church According to Recent Research: Results and Reflections', *SL* 11 (1976b), pp. 138–58.

Taussig, H., *In the Beginning was the Meal: Social Experimentation and Early Christian Identity* (Minneapolis, MN, 2009).

Taylor, J. E., 'The Women "Priests" of Philo's *De Vita Contemplativa*', in Schaberg, J., et al. (eds.), *On the Cutting Edge: The Study of Women in Biblical Worlds: Essays in Honor of Elizabeth Schüssler Fiorenza* (New York, NY, 2004), pp. 102–22.

Theiss, N., 'The Passover Feast of the New Covenant', *Interpretation* 48 (1994), pp. 17–35.

Theissen, G. (1982), *The Social Setting of Pauline Christianity* (Edinburgh, 1982) [compilation and translation by J. H. Schütz of articles previously published].

Thompson, M. B., 'The Holy Internet: Communication Between Churches in the First Christian Generation', in R. Bauckham (ed.), *The Gospels for all Christians: Rethinking the Gospel Audience* (Edinburgh, 1998), pp. 49–70.

Triacca, A. M. and Pistoia, A. (eds.), *Liturgie, spiritualité, culture: Conférences Saint-Serge, 30e Semaine d'Etudes Liturgiques, Paris, 29 juin-2 Juillet 1982* (Rome, 1983).

Tuckett, C. (ed.), *Feasts and Festivals* (Leuven, 2009).

Uro, R., 'Ritual, Memory and Writing in Early Christianity', *Temenos* 47 (2011), pp. 159–82.

Van der Meer, F., *Apocalypse: Visions from the Book of Revelation in Western Art* (London, 1978).

van der Ploeg, J., 'The Meals of the Essenes', *JSS* 2 (1957), pp. 163–75.

van de Sandt, H., '"Do not give what is holy to the dogs" (Did 9:5D and Matt 7:6A): the eucharistic food of the Didache in its Jewish purity setting', *VC* 56 (2002), pp. 223–46.

—'Was the Didache community a group within Judaism? An assessment on the basis of its Eucharistic Prayers', in M. Poorthuis and J. Schwartz (eds.), *A Holy People: Jewish and Christian Perspectives on Religious Communal Identity* (Leiden, 2006), pp. 85–107.

—'Why does the Didache conceive the Eucharist as a Holy Meal?', *VC* 65 (2011), pp. 1–20.

Vera, L. A., 'The Kiss of Peace: An Hispanic Understanding', *NTR* 17, 4 (2004), pp. 30–40.

Verheul, A., *Introduction to the Liturgy: Towards a Theology of Worship* (Collegeville, MN, 1968).

Visser, M., *The Rituals of Dinner: The Origins, Evolution, Eccentricities, and Meaning of Table Manners* (London, [first published 1991] 1993).

Vogel, C., 'Une mutation cultuelle inexpliquée: le passage de l'Eucharistie Communautaire a la Messe Privée', *RSR* 54 (1980), pp. 231–50.

—'La multiplication des messes solitarires au Moyen Age: Essai de statistique', *RSR* 55 (1981), pp. 206–13.

—'La vie quotidienne des moines-prêtres à l'époque de la floraison des messes privées', in A. M. Triacca and A. Pistoia (eds.), *Liturgie, spiritualité, culture: Conférences Saint-Serge, 30e Semaine d'Etudes Liturgiques, Paris, 29 juin-2 Juillet 1982* (Rome, 1983), pp. 341–60.

—'Deux Conséquences de l'eschatologie Grégorienne: La multipication des Messes Privées et les moines-prêtres', in J. Fontaine, R. Gillet and S. Pellistrandi (eds.), *Grégoire le Grand* (Paris, 1986), pp. 267–76.

Vogel, D. W. (ed.), *Primary Sources of Liturgical Theology: A Reader* (Collegeville, MN, 2000).

Wagner, P. M., 'Food as Ritual', in S. M. Farber and N. L. Wilson (eds.), *Food and Civilization* (Springfield, IL, 1966), pp. 60–82.

Walker, J. H. (1980), 'A pre-Marcan Dating for the Didache: Further Thoughts of a Liturgist', in E. A. Livingstone (ed.), *Studia Biblica 1978* (3; Sheffield, 1980), pp. 403–11.

Wandel, L. P., *The Eucharist in the Reformation: Incarnation and Liturgy* (Cambridge, 2006).

Wainwright, G., 'Any Advance on "BEM"? The Lima Text at Twenty-Five', *SL* 37 (2007), pp. 1–29.

Ward, W. A., 'Temples: Egypt', in D. N. Freedman (ed.), *The Anchor Bible Dictionary* (6; New York, NY, 1992), pp. 369–72.

Ware, K., 'Church and Eucharist, Communion and Intercommunion', *Sobornost* 7 (1978), pp. 550–67.

Weinfeld, M., 'Grace after Meals in Qumran', *JBL* 111 (1992), pp. 427–40.

Wenks, A. W., 'Eating and Drinking in the Old Testament', in D. N. Freedman (ed.), *The Anchor Bible Dictionary* (2; New York, NY, 1992), pp. 250–4.

Wilpert, J., *Fractio Panis: Die alteste darstellung des eucharistichen opfers in der 'Capella Greca'. entdeckt und erlautert* (Freiburg-im-Breisgau, 1895).

Wirzba, N., 'Thinking Theologically About Food', *BT* (Summer issue 2013), pp. 5–7.

Witczak, M. G., 'The Manifold Presence of Christ in the Liturgy', *TS* 59 (1998), pp. 680–702.

Witherington III, B., 'The Influence of Galatians on Hebrews', *NTS* 37 (1991), pp. 146–52.

—*Making a Meal of It: Rethinking the Theology of the Lord's Supper* (Waco, TX, 2007).

Wolter, M., 'Primitive Christianity as a Feast', in C. Tuckett (ed.), *Feasts and Festivals* (Leuven, 2009), pp. 171–82.

Woolley, R. M., *The Bread of the Eucharist* (London, 1913).

Yamauchi, E. M., 'The "Daily Bread" Motif in Antiquity', *WTJ* 27 (1964), pp. 145–56.

INDEX

Biblical and other Ancient Texts

GENERAL INDEX

Jennings, T. 191
Jeremias, J. 22, 27, 136, 157, 197
Jerusalem Bible 176
Jewett, R. 43, 169, 171
John the Baptist 73, 83, 169
John 'the beloved' 36
Johnson, M. 39, 145, 146, 148, 150,
    157, 169, 200
Jones. M. 52, 61
Josephus 131–5, 167
Judas Iscariot 113, 162
Jungmann, J. A. 34, 37, 38, 39, 40,
    182, 184
Justin 'martyr' 9–10, 79, 144, 154,
    157–8, 179

Kavanagh, A. 188
Keegan, J. 100
Keithley, G. M. 4, 5, 119, 153
Kershaw, S. 164
kerygma 24, 90, 125, 135, 153, 169
Kilmartin, E. J. 43, 47, 54, 187
Kirk, A. 18
kiss of peace 138
Kitzinger, E. 68
Klawiter, F. C. 162, 172, 177, 186
Klein, G. 52
Knight, F. 35
Kobel, E. 184, 186, 189
Koester, H. 9, 49, 118
koinonia 153
Kreider, E. 183
Kuijt, I. 107, 123

Ladner, G. 93
Laeuchli, S. 88, 100
Lammas Day 75
language 66–7
Last Supper 7, 17, 22–4, 33, 39–41,
    46, 51, 66, 69, 82, 86, 89, 90,
    113, 144, 149–50, 155, 168, 175,
    180–7, 190, 199
Lathrop, G. W. 89, 98, 130, 132
LaVerdiere, E. 22, 89
Lawlor, J. E. 172
leadership at Eucharist *see* 'ordination'
lex orandi ... 11
libations 99
Liberation Theology 78

Ligier, L. 5, 29, 88, 90, 158,
    180, 183
Lindbeck, G. 145
Liturgical Movement 23, 29
Liturgy of the Word 49, 192
Lohse, E. 47
Lord's Prayer 45, 107, 194
Lord's Supper (as title) 27, 29
Lughnasa 74
Luther, M. 57
Lysaght, P. 41

MacGregor, G. H. C. 184
Mac Neill, M. 75
McAdoo, H.R. 32
McCormack, J. 36
McGinnness, M. M. 37
McGowan, A. B. 85, 90, 91, 92, 147,
    155, 169, 175, 180
McGrail, P. 37
McPartlan, P. 156
Macy, G. 8, 30, 62
Marcus, J. 183
Marini, P. 199
Markus, R. A. 39
marriage 145
Marshall, M. 65, 68, 87, 135
Martène, E. 87
martyrdom 172
Mary, mother of Jesus 36
Mass (as title) 27–30, 55
Masses for the Dead 3, 17
Mazza, E. 45, 62, 77, 158
meals and liturgy 12–3, 85–88
meals *passim, and see* 'food'
meal sharing 70, 96, 103–5, 112–4
Meeks, W. A. 137
Meens, R. 107
Megivern, J. J. 171, 174, 175
Meier, J. P. 23, 72, 144, 168, 170,
    173, 183
memory 17–20, 24, 91, 96–7, 105,
    112, 118–21, 123–6, 143–4, 159
Méndes Montoya, A. F. 79, 107,
    177, 178
Mennonites 102, 179
Metzger, B. M. 73, 176
Meyers, C. 81
Middleton, R. D. 77

Uro, R.   151
Utraquism *see* 'Subutraquism'

van der Meer, F.   147
van der Ploeg, J.   115, 118
van de Sandt, H.   158, 161, 171, 195
Vatican II   3, 5, 14, 20, 27, 29, 37, 40,
    57, 59, 65, 156, 187, 199
Vera, L. A.   163
Verheul, A.   29
viaticum   38
Vincent of Lérins   7
Visser, M.   13, 64, 113
vocation of theologians   21–2
Vogel, C.   40
Vulgate   176

Wagner, P. M.   61
Wainwright, G.   89, 200
Walker, J. H.   44
Wandel, L. P.   157

War Stone, the   98
Ward, W. A.   74
Ware, K.   145, 146
water at Eucharist   169
weddings   114–5, 117, 136, 156
wedding cakes   113
Weinfeld, M.   52, 77, 115
Wenks, A. W.   79
Wilpert, J.   163, 164
Wirzba, N.   175
Witczak, M. G.   187
Witherington III, B.   22, 185, 189, 198
Wolter, M.   65, 86, 144, 153, 177
Woolley, R. M.   148, 164, 183
World Council of Churches   89

Xenophon   97

Yamauchi, E. M.   75

Zellentin, H.   83